Stepping Up Skills in Urban Ghana

DIRECTIONS IN DEVELOPMENT
Human Development

Stepping Up Skills in Urban Ghana

Snapshot of the STEP Skills Measurement Survey

Peter Darvas, Marta Favara, and Tamara Arnold

WORLD BANK GROUP

Contents

Boxes

Figures

Tables

Foreword

The past two decades in Ghana have been marked by steady economic progress, which has transformed the country into a lower-middle-income economy, accompanied by a decline in poverty, increases in incomes for families, improvements in health, and expanded educational opportunities. As Ghana looks forward to a future of economic growth, it needs to regain growth from the 2016 slowdown, including improving competitiveness and economic diversification and raising labor productivity. A well-equipped workforce will be key to obtaining these goals. The Government of Ghana and its development partners such as the World Bank have long recognized the importance of investments in human capital. Insufficient skills in young people will be an obstacle to improving competitiveness in all sectors across the economy, be they informal or formal, in traditional sectors or in the modern areas such as information and telecommunications technologies.

An agenda for improving skills in the workforce relies on being able to identify where the more practical and profitable investments in the current skills profile should be made. To that end, Skills Toward Employment and Productivity (STEP) is an innovative tool used across the world to assess the education, cognitive, work-related, and socioemotional skills stock in a population, as well as the impact of these traits on employment and earnings. Ghana is among the first two countries (along with Kenya) in Sub-Saharan Africa where this systematic assessment of skills has been carried out. The evidence collected through this assessment shows that the multidimensional nature of skills requires nurturing from early childhood education to school and university systems, as well as through school-based and on-the-job training. This broad concept of skills has a significant impact both on jobs and on earnings, and the relationship is also mutual: jobs attract and reward skills. The information from the *Stepping Up Skills in Urban Ghana* study provides detailed insights for policy makers. These insights cover areas including investments in early childhood education, the role of improvements in the quality of education, and the creation of incentives for economic actors to invest in on-the-job training to improve Ghana's competitiveness and the well-being of its citizens.

Henry Kerali
Country Director for Ghana
The World Bank

Jaime Saavedra Chanduvi
Senior Director, Education Global Practice
The World Bank

Acknowledgments

The authors thank Henry Kerali, World Bank Country Director for Ghana; Jaime Saavedra Chanduvi, Senior Director; Amit Dar, Director; Luis Benveniste, Director; and Peter Nicolas Materu, Meskerem Mulatu, and Halil Dundar, Managers of the World Bank Education Global Practice, for their overall leadership and management guidance. We would also like to thank Alexandria Valerio, Kathleen Beegle, Maria Laure Sanchez Puerta, and Omar Arias for peer reviews and technical guidance. The team also received valuable advice from Deborah Mikesell and Eunice Ackwerh.

The survey work was carried out by a team of the Institute for Social Statistical and Economic Research of the University of Ghana, led by Frank Ochere. The literacy assessment was completed with technical support by the Educational Testing Service (Princeton, New Jersey). Technical support to data management was provided by Tania M. Rajadel and Sebastian Monroy Taborda, both at the World Bank. Financial support was provided by the Multi-Donor Education Trust Fund and the Bank-Netherlands Partnership Support Program, both managed by the World Bank.

Editing and publishing support were provided by Jonathan Faull and Aziz Gökdemir. Janet Adebo provided invaluable administrative support throughout the process.

Overview

Introduction

Ghana stands at the cusp of extraordinary opportunity. Since the country's return to democratic rule and the advent of the Fourth Republic, per capita gross domestic product (GDP, current US$, PPP [purchasing power parity]) has increased almost fourfold, from US$375 in 1993 to US$1,442 in 2014. In 2011, Ghana was the only African economy to demonstrate double-digit economic growth, surpassing 14 percent that year. In the aftermath of the Chinese economic slowdown and the slump in global commodities markets, Ghana's growth tempered to 4 percent in 2014 but is expected to recover above 8 percent in the medium term as the country begins exploiting significant oil and gas resources.

Throughout the period of the Fourth Republic, fertility rates have remained relatively high, falling from 5.3 births per female in 1993 to 4.2 in 2014. Concurrently, the proportion of children under the age of 15 in the total population declined only marginally from 43 percent in 1993 to 39 percent in 2014. As a consequence, Ghana's labor force has grown rapidly, from approximately 6.5 million in 1993 to 11.3 million in 2014, and is expected to continue to grow in the coming decades.

Population growth has also contributed to an erosion of the effects of buoyant economic growth on poverty reduction. Although the country has made progress in reducing poverty—with the proportion of the population living below the government's poverty line falling from 32 percent in 2005 to 24 percent in 2012—stubborn disparities persist with regard to access to economic, social, and political opportunities.

Inequity is particularly evident in the differences between the populations of the poorer northern Savannah regions and the rest of the country. In the three northernmost administrative regions of the country, more than half, or

---

Unless stated, all statistics cited in the Introduction are drawn from the World Bank Group's Data Bank, accessible at data.worldbank.org (accessed March 23, 2016).

58 percent, of the population falls below the poverty line, compared to 19 percent in the seven administrative districts of the south of the country. The spatial distribution of poverty and economic opportunity, in turn, has led to significant migration from north to south, and a swelling of the ranks of the urban labor force.

Nevertheless, a significant economic dividend is implicit in Ghana's increasingly abundant urban labor force. If current and future generations of workers can be empowered to realize their potential in a vibrant and increasingly competitive economy, the prospect of sustained poverty reduction, further economic development, and the reaping of benefits associated with a demographic transition could profoundly reshape Ghana's society and economy for future generations.

Equipping current and future generations of workers with the skills they need to improve their livelihoods and to drive increases in national productivity and competitiveness requires that these workers have skills appropriately aligned with the needs of a growing economy. Some skills are innate, arbitrarily assigned through the accident of birth. Other skills are acquired through education, work, and life experience. The primary means through which a government can develop the skills of its labor force is through policies and strategies implemented through the education system.

Jobs form the foundation of economic development, rising living standards, increases in productivity, and improved social cohesion. Equipping people with appropriate skills to access meaningful work constitutes the means for achieving these objectives. This report, premised on the Skills Toward Employment and Productivity (STEP) framework, considers education the instrument for learning and acquiring skills and the key for accessing employment.

Although the Ghanaian government has made significant progress in expanding access to basic education, many challenges persist in the education sector. These include the low quality of learning in both basic and post-basic education, inequity of access, and the limited capacity of the education system to equip beneficiaries with skills aligned with increasing competitiveness and productivity in the economy. If education and training institutions are unable to provide the skills demanded by the market, economic inefficiencies could be compounded.

Skills development strategies can be effective only if they are appropriately calibrated to the needs of the economy and only if they take into account the current skills endowment of the existing labor force. The most effective skills development strategies are informed by evidence, and effective implementation requires the ongoing collection of data to gauge shifting demand for skills and the changing character of the labor force and economy at large.

To date, evidence regarding the stock of existing skills in Ghana's labor force is relatively underdeveloped. The precise measurement of the prevalence of different categories of skills within the population is required for the effective design of policy interventions that target improved training to reduce skill gaps aligned with the needs of specific sectors, improvement in productivity, and increased employability of workers. With the data it gathers, the first STEP household survey aims, in part, to address this deficiency through a rigorous analysis of the skills endowment of urban Ghanaian adults.

The STEP survey was carried out between September 2011 and December 2013 in Ghana, as part of the first wave of surveys initiated under the STEP Skills Measurement Program. The Ghanaian sample consists of about 3,000 individuals between 15 and 64 years of age, living in urban areas across 71 districts. In addition to standardized information captured at the household level, the STEP survey collects information regarding the level of skill, level of education completed, and work history. On skills, the STEP survey includes information about (i) self-reported cognitive skills (that is, a subjective assessment of an individual's use of foundation skills—reading, writing, and numeracy—at work and in daily life); (ii) assessed cognitive skills (that is, an objective assessment of reading literacy based on the International Adult Literacy Survey); (iii) socioemotional skills (that is, personality traits, behavior, and risk and time preferences); and (iv) job-specific skills (that is, an indirect assessment of skills used at work).

The STEP framework is structured according to five iterative steps and associated objectives: (i) getting children off to the right start; (ii) ensuring that all students learn; (iii) building job-relevant skills; (iv) encouraging entrepreneurship and innovation; and (v) facilitating labor mobility and job matching. Ultimately, if these five steps are achieved, Ghana will significantly advance the likelihood of realizing the potential of its labor force, with considerable positive implications for the livelihoods of its people, poverty reduction, improved productivity, economic development, and the betterment of society at large.

Objectives

This report is intended to complement and support the work of the Government of Ghana as it seeks to accelerate progress toward the achievement of the education-related Millennium Development Goals (MDGs) and the work of the Ministry of Education (MOE) and the Ghana Education Service (GES) in advancing the reforms envisaged by the Education Strategic Plan (ESP) for 2010–20.

This report is divided into eight chapters:

- Chapter 1 of the report describes Ghana's economic, social, and demographic trends and the current challenges faced by the education system. Chapter 2 outlines the report's framework for enquiry and a detailed description of the STEP framework. Chapter 3 provides an overview of the STEP survey's sampling methodology, a description of methodologies used to measure each subset of skills, and limitations to the analysis.

- Drawing on data collected through the STEP survey, chapter 4 describes the education profile of the urban adult population; explores trends in preschool, primary, secondary, and tertiary completion rates, disaggregated by age group, gender, and region; explores the effect of socioeconomic and demographic factors on educational attainment, dropout rates, and age of entry into the education system; and looks at the relationship between education attainment and inequality.
- Chapter 5 analyzes labor force participation, employment status, and underemployment; the correlation between labor market status and skills and education; and regional disparities in education and labor market opportunity.
- Chapter 6 focuses on the use of cognitive skills (both self-reported and assessed), socioemotional skills, and technical skills. The authors analyze the mismatch between self-reported and assessed cognitive skills and the mismatch between respondents who report high levels of education attainment but who performed poorly when these skills were tested and vice versa. This section of the report aims to answer the following research questions: How do socioemotional skills relate to cognitive skills? Does inequality with regard to years of schooling reflect inequality in cognitive skills? What are the characteristics of respondents who under- or over-report cognitive ability? Do incremental increases in educational achievement result in more developed skill sets?
- Chapter 7 looks at the association between education and skills and labor market opportunity. It discusses the extent to which it is worthwhile for individuals to invest in (or for others to subsidize) education and/or skills development and to what extent these investments inform the development of skills demanded by the economy. In so doing, this chapter aims to answer the following research questions: Does education lead to better job market opportunities? Do skilled (educated) workers demonstrate higher earnings? Does education inculcate job-relevant skills? Which skills matter the most for employability? How much of the wage premium accruing to educated people is explained by skills? Is training relevant in producing good skills?
- Section 8 quantifies the magnitude of unused skills and underexploited potential within the labor force, examines the proportion of the employed population who do not use their skills at work, and weighs evidence of skills and education mismatching in the labor market.

Key Findings

The Educational Profile of Ghana's Adult Urban Population

Ghana has made significant progress in expanding access to basic education, having achieved near universal access to primary education. However, challenges persist with regard to improving the quality of basic education to enhance learning outcomes and to expanding access to post-basic levels of education.

Moreover, a significant gender gap in educational achievement is evident for all levels of education in Ghana.

The expansion of early childhood education (ECE) in Ghana's urban areas has dramatically improved, and participation in ECE is positively correlated with household socioeconomic status and the intensity with which workers use basic skills. Only 30 percent of Ghanaians between ages 45 and 64 attended an ECE program compared to 87 percent of the youngest generation surveyed. Seventy-seven percent of adults living in households in the upper socioeconomic brackets had participated in an ECE program, compared to 49 percent of adults in the poorest households. Adults with ECE are more likely to read and write regularly and do so with greater intensity.

Approximately two-thirds of students who complete primary school do so without demonstrating proficiency in core subject areas. In terms of the quality of senior high school (SHS) programs, a large disparity in further educational attainment is evident between students attending the highest-performing schools and the rest of the sector.

The highest-performing 10 percent of high schools account for 90 percent of students entering university. There are significant regional, gender-based, and income-based disparities in access to and the returns accruing to post-basic education. Pass rates for the Basic Education Certificate Examination (BECE) vary greatly by region, with the poorest performance evident in the administrative regions of the north. The magnitude of difference in BECE pass rates for the north and south are upwards of 60 percent.

Access to tertiary education has not changed substantially over time. Over three generations, the percentage of people with a tertiary qualification increased by only two percentage points, from 11 percent for adults ages 45 to 64 to 13 percent for respondents in the generation ages 25 to 34.

A child's age on entry to the school system is correlated with educational achievement. Officially, children should commence formal schooling at the age of six; however, in practice many children enter school later, with negative implications for further education. Approximately 51 percent of those with incomplete primary education enrolled in primary school at eight years of age, whereas 89 percent of those with postsecondary education enrolled at the official age of entry.

Approximately one out of four members of the adult labor force dropped out of school prior to completing the highest grade of the level of education they had enrolled in, with the highest rates of dropout evident in the primary and junior high school (JHS) cycles of education. The most commonly cited reason for dropping out of school before the age of 16 is a lack of money for out-of-pocket expenses, regardless of the child's socioeconomic status.

Labor Force Participation and Employment Status Characteristics

The overall urban labor force participation rate in Ghana is 67 percent: 62 percent of respondents ages 15 to 64 years reported being employed, 5 percent reported being unemployed but looking for work, 23 percent were deemed economically inactive (22 percent in education, 1 percent had retired), and 10 percent fell into the category "Not in Education, Employment, or Training" (NEET).

A significant majority of the employed labor force works in the informal sector, primarily in self-employed work (66 percent) or as informal wage workers (20 percent). Only 15 percent of the employed population is engaged in salaried employment in the formal sector. However, these trends are changing, with younger generations less likely to be self-employed and more likely to hold salaried employment in formal or informal firms.

Although female workers are as likely to be employed as their male counterparts, a significant gender gap exists in the quality of employment enjoyed by male and female workers. Across all age groups, female workers are more likely than male workers to be self-employed. Approximately half of male workers are self-employed, with the remaining share split almost evenly between formal and informal wage employment. By contrast, 79 percent of female workers are self-employed, and only 7 percent are retained as employees in the formal sector.

A worker's level of education is strongly associated with employment status. Approximately 37 percent of workers holding a tertiary qualification work in the informal sector (20 percent as self-employed and 17 percent as informal employees), compared to 99 percent of workers with no formal education (86 percent as self-employed and 13 percent as informal employees). A key determinant of a worker's likelihood of accessing a job in the formal wage sector is education. Approximately 44 percent of workers in the formal sector have a tertiary education, 32 percent graduated from SHS, and 24 percent report JHS education or less.

The level of educational attainment is also strongly associated with employment in higher-skilled occupations. The majority of the employed population works in low-skilled occupations in the informal sector, and just 13 percent of the working population is employed in high-skilled occupations, concentrated in the formal sector. SHS and tertiary graduates are more likely to be employed in mid- or high-skilled occupations than are workers with lower levels of educational attainment. Approximately 29 percent of SHS graduates are employed in the high-value-added services sector, compared to just 3 and 8 percent of workers in this sector having terminated their education following the primary and JHS cycles, respectively.

The Skills Profile of Ghana's Adult Urban Population

As mentioned previously, the STEP survey collects information about cognitive skills by asking people about their use of numeracy, reading, and writing skills and through an objective assessment of their reading proficiency.

According to self-reporting by those surveyed, working-age Ghanaians use their numeracy skills on a regular basis, regardless of their level of education. At the same time, the use of reading and writing skills is significantly lower and strongly correlates with the level of education and with employment status. The intensity of the use of reading skills is higher among SHS graduates and highest for respondents with a tertiary qualification. All respondents who received tertiary education report using their reading and writing skills on a regular basis, and approximately 64 and 60 percent of the population with primary education report the regular use of reading and writing skills, respectively. Nevertheless, even among those who completed tertiary education, almost half write only with low intensity. Similarly, 84 percent of formal employees reported using their reading and writing skills on a daily basis, compared with approximately 41 percent of informal wageworkers and 21 percent of self-employed workers.

Overall, the use of reading and writing skills has intensified over time, with the youngest cohort surveyed reporting regular use of their writing (89 percent of respondents) and reading (90 percent) skills, compared to the oldest age cohort of workers who reported a lower regular use of reading (41 percent of respondents) and writing (41 percent). The results of the reading proficiency tests mirror the respondents' self-reported levels of skill use.

Educational attainment was highly predictive of relative success on the Core Literacy Test component of the survey. Ninety-three percent of those who failed the test reported educational attainment of JHS or less (42 percent report no formal education, and 33 percent attended JHS), whereas about 57 percent of those who passed the test have at least an SHS education and approximately 21 percent report having tertiary education.

Nevertheless, average performance across all three measures of reading is low. Respondents who reported using their reading and writing skills more frequently performed better in *sentence processing* and *passage comprehension* tests than those who did not. However, poor performance on the *print vocabulary* subcomponent of the reading assessment was relatively uniform across all subgroups. Respondents with higher reported levels of educational attainment performed better on all aspects of the reading component. Younger respondents were more likely to perform better in sentence and passage comprehension tests than older respondents.

Respondents with lower socioeconomic status, and for whom English was not their main language at home or at work, were less likely to pass the Core Literacy Test. Of those who passed the test, 73 percent reported using English as their primary workplace language, compared with 17 percent of those who failed the test. However, in light of the fact that the reading test was administered in English, it is not surprising that a higher percentage of those who passed the test report speaking English as their primary language at home and work than those who failed. Of the respondents who were employed, 81 percent of those who failed the reading test were self-employed and only 3 percent were formal wageworkers. By contrast, 38 percent of those who passed the reading assessment were self-employed and 34 percent were formal wageworkers, with one-third retained in high-skilled occupations. Respondents who passed the reading assessment earned on average 274 GHS (approximately US$80) per month more than those who failed the test.

Average performance on the Literacy Exercise Booklets section of the test, which allows for an in-depth analysis of reading ability, was very poor. Sixty-one percent of the subsample to whom the Literacy Exercise Booklets were administered scored on the lowest rung of proficiency. Respondents who attained higher scores were more likely to be younger, to have reported higher levels of educational attainment (SHS or tertiary), to work in the formal sector, to have reported the use of English as their primary home or workplace language, and to have reported using their reading and writing skills more intensively.

Finally, it is worth mentioning that the data show a substantial mismatch between self-reported use of skills and tested literacy: of the sample as a whole, approximately 69 percent of adults reported reading regularly, but only 42 percent passed the Core Literacy Test component of the literacy assessment. However, the poor results in the Core test may reflect poor English literacy rather than present a true measurement of general reading skills. Those who reported being able to read but who then failed the Core test are more likely to be women, more likely to work in low-skilled occupations and to be less educated, and less likely to work in the high-value-added sector. Respondents who reported being able to read but then failed the Core test also earn approximately 41 percent less than those who reported being able to read and who passed the Core test.

The analysis suggests that socioemotional skills are closely associated with educational attainment and labor market outcomes. Individuals with higher self-reported scores relative to the "Big Five" personality traits (stability, agreeableness, extraversion, conscientiousness, and openness) also had higher educational attainment. Similarly, individuals scoring higher on the Big Five personality traits, and who demonstrated lower levels of hostile bias, are less likely to be self-employed.

The association between socioemotional skills and labor market outcomes is reversed nevertheless when controlling for education. This finding confirms that education and socioemotional skills are (positively) correlated and also suggests that the development of socioemotional skills might be one of the channels through which education can contribute to better labor market outcomes.

Job-Specific Skills

Employment in the formal sector requires that a worker be capable of regularly learning new skills at work, more frequently involves the supervision of others' work, and more often requires workers to make presentations. Survey data demonstrate that work in the informal sector is less cognitively demanding, more repetitive, and more physically demanding. Self-employed workers reported greater autonomy at work and a greater incidence of repetitive tasks than did wage workers.

Further Education and Training

Approximately 32 percent of the population surveyed had actively engaged in activities to further develop their skills in the year prior to taking the survey. More than one in four respondents surveyed by STEP reported participating in an apprenticeship, and less than 7 percent had participated in a training course of 30 hours or more.

Apprenticeship-based training is more common among self-employed workers, whereas formal wageworkers are more likely to enroll in skills training courses. Approximately 26 percent of formal workers reported attending a work-related or personal skills training course in the year prior to the survey, compared to 3 and 6 percent of self-employed and informal wageworkers, respectively. On the other hand, approximately 38 percent of self-employed and 25 percent of wageworkers had participated in an apprenticeship in the 12 months prior to the survey.

Returns to Education and Skills

The analysis demonstrates that an additional year of education is associated with an increase of 6–10 percent in monthly earnings. After controlling for socioeconomic characteristics, primary education is associated with no distinguishable earnings premium for people with no formal education or incomplete primary education. On the contrary, the wage premium accruing to SHS and tertiary graduates is 29–79 percent (SHS) and 112–172 percent (tertiary) higher than the average wage of workers with no formal education or incomplete primary education. The premium for workers with JHS over workers with no formal education or incomplete primary education is much lower (35–59 percent).

Returns to education and skills vary by type of employment and with respect to the type of skill. An additional year of education increases the monthly earnings of informal wageworkers by 4–6 percent, compared to 7–10 percent for formal wageworkers. However, taking into account the individual's skills (cognitive, socioemotional, and job-related skills), the earnings premium associated with any additional year of education decreases by 2 percent.

The premium accruing to a female worker through an additional year of education is higher than that accruing to male workers (between 9 and 13 percent for female workers, compared to between 6 and 9 percent for men). For male workers, a pronounced premium associated with educational attainment becomes evident only at the tertiary level, whereas the data suggest that substantial payoffs accrue to female workers from JHS and above. Furthermore, with respect to skills, the pro-women gender gap is persistent at tertiary education (female workers with tertiary education make 164 percent more than those without compared to a 118 percent advantage for men). However, this apparent gender gap may be misleading because it does not take into account the fact that average labor market participation and educational attainments are lower for female workers.

Evidence of an Unrealized Potential in the Labor Force

An apparent mismatch between skills and their use at work could reflect unexploited human capital in the labor force. Within the overall population of employed adults, the evidence suggests that there is a subset of individuals who use their cognitive and computer skills at home but not at work. Moreover, there is a disproportionately large number of young workers who report being able to use a computer but who are not required to do so at work. The evidence suggests that the greatest residue of unexploited potential is located in low-skilled occupations and low-value-added sectors. Approximately 34 percent of self-employed workers report reading at home but never using this skill at work. On the other hand, only 6 percent of formal sector workers report this skills mismatch.

Abbreviations

ALL	Adult Literacy and Life Skills Survey
BECE	Basic Education Certificate Examination
ECE	early childhood education
ESP	Education Strategic Plan
GDP	gross domestic product
GES	Ghana Education Service
GLSS V	Ghana Living Standards Survey (Fifth Round)
GSS	Ghana Statistical Service
IALS	International Adult Literacy Survey
JHS	junior high school
MDG	Millennium Development Goals
MOE	Ministry of Education
NEET	not in education, employment, or training
OECD	Organisation for Economic Co-operation and Development
PIAAC	Programme for the International Assessment of Adult Competencies
PPP	purchasing power parity
SES	socioeconomic status
SHS	senior high school
SSA	Sub-Saharan Africa
STEP	Skills Toward Employment and Productivity
TVET	technical and vocational education and training
WAEC	West African Examinations Council
WASSCE	West African SHS Certificate Examinations

CHAPTER 1

Country Context

Economic, Social, and Demographic Trends

In the contemporary period, Ghana has achieved sustained economic growth and significant poverty reduction. The country has experienced 20 years of positive economic growth (in the range of 4–5 percent) and in 2011, with year-on-year growth of 14.4 percent, was one of only seven countries in the world, and the only country in Sub-Saharan Africa (SSA), to achieve double-digit economic growth (IMF 2012).[1]

Improved economic performance has been accompanied by significant poverty reduction, underpinned by rural development and increasing urbanization. In rural areas, small-scale agriculture has benefitted from improved agricultural productivity (notably in cocoa), rising incomes, and rising domestic demand. Concurrently, Ghana's rapidly growing urban centers have led to a significant expansion of the service sector and a growing labor force, inclusive of migrants from rural areas who have been absorbed into better-paying jobs in both the formal and the informal sectors of the economy.

Despite this impressive progress, deep inequity continues to characterize Ghanaian society and is reflected in significant disparities in access to economic, social, and political opportunities. This is especially evident when observing differences in access to opportunity between the populations of the poorer northern "Savannah regions" and the rest of the country.

The bulk of Ghana's poverty is concentrated in the three northernmost administrative regions of the country: the Upper East, Upper West, and Northern regions. These Savannah regions (home to approximately one quarter of the country's population) are the locus of an average poverty rate of 58 percent, compared to 19 percent in the seven administrative districts in the south of the country. Between 1995 and 2005, the number of people living in poverty fell by 2.5 million in the south. Over the same period the number of people living in poverty in the north increased by 0.9 million, although the poverty rate for this area declined because of an absolute increase in the population.[2]

Unemployment and underemployment in Ghana are structural in nature, which is not atypical in SSA. However, when demographic trends are taken into account, the structural nature of the challenges becomes more pronounced, with most economies on the continent being unable to generate sufficient rates of growth to create the jobs required to absorb the ever-increasing number of workers entering the labor force. The scale of the challenge is evident in the fact that formal private sector employment accounts for only a small proportion of available manpower.

To sustain and accelerate economic growth and poverty reduction, Ghana's education strategy is focused on building the skills profile of the youth demographic (IMF 2012). The urgent need to intervene in this regard is underlined by a national median age of approximately 20 years (UNDP 2011). Although the country's youth demonstrate the highest levels of educational attainment relative to older generational cohorts, younger workers also depend most on salaried employment because of the inability of rural agriculture to sustain workers and their families and the contingent movement of migrants from the countryside to Ghana's urban centers.

From a developmental perspective, the most important demographic trend is the pace and character of migration from the northern regions of the country to the south (figure 1.1). Migrants to cities in search of jobs, education, skills, and business opportunities disproportionately include large family groups with children of school-going age and unemployed youth with poor educational attainment.

Figure 1.1 Net Migration Rate, by Region

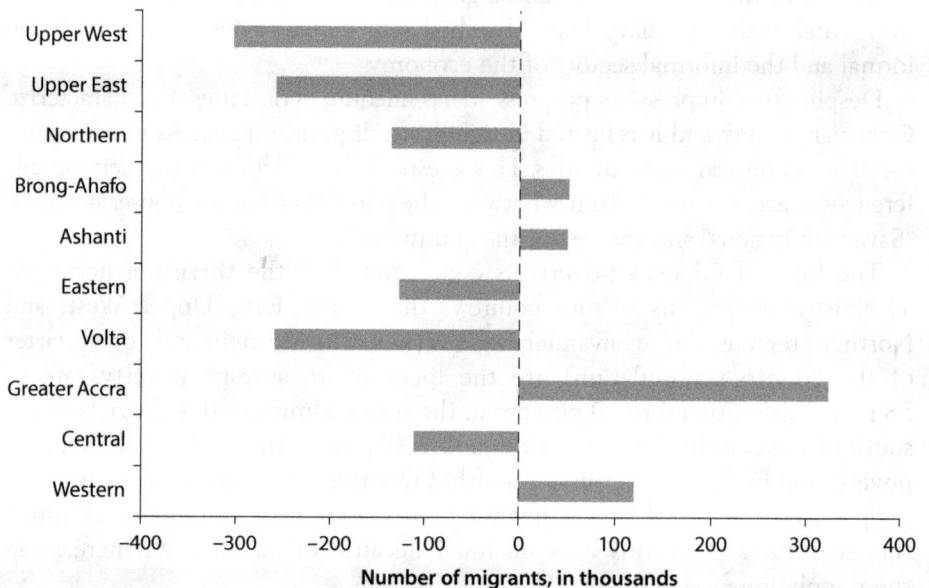

Source: GSS 2013.

Education and Skills

Ghana has made significant progress in expanding access to basic education over the course of the past 15 years. Having achieved near universal access to primary education, the country now faces two new urgent challenges: (i) improving the quality of basic education to enhance learning outcomes and (ii) expanding access beyond basic levels of education.

The majority of students receiving upper secondary education in Ghana are enrolled in three-year senior high schools (SHS), following the completion of 11 years of basic education (comprising preprimary school, primary school, and junior high school [JHS]) (see box 1.1 for more information on Ghana's education system). The government intends to universalize access to upper secondary education by enabling students who are unable to afford fees to attend secondary school at no charge.

Informal apprenticeships currently equip many more workers with skills than do formal public technical and vocational education and training (TVET) programs.[3] Fewer than 10 percent of workers with technical and vocational skills acquired their skills through public TVET institutions. Moreover, there are approximately one and a half times as many trainees enrolled in private TVET institutions as in public institutions, and the number of students engaged in informal apprenticeships is 10 times that of students enrolled in the formal TVET sector.

Box 1.1 The Ghanaian Education System

In theory, the age range for children and young people engaged in the Ghanaian education system spans from 3 to 21 years. The educational system in Ghana consists of the following cycles or levels of education:

- Preschool, equivalent to U.S. kindergarten (ages 4–5)
- Primary school (ages 6–11)
- Junior high school (JHS), equivalent to U.S. middle school (ages 12–14)
- Senior high school (SHS), equivalent to U.S. high school (ages 15–17)
- Tertiary education/institution, equivalent to U.S. college/university (ages 18–21)

A full cycle of basic education is optimally provided over the course of 11 years, comprising two years of kindergarten, six years of primary school, and three years of JHS. Ghanaian children enter class one (first grade) during the calendar year in which they reach their sixth birthdays. During the first three years, the medium of instruction is either English or a combination of English and local languages.

JHS education comprises forms 1 through 3 (U.S. grades seven through nine). Admission to JHS is open to any student who has completed primary class six. There is no entrance exam, and JHS education is considered integral to the country's nine-year cycle of basic education, to which all Ghanaian children are entitled. At the end of JHS form 3 (ninth grade), students sit

box continues next page

Box 1.1 The Ghanaian Education System *(continued)*

for the Basic Education Certificate Examination (BECE) in nine or ten subjects. The BECE is administered and graded by the West African Examinations Council (WAEC).

Admission to SHS is based exclusively on a student's BECE results. After JHS, students may choose to go into different streams within the SHS system or to pursue further skills acquisition through an apprenticeship scheme with some support from the government. All SHS courses prepare students for university education, but most TVET students are likely to join the labor market once they graduate.

SHS consists of forms 4 through 6 (equivalent to U.S. grades 10 through 12). The core SHS curriculum comprises six subjects—English, science, mathematics, social studies, physical education, and religious and moral education—which are studied throughout the three-year SHS cycle. Students undergo examinations only in the first four of these subjects. To complete a full course of SHS education, each student must choose—in addition to the core curriculum—one program (general arts, general science, agriculture, economics, business, or technical and vocational) and three or four elective subjects from within that chosen program.

At the end of the three-year SHS cycle, all students are required to sit the West African Senior School Certificate Examinations (WASSCE). Usually, the student's overall score is determined by aggregating the student's grades in his or her elective subjects and then adding this score to the aggregate score of the student's best "core" subjects, with scores in English and mathematics considered first. The Ministry of Education considers any SHS graduate with an aggregate score of 24 (a D average) or better to be a successful school-leaver, equivalent to a graduate of a U.S. high school. Entrance to universities is by examination following the completion of SHS. Students obtaining aggregate scores of 36 or above (six subjects) on the WASSCE can enter university. After completing SHS, students also have the option to pursue further education through a polytechnic.

Persistent Challenges in Education

Despite Ghana's steady economic growth and improved access to basic education, many challenges persistent in the education sector. Among other things, the primary challenges concern

- The poor quality of learning outcomes, in both basic and post-basic education;
- Inequity of access, especially in secondary education; and
- The limited capacity of the education system to create relevant skills aligned with increasing competitiveness and productivity within the economy.

The National Education Assessment carried out biannually since 2005 shows a persistent trend: approximately two-thirds of students who complete primary school do so without demonstrating proficiency in core subject areas. In terms of the quality of SHS programs, the annual WASSCE demonstrates a large disparity in further educational attainment between students attending the 100 highest-performing schools and the rest of the sector. The highest-performing 10 percent of high schools account for 90 percent of students entering university. Approximately 65–70 percent of SHS graduates do not continue education at the tertiary level. Students exiting the SHS cycle with low WASSCE scores are unable to access tertiary education, with many of these graduates going on to enroll in some form of training or apprenticeship program.

There are significant regional, gender-based, and income-based disparities in access to, and the relevance of, post-basic education. The 2010 Population and Housing Census and the 2013 Ghana Living Standards Survey (GLSS) demonstrate very low pass rates for the BECE in the Upper East (11 percent), Volta (17 percent), and Northern and Upper West (both 22 percent) administrative regions, compared to high pass rates in the Greater Accra (90 percent), Western (88 percent), Brong-Ahafo (86 percent), and Ashanti (81.5 percent) regions (GSS 2013, 2014).

Survey data also demonstrate that the limited capacity of Ghana's education and training systems inhibits their ability to produce human capital of sufficient quality to meet the needs of the labor market and to drive a more competitive and diversified economy. Many JHS and SHS graduates are unable to find jobs in the formal sector, or are unable to pursue further education and training because of poor performance in exit examinations, a lack of information, and/or the suboptimal supply of training providers. Consequently, many JHS and SHS graduates are limited to self-employment or finding employment in the informal sector. According to data from the most recent National Census (2010), approximately two-thirds of the adult population is self-employed, and the proportion of employment accounted for by the formal private sector has declined since 2000 (GSS 2013). Formal (public or private) employment accounts for only 17 percent of total employment and is disproportionately concentrated in urban areas, although a relatively large minority of public employees—primarily teachers—are present in rural areas.

Skills development in Ghana encompasses the inculcation of foundational, or basic, skills (literacy, numeracy); transferable and soft skills; and technical and vocational skills. These skills are acquired over the course of a lifetime through formal education, training, and higher education; through on-the-job and professional training; and through the family, community, and media. The majority of young Ghanaians acquire technical and vocational skills through informal on-the-job apprenticeships (Darvas and Palmer 2014). Although the scale and scope of Ghana's TVET systems are difficult to measure, clear opportunities exist for further skills development at the intersection of education, youth, and the needs of the labor market (Darvas and Palmer 2014).

Enterprise surveys demonstrate mixed perceptions on the part of firms with respect to the quality of workers' skills and the extent to which poor skills act as a constraint to improved economic performance (Darvas and Palmer 2014). However, in light of the demonstrable inadequacy of the supply of relevant and quality skills to the economy, a more deliberate analysis of enterprise survey data is required to more effectively understand the underlying causes of the apparent low demand for skills. If strategies for the further development of Ghana's human capital and economic development are to be successful, it is imperative that skills development strategies are premised on a thorough understanding of the existing supply of and demand for skills, as well as of the use of skills in the economy, in order to more effectively match the supply of skills to demand (Campbell 2012; Darvas and Palmer 2014).

Despite the central role skills play in shaping employment outcomes, there is very little information about the distribution of different types of skills in the Ghanaian labor force or of their contribution to labor market outcomes. Ultimately, the paucity of relevant information undermines the design of more effective skills development policies and programs (World Bank 2014). The Skills Toward Employment and Productivity (STEP) project—through its use of a framework enabling the analysis of Ghana's labor market conditions based on internationally comparable skills data—will help to address this knowledge gap and assist in the development of policies aligned to the needs of the economy.

Notes

1. Real gross domestic product (GDP) growth was 8 percent in 2010, 4 percent in 2009, 8.4 percent in 2008, 6.5 percent in 2007, 6.1 percent in 2006, 6 percent in 2005, 5.3 percent in 2004, 5.1 percent in 2003, and 4.5 percent between 1993 and 2002 (IMF 2012b, 196; IMF 2011, 185).

2. Calculations based on the Ghana Living Standards Surveys GLSS3, GLSS4, GLSS5 available at http://documents.worldbank.org/curated/en/2011/03/14238095/tackling -poverty-northern-ghana.

3. This report uses the terms "technical and vocational education and training (TVET)" and "technical and vocational skills development" interchangeably.

References

Campbell, M. 2012. "Skills for Prosperity? A Review of OECD and Partner Country Skill Strategies." LLAKES Research Paper 39, University of London, United Kingdom.

Darvas, P., and R. Palmer. 2014. *Demand and Supply of Skills in Ghana: How Can Training Programs Improve Employment?* Washington, DC: World Bank.

GSS (Ghana Statistical Service). 2013. *2010 Population & Housing Census: National Analytical Report.* Accra: GSS.

———. 2014. *Ghana Living Standards Survey Round 6 (GLSS 6): Main Report.* Accra: Ghana.

IMF (International Monetary Fund). 2012. "Ghana: Poverty Reduction Strategy Paper." IMF Country Report 12/203, IMF, Washington, DC.

UNDP (United Nations Development Programme). 2011. *Human Development Report 2011. Sustainability and Equity: A Better Future for All.* New York: UNDP.

World Bank. 2014. "STEP Skills Measurement Program." World Bank, Washington, DC. http://microdata.worldbank.org/index.php/catalog/step/about.

CHAPTER 2

Conceptual Framework: Why Is It Important to Focus on Skills?

Introduction

It is generally recognized that there is a strong positive correlation between the educational and skills profile of the workforce and a country's per capita gross domestic product (GDP)—which is intended here as a proxy of productivity. Thus, education and training are the foundations for a skilled workforce and would benefit not only individuals but also the economy as a whole.

If the education and the training system are of low quality, however, workers will be ill-prepared for the labor market. This could lead to several types of mismatches. For example, the education level of an individual may not match his or her skills, or individuals may overrate their own skills, thus leading to a mismatch between self-reported skills and tested skills. In another type of mismatch, workers may lack the skills required for available jobs or lack access to high-quality training programs that would increase their skill level and enable them to apply for higher-productivity jobs. As a result, many employees are either under- or overqualified for their occupations. These mismatches lead to a loss of human capital and show that having post-basic or higher education does not automatically translate into getting a good job. In all of these cases of mismatch, investments in education may not pay off.

Education policy makers and other education stakeholders in Ghana are paying more attention to learning outcomes by testing all students from early grades through basic and post-basic education. Various research and diagnostic work has highlighted the fact that the reading and mathematics proficiency of Ghana's students continues to be below acceptable levels. This means that most of them are unable to reach important milestones in literacy, to access post-basic education, or to develop a foundation for lifelong learning. As a result, their employment prospects are limited. Policy makers have identified the low quality of inputs and the limited relevance of science and technology education as being among the main causes of these limited prospects. Policy makers also highlight Ghana's large disparities in learning outcomes and related inequalities in the delivery of education services.[1]

Furthermore, policy makers and researchers have also homed in on several persistent challenges on the demand side. Not only do services and educational performance vary greatly by students' social and economic status and by geography, but demand for skills, job opportunities, productivity, and expectations also vary widely and are affected by similar disparities.

Despite the central role played by skills in improving employment outcomes and increasing productivity and growth in Ghana, information about the supply and demand of skills is sparse. Assessments of supply have largely focused on the outputs of mostly school and tertiary-level education and training institutions, whereas assessments of demand rely only on the responses to a few questions in enterprise surveys and rate-of-return analyses based on the last three Ghana Living Standard Surveys (GLSS) carried out in 1995, 1999, and 2005.[2] Recently, more systemic analyses, surveys, and impact evaluations have been initiated, and we hope their results will inform future policy making.

The lack of data and information on the skills endowment has made it difficult to design skills development policies and programs in Ghana, as in many other Sub-Saharan African (SSA) countries. Precise measurement of the prevalence of different types of skills among the population is needed to inform the design of public policies to reduce skill gaps in specific sectors, to increase the employability of the population, to improve training, and to enhance productivity.

The Skills Toward Employment and Productivity (STEP) framework considers education as the instrument that enables individuals to learn and acquire skills, and subsequently access employment (box 2.1). Jobs are the foundation of economic development, improved standards of living, improved productivity,

---

Box 2.1 Skills Toward Employment and Productivity (STEP)

The STEP framework (see figure B2.1.1) is informed by the following five interlinked steps:

- *Step 1. Getting children off to the right start*—by developing the technical, cognitive, and behavioral skills conducive to high productivity and flexibility in the work environment through early child development (ECD), emphasizing nutrition, stimulation, and basic cognitive skills. Research shows that the handicaps built early in life are difficult if not impossible to remedy later in life and that effective ECD programs can have a very high payoff.
- *Step 2. Ensuring that all students learn*—by building stronger systems with clear learning standards, good teachers, adequate resources, and a proper regulatory environment. Lessons from research and ground experience indicate that key decisions about education systems involve how much autonomy to allow and to whom, accountability from whom and for what, and how to assess performance and results.

box continues next page

Box 2.1 Skills Toward Employment and Productivity (STEP) *(continued)*

Figure B2.1.1 The Skills Toward Employment and Productivity (STEP) Framework

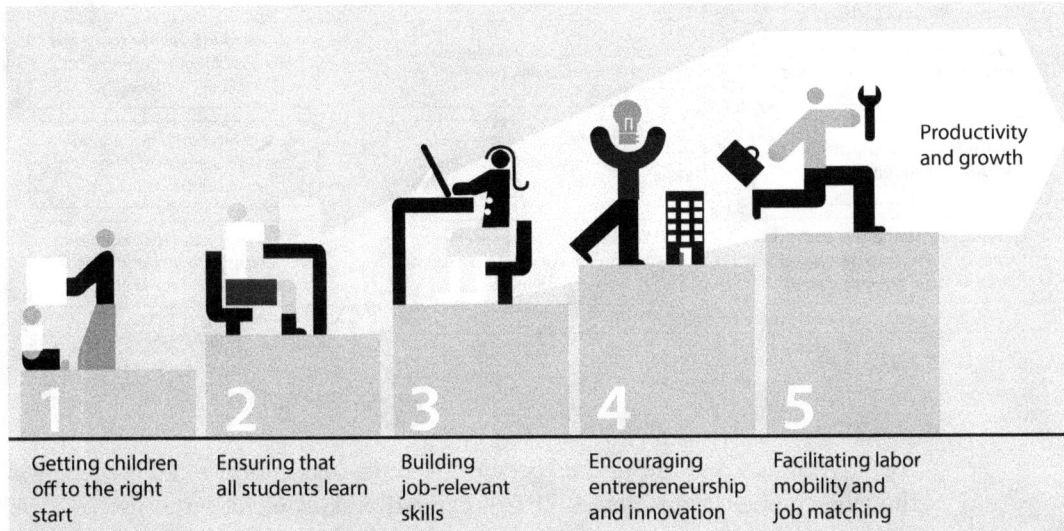

Productivity and growth

1	2	3	4	5
Getting children off to the right start	Ensuring that all students learn	Building job-relevant skills	Encouraging entrepreneurship and innovation	Facilitating labor mobility and job matching

Source: Banerji et al. 2010.

- **Step 3. Building job-relevant skills that employers demand**—by developing the right incentive framework for both pre-employment and on-the-job training programs and institutions (including higher education). There is accumulating experience showing how public and private efforts can be combined to achieve more relevant and responsive training systems.
- **Step 4. Encouraging entrepreneurship and innovation**—by creating an environment that encourages investments in knowledge and creativity.
- **Step 5. Matching the supply of skills with the demand**—by moving toward more flexible, efficient, and secure labor markets. Avoiding rigid job protection regulations while strengthening income protection systems, complemented by efforts to provide information and intermediation services to workers and firms, is the final complementary step transforming skills into actual employment and productivity.

Source: Banerji et al. 2010.

and social cohesion. As a consequence, equipping people with the right mix of skills is the means for achieving these objectives.

Which Skills Are Relevant?

A worker's skill set comprises different categories of skills, including cognitive skills, social and behavioral skills, and technical skills (see figure 2.1). These categories of skills relate to job skills relevant to specific occupations as well as to

Figure 2.1 Skills Classification

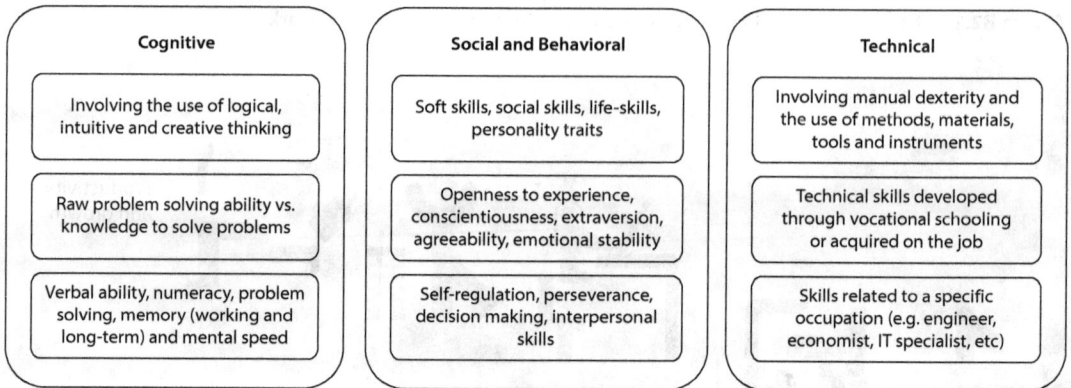

Cognitive	Social and Behavioral	Technical
Involving the use of logical, intuitive and creative thinking	Soft skills, social skills, life-skills, personality traits	Involving manual dexterity and the use of methods, materials, tools and instruments
Raw problem solving ability vs. knowledge to solve problems	Openness to experience, conscientiousness, extraversion, agreeability, emotional stability	Technical skills developed through vocational schooling or acquired on the job
Verbal ability, numeracy, problem solving, memory (working and long-term) and mental speed	Self-regulation, perseverance, decision making, interpersonal skills	Skills related to a specific occupation (e.g. engineer, economist, IT specialist, etc)

Source: Pierre et al. 2014.

cognitive ability and the various personality traits that inform relative success in the labor market (Pierre et al. 2014). Cognitive skills include the use of logic, intuition, and critical thinking, as well as problem-solving skills deployed using acquired knowledge. They also include literacy, numeracy, and the ability to understand complex ideas, to apply lessons accrued through experience, and to analyze problems using logical thought processes. Social and behavioral skills relate to personality traits that are linked to labor market success, such as an individual's relative openness to new experiences, conscientiousness, extraversion, agreeability, and emotional stability. Technical skills range from manual dexterity in the use of complex tools and instruments to occupation-specific knowledge and skills for use in professional and technical occupations such as engineering or medicine.

How Are Cognitive, Behavioral, and Technical Skills Formed?

The process of skills formation should be considered as a continuum spanning an individual's life, with critical stages for the development of both cognitive and socioemotional skills. Four features of skills formation are particularly relevant to the development of a skills strategy:

1. Foundational cognitive and behavioral skills are formed early in an individual's life and serve as a platform upon which other skills are developed. Children who fall behind early face significant disadvantages in catching up with their peers. Non-cognitive skills appear to be more malleable throughout life, but early interventions appear to have significant positive effects for their further development in the longer term.

2. Aggregate skills formation and development benefit from previous investments in skills development and are cumulative over an individual's life. For example, a child who has learned to read fluently by second grade will be able

to absorb more in third grade than a child of equivalent age who cannot read at the commencement of grade three. This implies that early investments in skills development are likely to have a greater longer-term impact on aggregate skills formation because it is easier and less costly to develop these skills when children are young and most receptive to learning.

3. Social and behavioral skills are particularly valuable early in a child's life because they support, and benefit from, the development of cognitive skills. For example, children who are open to new experiences are more likely to be imaginative and creative and to apply themselves at school.

4. The acquisition of technical and job-specific skills is facilitated by strong cognitive and behavioral skills acquired earlier in the education system. These skills are often acquired last, through technical and vocational education and training (TVET), higher education, and on-the-job learning. The skills learned in formal education help workers to continuously update their technical skills during their working lives.

Understanding the Focus on Adults and Urban Areas

Early investments are smart and cost-effective and prepare future generations of workers for the labor market. However, skills development strategies should also focus on maximizing the potential of current generations of workers.

In recent decades Ghana has experienced large-scale migration from more rural and comparatively impoverished areas to Ghana's more prosperous and urban areas. Migrants are disproportionately young adults who are motivated by educational opportunities and jobs in cities. Urbanization represents both a challenge and an opportunity for development because it has been associated with rising per capita income in Europe, Latin America, and, more recently, Asia. However, Africa has been an exception in this regard, because of the fact that in many African countries, including Ghana, industrialization has generally not accompanied urbanization.

The majority of migrants to Ghana's urban areas find employment in the comparatively poorly productive informal sector. However, even informal employment is, in many instances, much more than migrants could aspire to in their home regions. Equipping migrants with skills aligned with the needs of the urban labor market would give them a further opportunity for self-improvement.

Accurately measuring the skills of the adult population is critical for informing policies aimed at increasing the productivity of those already in the labor force. Understanding the demographic structure and the socioeconomic status of the adult population in Ghana, as well as the associations between levels of education and an individual's skills endowment, will help to inform the development of effective nonformal education and skills development programs aligned with the specific contextual characteristics of Ghanaian society and the labor force. It is for this reason that the STEP Skills Measurement Survey (discussed in the next chapter) is premised on gathering information about the skills endowment of the adult urban population.

Notes

1. References on equity, demand and supply work, and other analyses include Balwanz and Darvas (2014) and Darvas and Palmer (2014).
2. The GLSS 6 survey results have just been released, and a later version of this report will also analyze these results (GSS 2014).

References

Balwanz, David, and Peter Darvas. 2014. *Basic Education beyond the Millenium Development Goals in Ghana: How Equity in Service Delivery Affects Educational and Learning Outcomes*. Washington, DC: World Bank.

Banerji, Arup, Wendy Cunningham, Ariel Fiszbein, Elizabeth King, Harry Patrinos, David Robalino, and Jee-Peng Tan. 2010. *Stepping Up Skills for More Jobs and Higher Productivity*. Washington, DC: World Bank.

Darvas, Peter, and Robert Palmer. 2014. *Demand and Supply of Skills in Ghana: How Can Training Programs Improve Employment?* Washington, DC: World Bank.

GSS (Ghana Statistical Service). 2014. *Ghana Living Standards Survey Round 6 (GLSS 6): Main Report*. Accra: Ghana.

Pierre, Gaëlle, Maria Laura Sanchez Puerta, Alexandria Valerio, and Tania Rajadel. 2014. *STEP Skills Measurement Surveys: Innovative Tools for Assessing Skills*. Social Protection and Labor Discussion Paper 1421. Washington, DC: World Bank.

CHAPTER 3

Skills Toward Employment and Productivity Data

Introduction

The Skills Toward Employment and Productivity (STEP) survey provides a unique opportunity to collect information on the use of skills and skills proficiency in Ghana. The objective of the study is to yield a clearer understanding of the complex relationship between skills, employment, and productivity. This chapter discusses the characteristics of the sample used in the Ghana STEP survey, the data arising from the survey, and the definitions of skill and other variables used in this analysis.

Data and Sample Characteristics

This household survey was carried out in Ghana as part of the first wave of surveys under the STEP Skills Measurement Program between September 2011 and December 2013. The Ghanaian sample was gathered through a two-stage random sampling of households and individuals. It consists of 2,987 individuals between 15 and 64 years of age. Table A.1 in appendix A provides a complete description of the sample in terms of demographic characteristics, education, language, labor and employment status, economic sector and occupation, and geographic region.

It is important to note that the weighted sample represents only the urban population. Therefore, the findings of this report cannot be extended to the national level because the urban population is likely to differ from the rural population along many dimensions. For example, workers in the urban areas are likely to have higher education levels and to be relatively more concentrated in the services sector than workers in the rural areas.

Along with the standard information captured at the household level, the STEP survey collects extensive information on the skills level, education, and work history of one individual between ages 15 and 64 randomly selected from

Figure 3.1 The STEP Household Survey Instrument

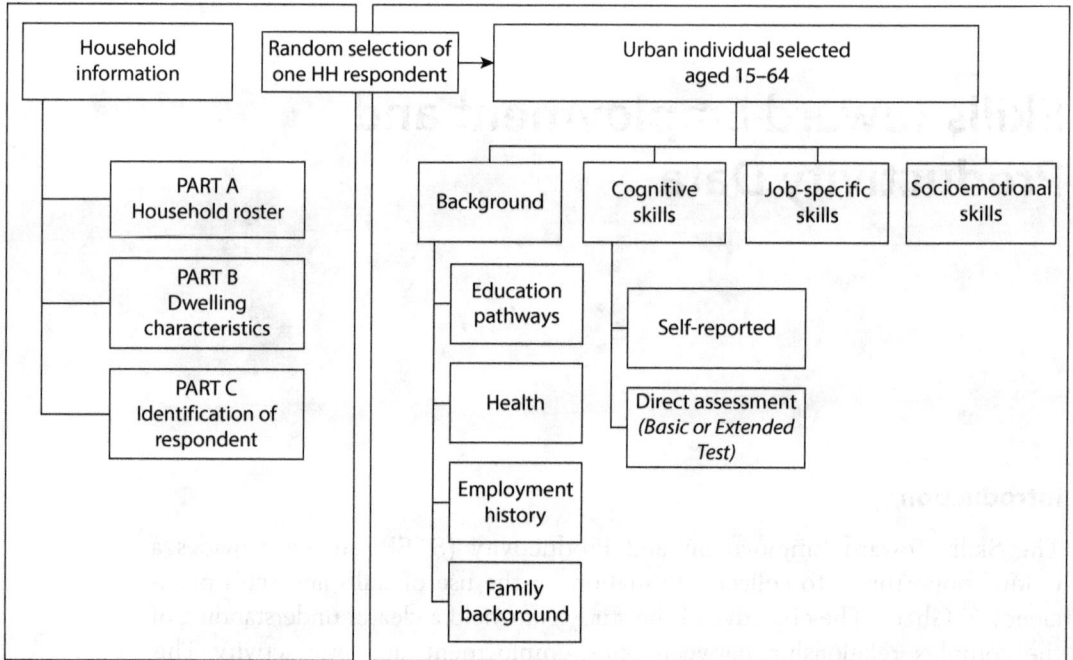

Source: Banerji et al. 2010.
Note: HH = household; STEP = Skills Toward Employment and Productivity.

each sampled household (figure 3.1). The survey includes three innovative modules on skills: (i) a specially designed assessment of reading literacy and competence to access, identify, integrate, interpret, and evaluate information, scored on the same scale as the test in the Program for the International Assessment of Adult Competencies (PIAAC) of the Organisation for Economic Co-operation and Development (OECD); (ii) a battery of questions capturing self-reported information on personality traits and behaviors; and (iii) a series of questions on job-specific skills that the respondent possesses or uses in his or her jobs. The skills of the entire sampled population are captured, irrespective of their labor force status (employed, unemployed, or inactive) or sector of employment.

Types of Skills Measured

The STEP survey evaluates three categories of skill: (i) cognitive (self-reported and direct assessment); (ii) socioemotional skills; and (iii) job-specific skills. Table 3.1 and appendix B summarize the dimensions of skills captured in each category, and the corresponding survey questions used to create the relevant variables for analysis.

Table 3.1 Definitions of Skill Types

Skills type	Definition	Measure	Skills
Cognitive	The "ability to understand complex ideas, to adapt effectively to the environment, to learn from experience, to engage in various forms of reasoning, [and] to overcome obstacles by taking thought"[a]	Indirect assessment (self-reported) of individual's use of foundation skills at work and in daily life	Reading Writing Numeracy
		Direct assessment of reading literacy based on the International Adult Literacy Survey (IALS) using the same scale as the Programme for the International Assessment of Adult Competencies (PIAAC)	Reading proficiency
Socioemotional skills	Related to traits covering multiple domains (social, emotional, personality, behaviors, attitudes, and so on)	Personality traits	Openness Conscientiousness Extraversion Agreeableness Emotional stability Persistence
		Behavior	Decision making Hostility bias
		Risk and time preferences	Risk-taking preferences Time preferences
Job-specific skills	Task related and build on a combination of cognitive and noncognitive skills	Qualifications required for the job and job learning times	Qualification requirement for current job Learning times
		Indirect assessment of skills used at job	Autonomy and repetitiveness Computer use Contact with clients Solving and learning Supervision Physical tasks

Note: For further details, see appendix B and Pierre et al. 2014.
a. Neisser et al. 1996.

Cognitive Skills

The STEP survey measures cognitive skills in two ways: First, respondents are asked to report whether and with what intensity they use their reading, writing, and numeracy skills in daily life and at work (if they work). These measures are likely to capture a combination of an individual's actual ability to conduct tasks involving these skills and their motivation or opportunity to do so. Second, the survey makes use of an objective literacy assessment to directly measure cognitive skills. The self-reported questions capturing the use of reading and writing skills may substantively differ from an individual's actual ability to read or write.

The STEP literacy test has been aligned with a series of large-scale international surveys, such as the International Adult Literacy Survey (IALS), the Adult Literacy and Life Skills Survey (ALL), and the PIAAC. The assessment consists of three parts: Reading Components, the Core Literacy Test, and the Literacy Exercise

Booklets, as shown in figure 3.2. The Reading Components focus on foundational reading skills, including a respondent's ability to assess word meaning, process sentences, and comprehend passages. The Core Literacy Test consists of eight literacy questions, which function as a screen to sort the least literate respondents from those with the highest literacy skills. Only respondents who were capable of answering two or more questions of the Core Literacy Test correctly are asked to complete the Literacy Exercise Booklets. The Booklets are broken down into four parts with a total of 18 questions, which allow for a more granular evaluation of reading skills among the relatively more literate respondents. All tests are conducted in English (see box 6.1 for further discussion).

Cumulatively, the data gathered by the STEP survey consist of: (i) the Reading Components score(s),[1] (ii) pass/fail information for the Core Literacy Test, and (iii) the score obtained in the Exercise Booklets grouped into five levels of competency (table 3.2), inclusive of descriptions of basic literacy skills from 1, the lowest level, to 5, the most advanced level.

Socioemotional Skills

Socioemotional skills refer to skills and traits that are not directly related to intelligence, such as social, emotional, personality, behavioral, and attitudinal skills. The measures used to capture behavioral attributes are less established

Figure 3.2 Workflow for the STEP Skills Measurement Survey

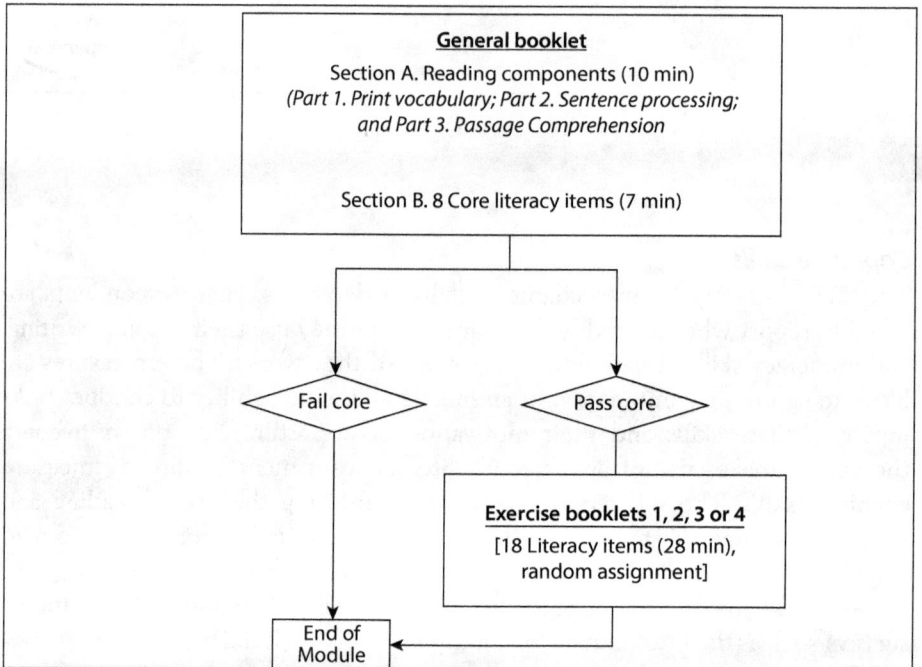

Source: Pierre et al. 2014.

Table 3.2 Levels of Reading Proficiency

Literacy Below Level 1 (0–175)

The tasks at this level require the respondent to read brief texts on familiar topics in order to locate a single piece of specific information. Only a basic knowledge of vocabulary is required to complete these tasks, and the reader is not required to understand the structure of sentences or paragraphs or make use of other text features. There is seldom any competing information in the text, and the requested information is identical in form to information in the question or directive. Although the texts can be continuous, the information can be located as if the text were noncontinuous. Tasks below level 1 do not make use of any features specific to digital texts.

Literacy Level 1 (176–225)

Respondents are required to read relatively short digital or continuous print, noncontinuous print, or mixed texts to locate a single piece of information that is identical to, or synonymous with, the information given in the question or directive. Some tasks may require the respondent to enter personal information into a document, in the case of some noncontinuous texts. Little, if any, competing information is present. Some tasks may require simple processing of more than one piece of information. Tasks at level 1 require knowledge and skill in recognizing basic vocabulary, evaluating the meaning of sentences, and reading paragraph text.

Literacy Level 2 (226–275)

At this level the relative complexity of the text increases. Texts may be digital or printed, and may comprise continuous, noncontinuous, or mixed types of text. Competing pieces of information may be present. The completion of level 2 tasks requires respondents to match the text to information and may require the ability to paraphrase or make low-level inferences. Tasks require the respondent to

- Cycle through or integrate two or more pieces of information against given criteria;
- Compare, contrast, and/or reason about information requested in the question; or
- Navigate within digital texts to access and identify information from various parts of a document.

Literacy Level 3 (276–325)

Texts at this level are comparatively dense and lengthy, and include continuous, noncontinuous, mixed, and/or multiple pages. Respondents must demonstrate an understanding of textual and rhetorical structures to successfully complete tasks, especially in the navigation of complex digital texts. Tasks require the respondent to identify, interpret, or evaluate one or more pieces of information, and often require varying levels of inference. Many tasks require the respondent to construct meaning across larger chunks of text, or perform multistep operations in order to identify and formulate responses. Tasks may also require that the respondent disregard irrelevant or inappropriate text to answer the question accurately. Competing information is present, but it is not more prominent than correct information.

Literacy Level 4 (326–375)

Tasks at this level require respondents to perform multiple-step operations to integrate, interpret, and/or synthesize information from complex or lengthy continuous, noncontinuous, mixed, or multiple-page texts. Complex inferences and the application of background knowledge may be needed to perform successfully. Many tasks require the identification and understanding of one or more specific, noncentral ideas in the text to interpret or evaluate subtle evidentiary claims or persuasive discursive relationships. Conditional information is frequently present in tasks at this level and must be taken into consideration by the respondent. Competing information is present and may be as prominent as correct information.

Literacy Level 5 (376–500)

At this level, tasks may require the respondent to search for and integrate information across multiple, dense texts; construct syntheses of similar and contrasting ideas or points of view; and/or evaluate evidence-based arguments. Application and evaluation of logical and conceptual models of thinking may be required to accomplish tasks. Evaluating the reliability of evidentiary sources and selecting key information is frequently a requirement to successfully complete tasks. Level 5 tasks require respondents to be aware of subtle, rhetorical cues, to make high-level inferences, and/or to use specialized background knowledge.

Source: Adapted from Valerio et al. 2014.
Note: Scores are out of a possible 500.

than those used to measure cognitive skills, in part because of the absence of a consensus on the structure and evolution of personality. STEP builds on the "Big Five" personality traits (openness, conscientiousness, extraversion, agree-ableness, and stability), a widely accepted taxonomy for capturing personality traits. This taxonomy has been found to be replicable across cultures and can be used to capture the evolution of a personality over an individual's lifetime (John and Srivastava 1999). Measures of grit and hostility bias were also included. The survey of socioemotional skills includes a module aimed at assessing respondents' time and risk preferences.

Job-Specific Skills

Job-specific skills are task related and build on a combination of cognitive and noncognitive skills. The STEP survey asks individuals about specific tasks they perform and the skills that they use in their current job. Questions on job-specific skills are intended to capture an individual's technical skills, reflecting his or her acquired knowledge in particular areas. Because technical skills are often specific to a certain discipline, they are difficult to capture using a survey instrument aimed at the general population. As a consequence, the STEP survey focuses on a range of skills relevant to performance in multiple jobs.

Methodology

This report uses a combination of descriptive statistics, simple probability models (to estimate what determines the probability of acquiring education and skills and of finding employment), and the Mincer equation (to estimate the returns to education and skills). The descriptive analysis includes simple distributions of the use and intensity of use of skills across genders, age cohorts, different socio-economic statuses, and regions. The estimation is done using the sample weights, and the results are representative for the urban population of Ghana. The returns to education are estimated using a Mincerian wage regression. The total log monthly earnings of the main and second occupation are estimated as a function of education and a number of control variables (as detailed in appendix C). The sample is restricted to those individuals with monthly earnings different from zero, and models are estimated using ordinary least squares (OLS) with robust standard errors. For all skills, dummies of nonresponse (missing variables) have been included in the regression.

These models describe associations between earnings and education or skills but do not claim any causal relation. If a person with a college degree earns more than a person with lower education it does not necessarily mean that the college education is the cause of the difference in pay. Rather, the person who went to college might have some characteristics that make him or her more productive in the labor market, thus resulting in higher earnings. It is possible, for example, that high-ability people self-select themselves into college. Thus, higher productivity might be the result of this selection rather than the consequence of the education level achieved. Therefore, it is uncertain whether the education premium reflects the returns to education or a higher market value of unobserved skills. In an attempt to alleviate this selection problem, the regression model included a broad set of controls. Nevertheless, there are many other observable and unobservable factors that might affect both the probability of being employed and of working in specific sectors and occupations and the returns to education.

Note

1. The scores for Reading Components will depend on whether there are sufficient data to report three subscales or just a single reading components score.

References

Banerji, Arup, Wendy Cunningham, Ariel Fiszbein, Elizabeth King, Harry Patrinos, David Robalino, and Jee-Peng Tan. 2010. *Stepping Up Skills for More Jobs and Higher Productivity*. Washington, DC: World Bank.

Carroll, J. B. 1993. *Human Cognitive Abilities: A Survey of Factor-Analytic Studies*. New York: Cambridge University Press.

Cattell, R. B.1971. *Abilities: Their Structure, Growth, and Action*. Boston, MA: Houghton, Mifflin.

Horn, J. L., and R. B. Cattell. 1967. "Age Differences in Fluid and Crystallized Intelligence." *Acta Psychologica* 26: 107–29.

John, O. P., and S. Srivastava. 1999. "The Big Five Trait Taxonomy: History, Measurement and Theoretical Perspectives." In *Handbook of Personality: Theory and Research*, edited by L. A. Pervin and O. P. John. New York: Guilford Press.

Neisser, U., G. Boodoo, T. J. Bouchard, Jr., A. W. Boykin, N. Brody, S. J. Ceci, D. F. Halpern, J. C. Lochlin, R. Perloff, R. J. Sternberg, and S. Urbina. 1996. "Intelligence: Knowns and Unknowns." *American Psychologist* 51 (2): 77–101.

Pierre, Gaëlle, Maria Laura Sanchez Puerta, Alexandria Valerio, and Tania Rajadel. 2014. *STEP Skills Measurement Surveys: Innovative Tools for Assessing Skills*. Social Protection and Labor Discussion Paper 1421. Washington, DC: World Bank.

Valerio, Alexandria, Maria Laura Sanchez Puerta, Gaelle Pierre, Tania Rajadel, and Sebastian Monroy Taborda. 2014. *STEP Skills Measurement Program: Snapshot 2014*. Washington, DC: World Bank.

CHAPTER 4

Education Issues in Ghana

Foundational Skills: Early Childhood Education

Early childhood is a critical stage for long-lasting skills development. Investment in children between the time of birth and the beginning of primary education is a major determinant of their future school performance and labor market success. Various studies find a strong association between cognitive and socioemotional skills gained at a young age and school achievement, graduation rates, and employment outcomes.

Provision of early childhood education (ECE) in Ghana has dramatically increased since 2000. Only 30 percent of Ghanaians between the ages of 45 and 64 attended an ECE program (kindergarten, crèche, day care, and/or nursery school) against 87 percent of the youngest generation ages 15–19 years old. Interestingly, there are no significant differences in ECE participation between males and females.

Participation in preschool is positively correlated with household socioeconomic status. Seventy-seven percent of adults living in households in the upper socioeconomic brackets participated in an ECE program as compared to 49 percent of individuals from the poorest households (figure 4.1). This is consistent across all age cohorts.

Adults who received ECE are more likely to read and write regularly. Adults who did not attend preschool programs report lower levels of reading and writing regularly (47 and 45 percent, respectively) compared with 82 and 77 percent of those who benefitted from ECE (figure 4.2). Almost all of the population reported using their numeracy skills on a daily basis. Figure 4.3 demonstrates that those who participated in ECE also use their reading, writing, and numeracy with more intensity. Only 27 percent of the adult population of Ghana uses a computer. A third of those who attended ECE programs use one, whereas only one in every ten adults who did not attend ECE uses one.

Over time, access to primary and secondary education has substantially increased. In fact, most of the population has completed at least primary education (80 percent) and junior high school (JHS) (69 percent) (figure 4.4).

Figure 4.1 Participation in Early Childhood Education in Ghana

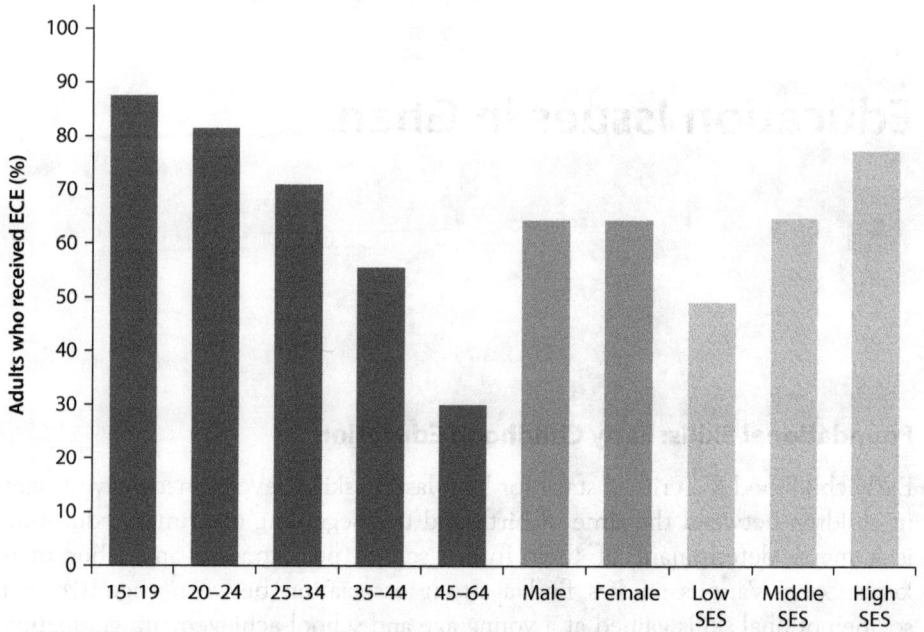

Note: The figure includes people currently attending school. ECE = early childhood education; SES = socioeconomic status.

Figure 4.2 Regular Use of Reading, Writing, Numeracy, and Computer Skills in Ghana

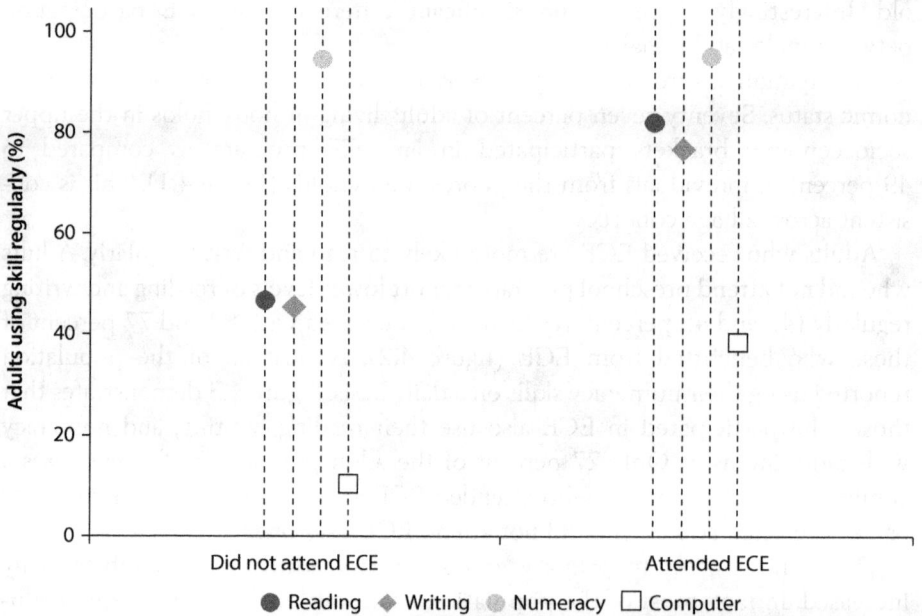

Note: The regular use of skills is defined on the basis of general questions about daily activities that involve the use of skills at work and outside work. The figure includes people currently attending school. ECE = early childhood education.

Figure 4.3 Intensity of Skill Use in Ghana

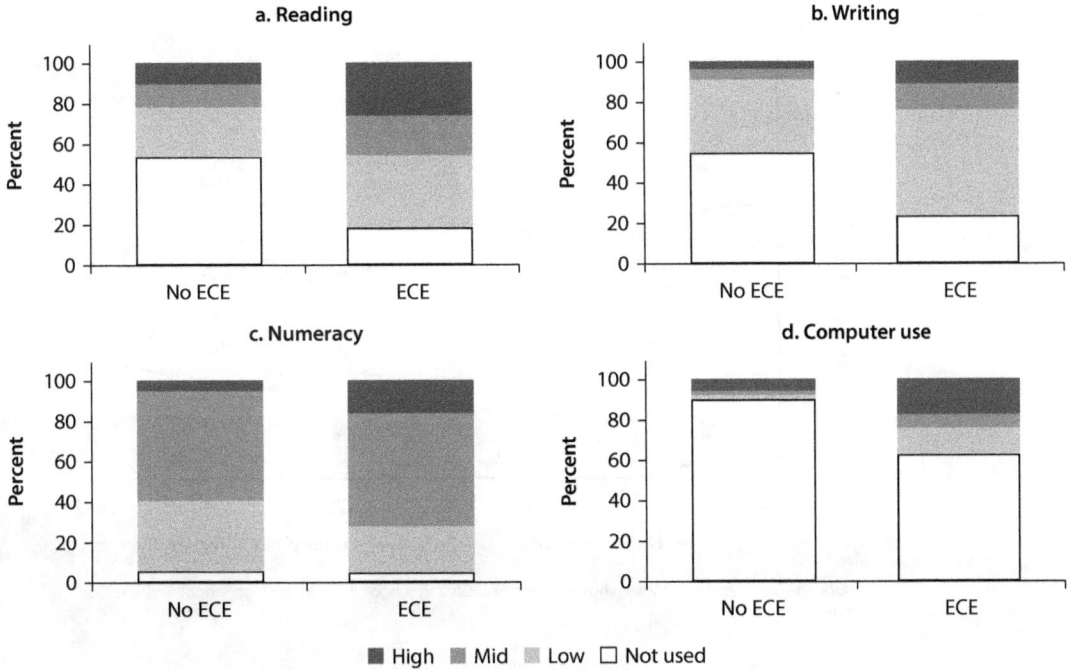

a. Reading

b. Writing

c. Numeracy

d. Computer use

■ High ▨ Mid ▨ Low ☐ Not used

Note: Intensity of skill use is defined as follows: High = more than 25 pages a week; Medium = 6–25 pages; Low = 1–5 pages requiring the use of skills at work and outside work. The figure includes people currently attending school. ECE = early childhood education.

Figure 4.4 Educational Attainment in Ghana

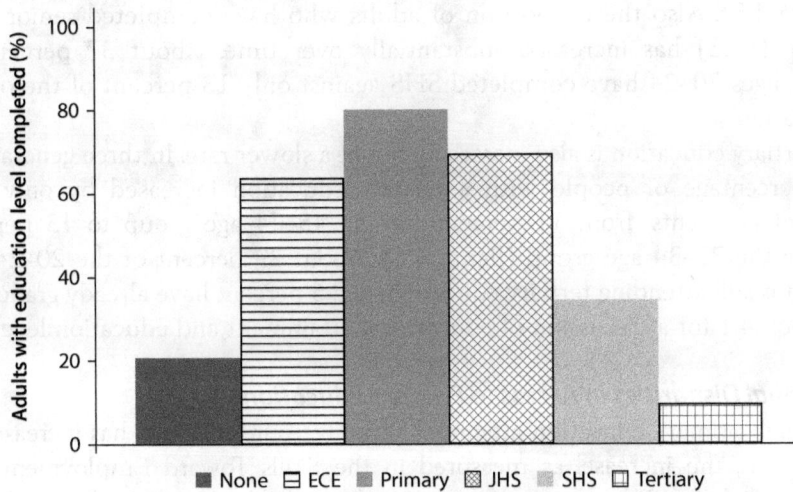

■ None ▤ ECE ■ Primary ▧ JHS ▨ SHS ▦ Tertiary

Note: Attainment is the ratio of the population who complete a specific level of education to the population who could have finished this level of education (see box 4.1). The figure includes people currently attending school. ECE = early childhood education; JHS = junior high school; SHS = senior high school.

Figure 4.5 Educational Level in Ghana, by Age Groups

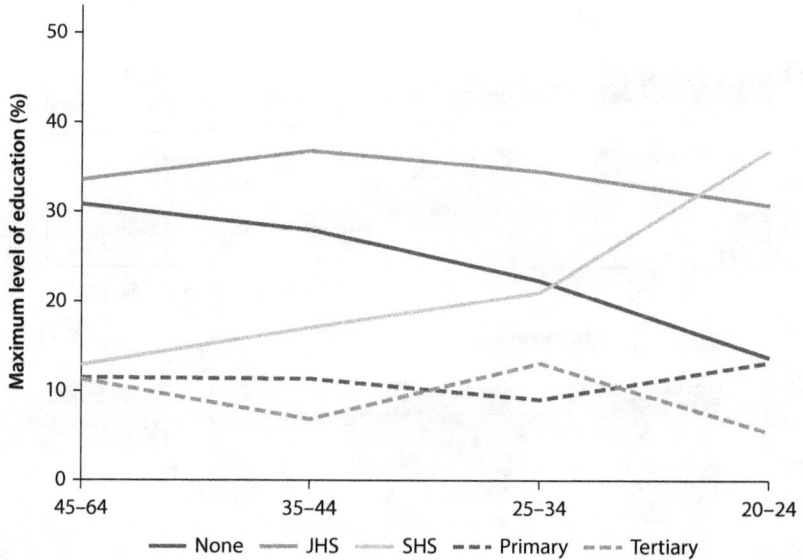

Note: The figure excludes those who are currently attending school. JHS = junior high school; SHS = senior high school.

In general, younger generations have more years of schooling than their elders. Whereas adults in the 45–64 age cohort have an average of 7.4 years of education, adults ages 20–24 have 2.6 more years of schooling. About 14 percent of adults ages 20–24 report not having completed primary education, but the equivalent figure was 31 percent among the oldest generation (ages 45–65) (figure 4.5). Also the proportion of adults who have completed senior high school (SHS) has increased substantially over time. About 37 percent of adults ages 20–24 have completed SHS against only 13 percent of the oldest generation.

Tertiary education is also increasing but at a slower rate. In three generations the percentage of people with a tertiary education increased by only two percentage points, from 11 percent for the 45–64 age group to 13 percent among the 25–34 age group (figure 4.5). About 29 percent of the 20–24 age cohort is still attending tertiary education, and 5 percent have already graduated (see box 4.1 for a discussion of educational attainment and education levels).

Regional Disparities in Access to Primary Education

Although primary education attainment among younger adults has increased in all regions, the increase, as measured in the Skills Toward Employment and Productivity (STEP) survey, was more significant in the Northern, Brong-Ahafo, and Volta regions. Nevertheless, it is worth remembering that, although similar trends are likely to have occurred in the Upper West and Upper East, the STEP

Box 4.1 Definitions of Education Variables

The education variables include five subgroups of respondents: (i) those with no formal education or incomplete primary (henceforward called the "No education" or "None" subgroup); (ii) those with complete primary education; (iii) those who completed junior high school (JHS); (iv) those who completed senior high school (SHS); and (v) those who completed tertiary education.

We define two variables for education: educational attainment and educational level. *Educational attainment* identifies the percentage of the population that has completed a specific education level whereas *education level* identifies the maximum level of education achieved. For example, someone whose education level is tertiary has attained primary, secondary, high school, and tertiary education. Thus, tertiary attainment is the ratio of those with tertiary-level education to all those who achieved (or are currently attending) a lower level of education. Notably, educational attainment is age independent. Indeed, at the denominator, it takes into account only those who, given their age, might have achieved the same level of education. Thus, for example, tertiary education attainment is the ratio of individuals at least 21 years of age having completed tertiary education to the same age-specific group with lower educational attainment. The age references for each educational level are defined as following: 11 years old and above for primary level, 14 years old and above for JHS, 17 years old and above for SHS, and 21 years old and above for tertiary level.

Educational attainment is therefore useful for understanding the coverage of a specific education level within a population. For instance, if 80 percent of the population in a country has attained primary education, this includes those who have also achieved higher levels of education. In contrast, when analyzing educational level, the focus is on the highest level completed by the population. Educational level is useful for analyzing how the overall years of education completed by individuals might be correlated with their labor force participation, health, and life outcomes.

---

survey's small sample of urban households made it impossible to measure them. In the Northern region the proportion of people who attained (or currently attend) primary education increased from 22 percent among adults ages 45–65 to 100 percent among the youngest population. Similarly, in Brong-Ahafo only 42 percent of the 45–64 cohort attained primary education compared to 96 percent of the youngest cohort. The Central region is the only region that is lagging behind, with only 83 percent of those 15–19 years old having attended primary education (figure 4.6).

Socioeconomic Disparities

As might be expected, educational attainment increases with household wealth. More than 36 percent of individuals from the lowest quintile have not completed formal education compared with only about 19 percent of individuals from the highest income quintile (figure 4.7).

Figure 4.6 Regional Disparities in Changes in the Primary Completion Rate

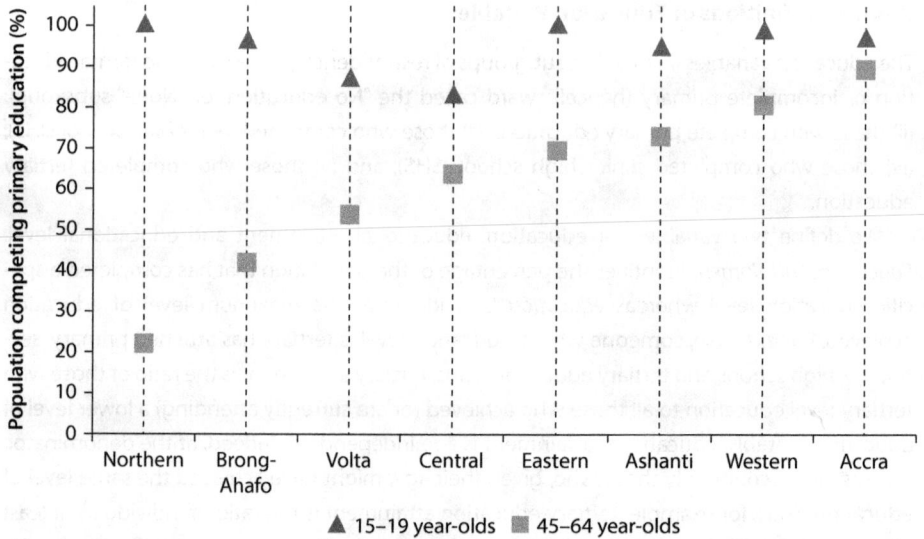

Note: The figure includes those who are currently attending school. Upper West and Upper East not reported because of their small sample size.

Figure 4.7 Education Level Attained in Ghana, by Socioeconomic Status

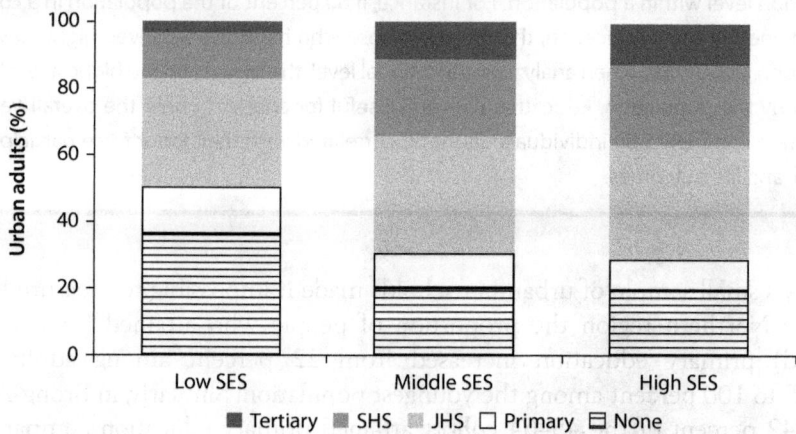

Note: The figure excludes those who are currently attending school and uses a subjective measure of socioeconomic status (SES) at age 15. JHS = junior high school; SHS = senior high school.

Nevertheless, Ghana is far from universal attainment in basic education, even among the urban population, and the education disparity is increasing. The richest segment of the population has been driving most of the improvement in education achievement—especially at the secondary level. Educational level has increased more quickly among the wealthiest, thus increasing the education gap between the poor and the wealthy (figure 4.8).

Figure 4.8 Evolution of Educational Profile in Ghana, by Socioeconomic Status

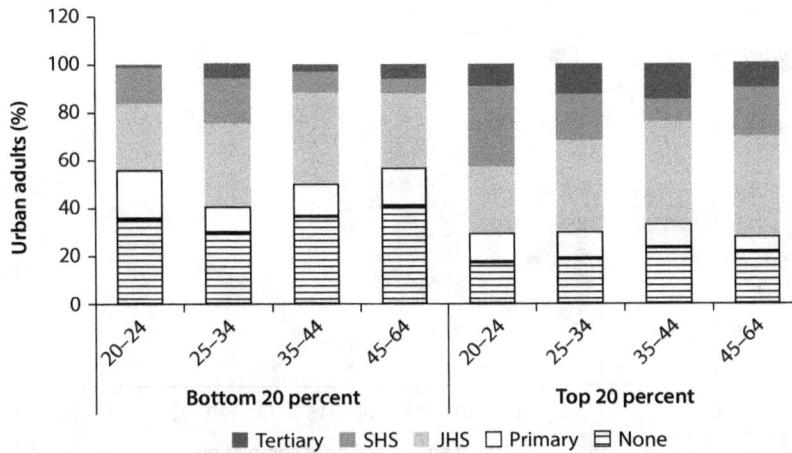

Note: The figure excludes those who are currently attending school and uses a subjective measure of socioeconomic status at age 15. JHS = junior high school; SHS = senior high school.

Constraints for Education: Late Entry, Completion Delay, and Dropouts

Delaying school entry correlates to educational achievement. The average age for starting school for all Ghanaians is 7 years even though the official entry age is 6 years old. On average, those who completed a higher level of education began school around the official age of entry. About 51 percent of those who never complete primary education enroll in school at age 8, whereas 89 percent of those with a post-secondary education enrolled at the official entry age. Figure 4.9 shows the average age of school entry and completion for each level of education achieved compared with the official ages for entry and graduation.

Although education attainment is increasing, delays in completion remain prevalent. Primary school should be completed by age 11, JHS by age 14, and SHS by age 17. However, those whose maximum level of education is primary graduate at an average age of 16.4. Considering their late entry, it takes them almost nine years to complete this level, four years more than expected (figure 4.9). For JHS and SHS, the difference between the actual and expected ages of graduation decreases, with the difference being about three years for both JHS and SHS. However, students are graduating from SHS at the age at which they should be finishing tertiary education instead. Tertiary education is the level with the highest delay in completion: although the expected age of completion is 21, the graduation age is on average almost six years later.

Almost one out of four adults dropped out of school. The dropout rate is highest during primary education and JHS: among dropouts, 44 percent left school before completing primary education, 37 percent while attending JHS, 16 percent while attending SHS, and 4 percent during tertiary education. Among those starting primary education, 82 continue with a higher level of education; for 8 percent, primary education is their highest level of education, and 10 percent dropped out of primary education before completing it (figure 4.10, panel a).

Figure 4.9 Delay in the Official Age of School Entry and Graduation

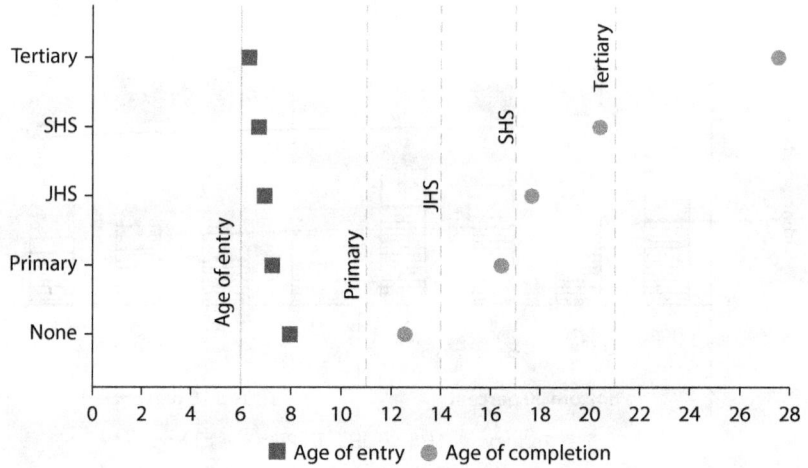

Note: The figure excludes those who are currently attending school. The dash lines indicate the expected age of completion for each education level. JHS = junior high school; SHS = senior high school.

Figure 4.10 Dropped Out of Highest Educational Level Started, by Maximum Level of Education Completed and Socioeconomic Status

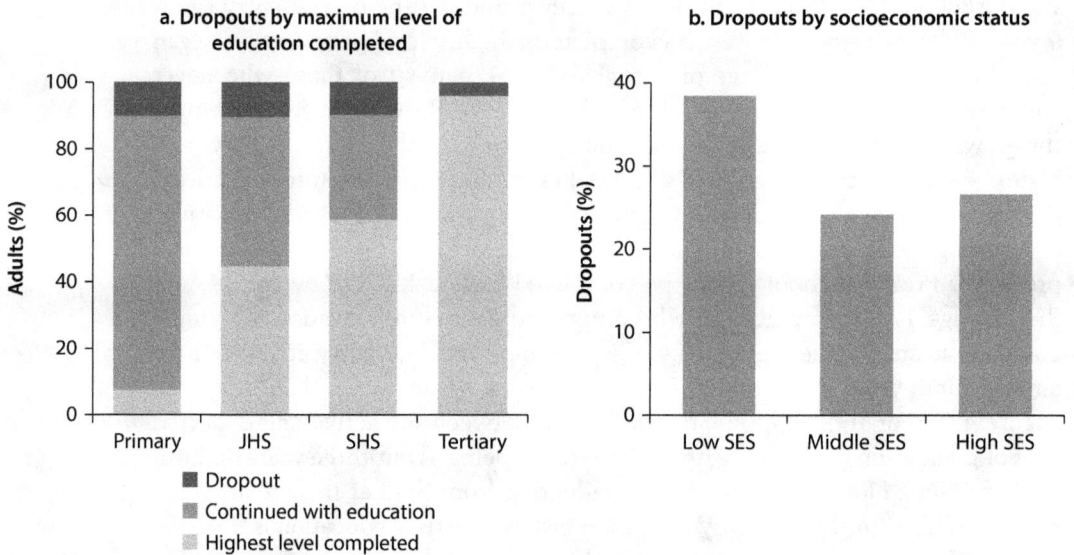

Note: The figure excludes those who are currently attending school. JHS = junior high school; SES = socioeconomic status; SHS = senior high school.

Among those starting JHS, 10 percent dropped out before completing this level; 9 percent of SHS students dropped out before completing SHS. Most of the dropouts belonged to households with low socioeconomic status when they were 15 years old. Whereas the dropout rate for individuals from the richest households is about 26 percent, this rate increases to 38 percent among the poorest households (figure 4.10, panel b).

Figure 4.11 Main Reason for Dropping Out

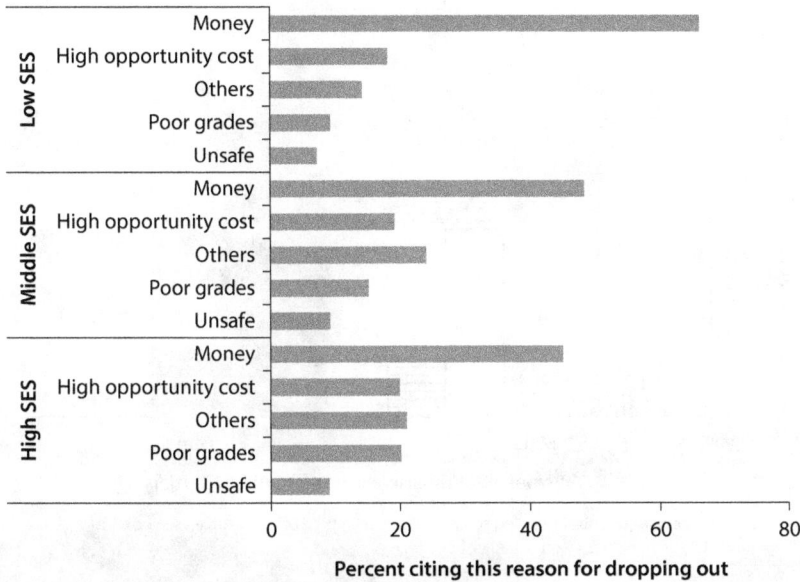

Note: The figure excludes those who are currently attending school and uses a subjective measure of socioeconomic status (SES) at age 15.

The lack of money for out-of-pocket expenses is the top reason for dropping out at age 15 for all households, regardless of their socioeconomic status. Among the poorest households, which suffered the highest dropout rate, 66 percent mentioned lack of money for fees, uniforms, or school materials as a reason for dropping out (figure 4.11). High opportunity costs were the second most frequently mentioned reason. These high opportunity costs stemmed from the fact that students with lower qualifications might (relatively) easily find self-employment in the informal sector.

The Gender Gap in Education

The gender gap in education attendance is significant for all levels of education in Ghana (figure 4.12). For example, at 26 percent, the proportion of female students completing SHS education is significantly lower than the completion rate of male SHS students, at 47 percent. Moreover, in primary education, 74 percent of female students enrolling in primary education complete a full course of primary education, compared to 88 percent for their male counterparts. The gender gap in the primary completion rate is still significant. Females make up a larger proportion of adults with no formal education. About 13 percent of men and 26 percent of women have no or an incomplete primary education.

Nevertheless, women's educational attainment at both the primary and secondary level is increasing over time (figures 4.13 and 4.14). Within the oldest generation,

Figure 4.12 Educational Attainment, by Gender

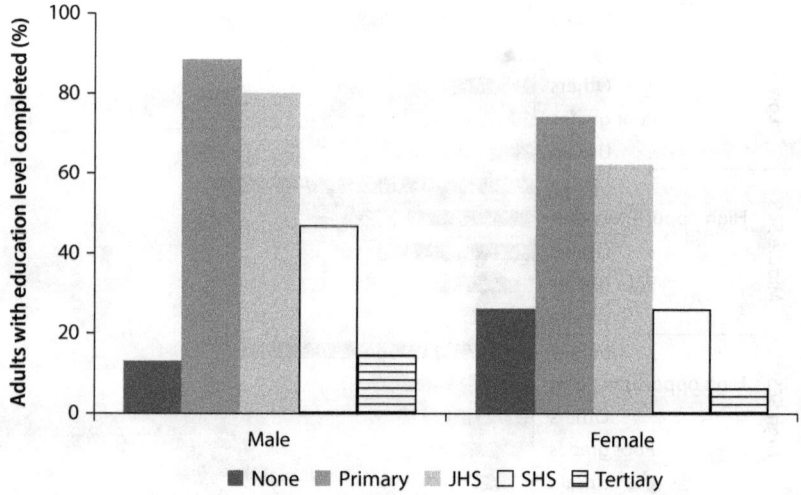

Note: Includes people currently attending school. For the definitions of the variables, see box 4.1.
JHS = junior high school; SHS = senior high school.

Figure 4.13 Educational Composition: Is the Gender Gap Narrowing?

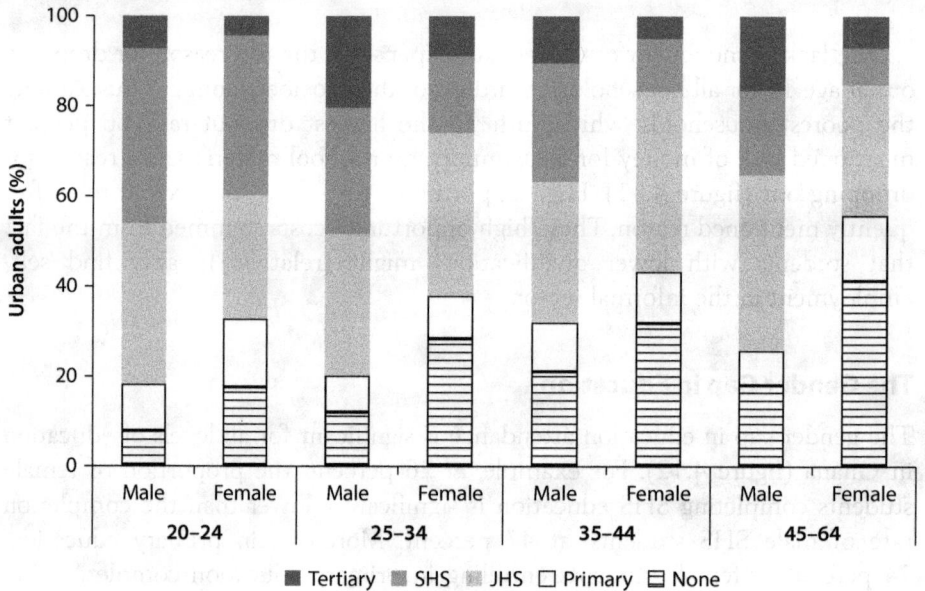

Notes: The figure excludes those who are currently attending school and uses a subjective measure of socioeconomic status
at age 15. JHS = junior high school; SHS = senior high school.

Figure 4.14 The Gender Gap in Educational Attainment (Male–Female), by Age Group

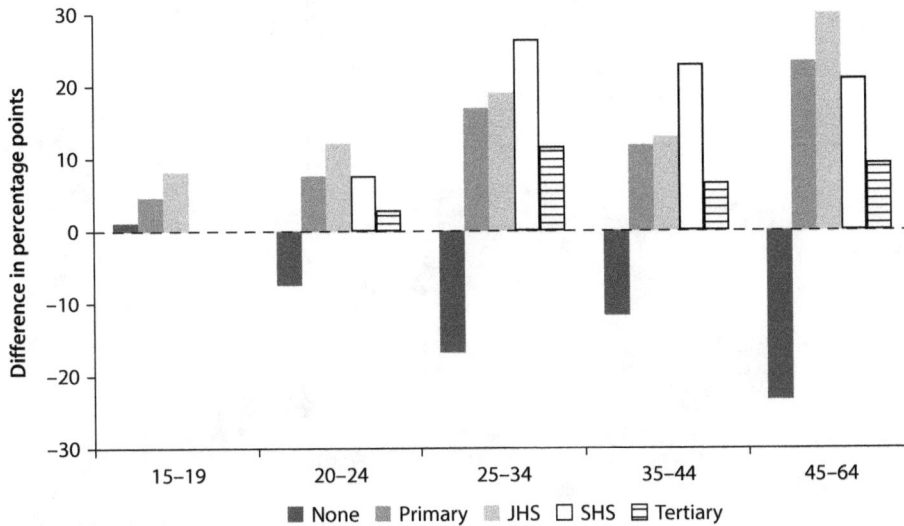

Note: The figure excludes those who are currently attending school.

41 percent of women have no formal education (compared with 18 percent of men), but this proportion is 23 percentage points lower among the youngest cohort. Similarly, only 8 percent of women ages 45–64 have SHS education against an SHS completion rate of 35 percent among the youngest.

In sum, the STEP survey data show a clear trend of increases in education attainment across generations. Although driven mostly by deprived regions catching up with the rest of the country, these increases were also led by the highest-income groups. Despite improvements, inequality persists because lower-income groups continue to have high opportunity costs.

Reference

World Bank. 2014. "STEP Skills Measurement Program." World Bank, Washington, DC. http://microdata.worldbank.org/index.php/catalog/step/about.

CHAPTER 5

Labor Market Participation

Introduction

Following the analysis of education attainment based on the Skills Toward Employment and Productivity (STEP) survey, we analyze the survey's data on labor force participation and employment. The labor force participation rate in Ghana is 67 percent, with 62 percent reported to be working and only 5 percent to be unemployed (figure 5.1, panel a). About 23 percent of the population are inactive either because they are enrolled in school[1] (22 percent) or because they are retired (1 percent). The remaining 10 percent are "Not in Education, Employment, or Training" (NEET) (see box 5.1 for definitions of various labor market terms). The most common reasons that respondents gave for being NEET were being a housewife, being unfit to work, or having been discouraged from working (figure 5.1, panel b).

Unemployment rates are generally low, and inactivity varies very little across levels of education achieved. Unemployment is up to 6 percent for those with tertiary education, and the rate of NEET varies between 11 percent for people with no formal education and those with senior high school (SHS) education and 6 percent among tertiary graduates (figure 5.2).

The transition from school to work is very slow. Individuals ages 35–44 have the highest employed rate. Whereas unemployment and NEET rates vary little across age groups, inactivity declines significantly (by about 28 percentage points) between the age 20–24 and 25–34 cohorts and falls by 7 additional percentage points for those ages 35–44 (figure 5.3). Although this trend might be explained by a change over time of the labor market structure, it also shows (together with the prevalence of late school entry and late completion) a slow transition from school to work.

Figure 5.1 Labor Force Participation and Nonparticipation in Ghana
percent

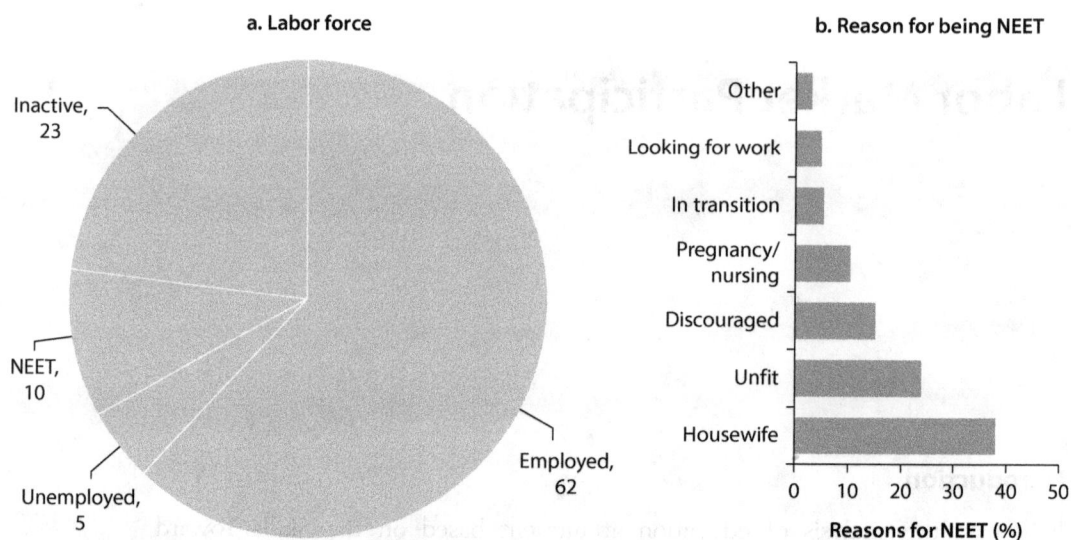

a. Labor force

b. Reason for being NEET

Note: NEET = Not in Employment, Education, or Training.

Box 5.1 Definitions of Labor Market Terms Used in the Skills Toward Employment and Productivity (STEP) Survey

Ghana's labor force includes people ages 15–64, both employed and unemployed (and those seeking a job). The *employed labor force* includes those working for pay, those who have found a job but are not working because they are sick or waiting to start their new job, those working for profit, and those in apprenticeships. The *unemployed labor force* includes those who are looking for job and who have been laid off for 30 days or less. The employment/unemployment rate can be computed as share of employed/unemployed people over the whole population aged 15–64 or over the labor force (which excludes the inactive population).

The *inactive population* includes people enrolled in school and those who are "Not in Education, Employment, or Training," or *NEET*. The NEET rate is defined as a share of NEET over the 15- to 64-year-old population, including both the active and inactive population. The inactive subgroup is ultimately broken down to distinguish between married and unmarried people.

The *underemployed* are those working less than 40 hours a week (considering the primary and secondary occupations together) and willing to work more hours. Underemployment is defined both as a share of the active labor force and as a share of the employed labor force only.

A further distinction is made between those employed in the *formal sector* and those working in the *informal sector*. The STEP survey defines informal sector workers as unpaid workers (mainly employed in family businesses), the self-employed and wageworkers who report not having any social security or benefits, or informal wageworkers. The rest of the employed population constitutes the formal sector, made up predominantly of wageworkers.

box continues next page

Box 5.1 Definitions of Labor Market Terms Used in the Skills Toward Employment and Productivity (STEP) Survey *(continued)*

Occupations are classified into three categories on the basis of the level of skills required. *Low-skilled occupations* include agricultural, forestry, and fishery workers; craft and related trades workers; plant and machine operators and assemblers; and elementary occupations. *Mid-skilled occupations* include technicians and associate professionals; clerical support workers; and service and sales workers. *High-skilled occupations* include managers and professionals.

Finally, the *economic sectors* are classified in four groups: (i) agriculture, fisheries, and mining; (ii) manufacturing; (iii) low-to-mid-value-added services; and (iv) high-value-added services. The low-to-mid-value-added services sector includes electricity, gas, steam, and air conditioning supply; water supply and sewage; waste management; construction; the wholesale and retail trade; transportation and storage; accommodation and food services; information and communication; arts, entertainment, and recreation; other services activities; and the activities of households and extraterritorial organizations and bodies. The high-value-added services sector includes financial and insurance activities; real estate activities; professional, scientific, and technical activities; administrative and support service activities; public administration and social security; and education, human health, and social work activities.

Figure 5.2 Labor Status, by Educational Level

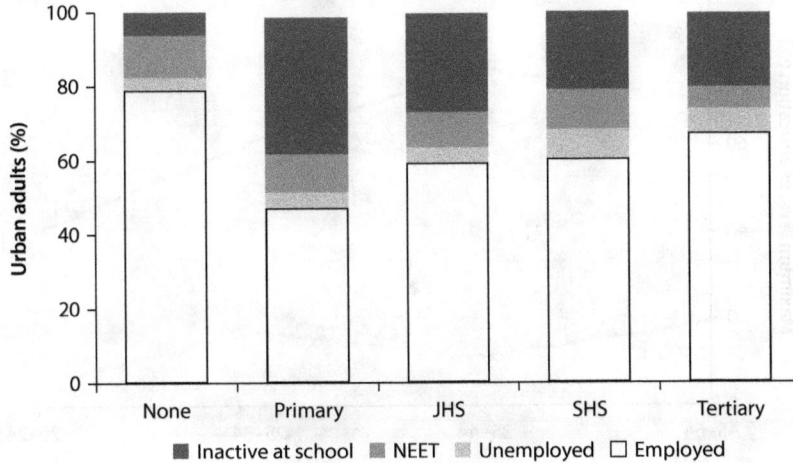

Note: The figure includes people currently studying but not inactive retired people. JHS = junior high school; NEET = Not in Education, Employment, or Training; SHS = senior high school.

Wage Employment, Self-Employment, and Formality

Most of the employed labor force works in the informal sector, either as self-employed (66 percent) or as informal wageworkers (20 percent).[2] In fact, only 15 percent of the employed population works as salaried workers in the formal sector. However, this trend is changing: younger generations are less likely to be self-employed and more likely to be salaried workers, with either formal or

Figure 5.3 The (Slow) Transition from School to Work: Labor Status, by Age Group

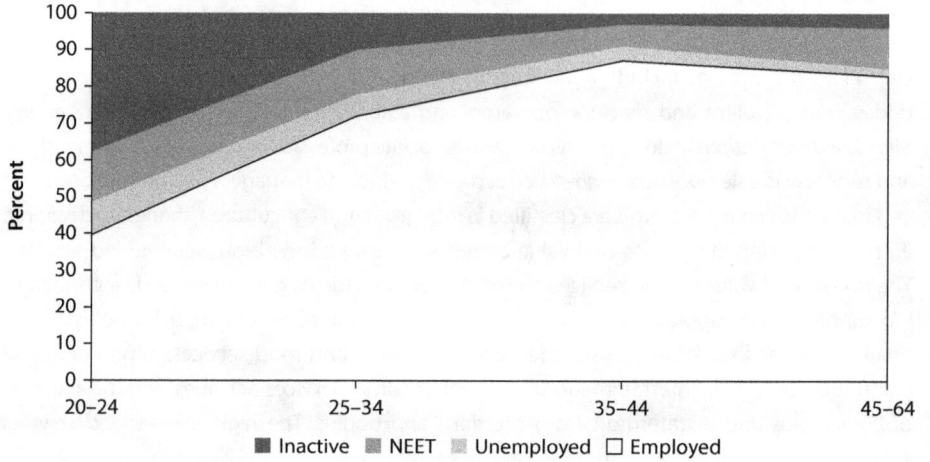

Note: The figure includes people who are currently studying. NEET = Not in Education, Employment, or Training.

Figure 5.4 Employment Status, by Age Group

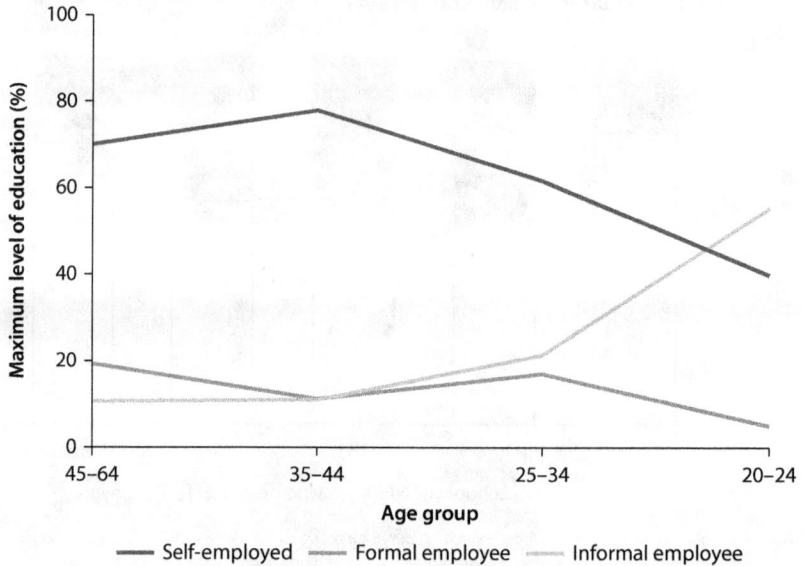

Note: The figure excludes people currently studying.

informal firms. Nevertheless, still more than 95 percent of the youngest age cohort (20- to 24-year-olds) work in the informal sector, most of them as informal wageworkers rather than self-employed (55 percent) (figure 5.4).

Education is strongly associated with employment status, as shown in figure 5.5. About 37 percent of those with a tertiary education work in the informal sector (20 percent as self-employed and 17 percent as informal employees), and this

Figure 5.5 Employment Status, by Education Level

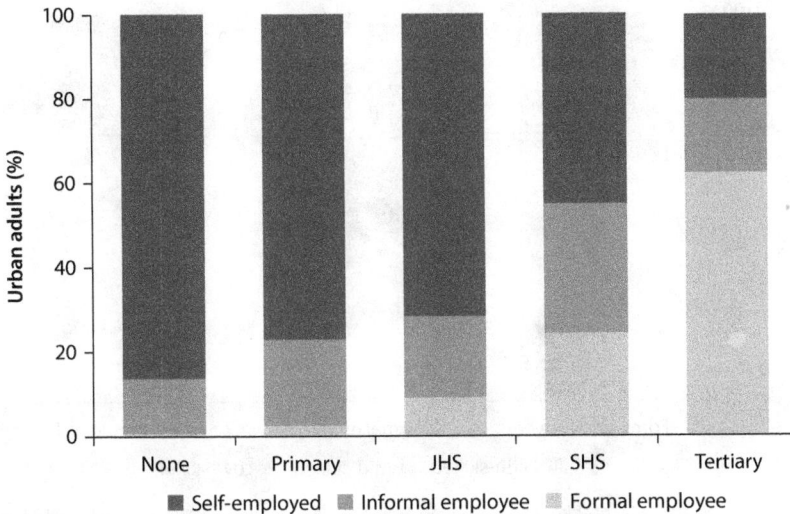

Note: The figure excludes people who are currently studying. JHS = junior high school; SHS = senior high school.

share increases to 99 percent for those who do not have any formal education (86 percent as self-employed and 13 percent as informal employees).

Occupation Type

Informality is synonymous with low-skilled occupations. Only 13 percent of the employed population works in high-skilled occupations, mainly in the formal sector (figure 5.6). Conversely, the majority is employed in low-skilled (39 percent) and mid-skilled occupations (48 percent). The prevalence of workers employed in low- or mid-skilled occupations is relatively higher among the self-employed than among informal wageworkers.

Increasing education leads to better occupations. Nevertheless, although this is true for SHS and/or tertiary graduates, those with primary education and those with no formal education are equally distributed among low-skilled or mid-skilled jobs (figure 5.7). Junior high school (JHS) graduates do slightly better, with about 2 percent more working in mid-skilled occupations and about 4 percentage points fewer in low-skilled occupations. The scenario changes for those with an SHS education, with 18 percent working in high-skilled occupations and only 32 percent in low-skilled occupations. The contrast in terms of high-skilled jobs is even more pronounced for those with a tertiary education, for whom the figure reaches 70 percent, with only 6 percent working in low-skilled occupations.

Economic Sector of Occupation

The largest share of the employed population works in services (61 percent in low-to-mid-value-added services and 17 percent in high-value-added services). The smallest share works in manufacturing (about 10 percent), followed by

Figure 5.6 Type of Occupation, by Employment Status

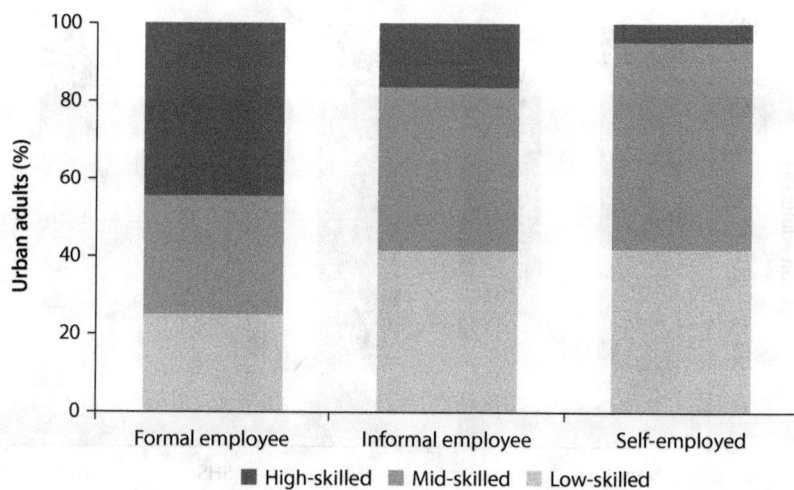

Note: The figure excludes people currently studying.

Figure 5.7 Type of Occupation, by Education Level

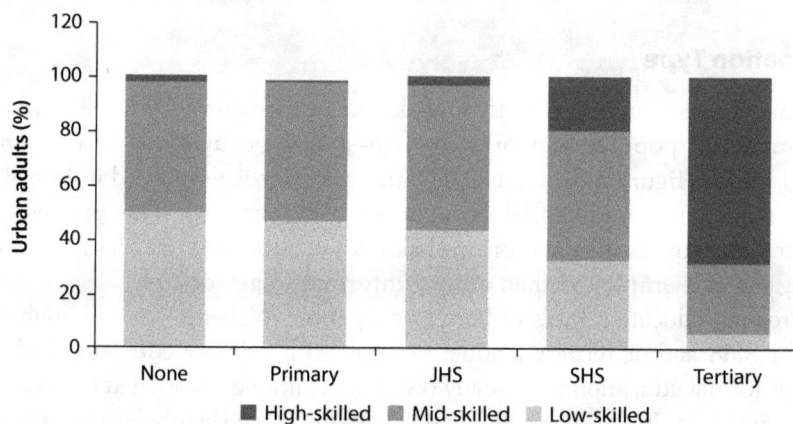

Note: The figure excludes people currently studying. JHS = junior high school; SHS = senior high school.

11 percent in agriculture, fishery, and mining combined. Almost all of the occupations in the manufacturing sector and the agriculture, fishery, and mining sector are low-skilled occupations (figure 5.8).

Education attainment increases in line with employment in higher-value economic sectors. Almost half of the workers in the agriculture, fishery, and mining sector have no formal education (53 percent) compared to 21 percent in the manufacturing sector and 28 percent in the low-to-mid-value-added services sector (figure 5.9). The education level of employees in the manufacturing sector is very similar to that of workers in the low-to-mid-value-added services sector.

Figure 5.8 Type of Occupation, by Economic Sector

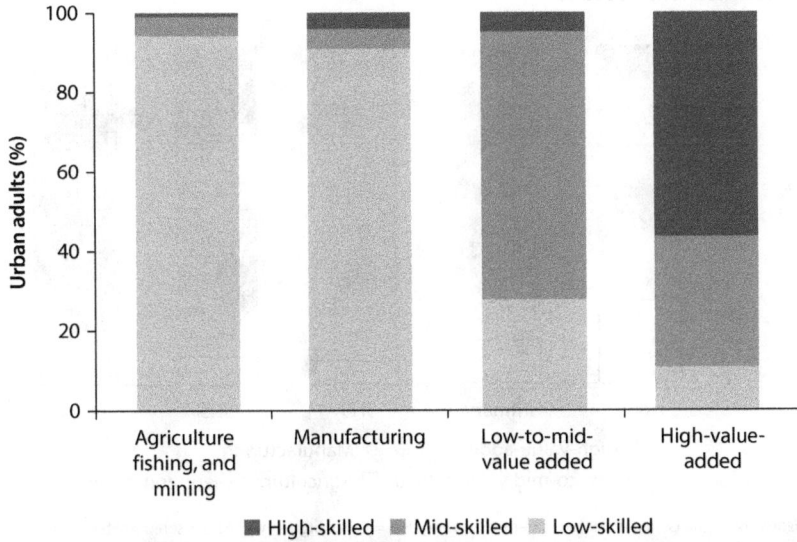

Note: The figure excludes people currently studying.

Figure 5.9 Characterizing Each Economic Sector by the Education Level of Its Labor Force

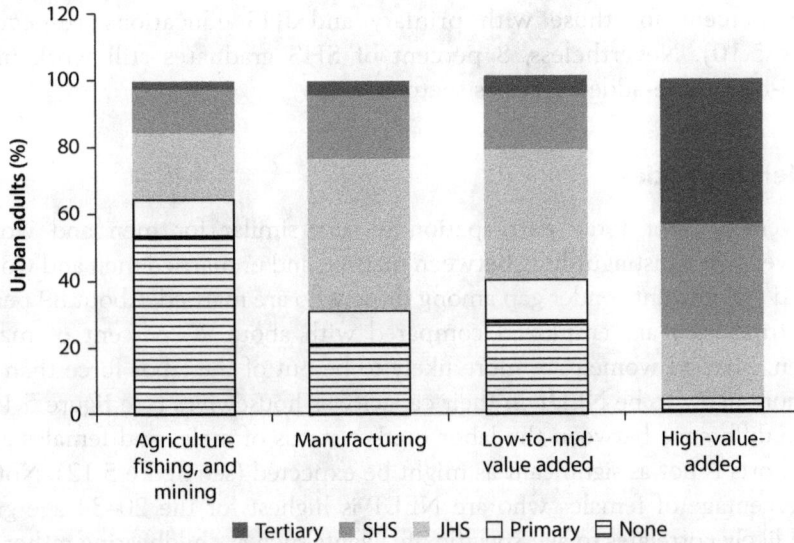

Note: The figure excludes people currently studying. JHS = junior high school; SHS = senior high school.

The pool of people with tertiary education is concentrated in the high-value-added services sector (43 percent).

Although completing primary education reduces the probability of working in agriculture, the picture for those with a primary education and those with a JHS education is again very similar (figure 5.10). Conversely,

Figure 5.10 How People with Different Levels of Education Are Distributed across Economic Sectors

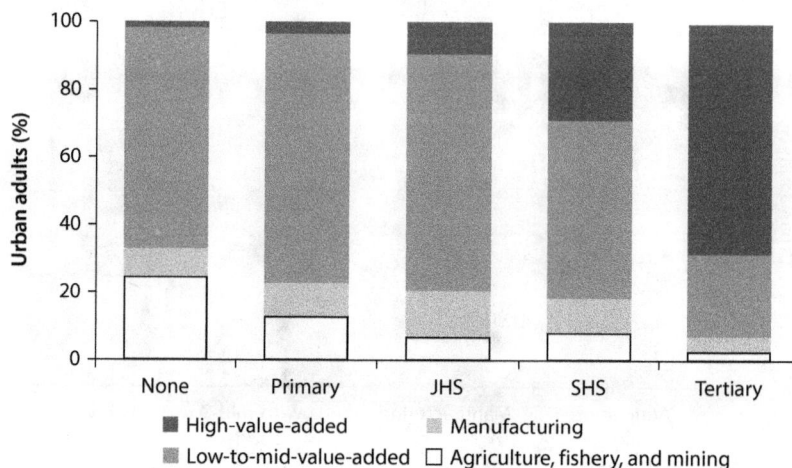

Note: The figure excludes people currently studying. JHS = junior high school; SHS = senior high school.

completing SHS makes a difference, given that about 29 percent of SHS graduates work in the high-value-added services sector compared with 3 and 8 percent for those with primary and JHS educations, respectively (figure 5.10). Nevertheless, 8 percent of SHS graduates still work in the low-to-mid-value-added services sector.

Gender Disparities

On average, labor force participation is very similar for men and women. However, when distinguishing between married and unmarried men and women, we find a significant gender gap among those who are married. About 89 percent of married men are employed compared with about 77 percent of married women. Married women are more likely to be out of the labor force than men and more likely to be NEET in their capacity as housewives (see figure 5.11).

The difference between the labor market status of males and females across age cohorts is not as significant as might be expected (see figure 5.12). Notably, the percentage of females who are NEET is highest for the 20–34 age group, which likely correlates to age-specific life events such as childbearing rather than a change over time in the women's labor market status. Increasing access to childcare and flexible work options might help to expand labor market participation and opportunities for women.

Although women are as likely as men to be employed, the gender gap is very pronounced in the quality of employment. At all ages, females are more likely to be self-employed than men. About half of the male working population is

Figure 5.11 Employment Status, by Marital Status

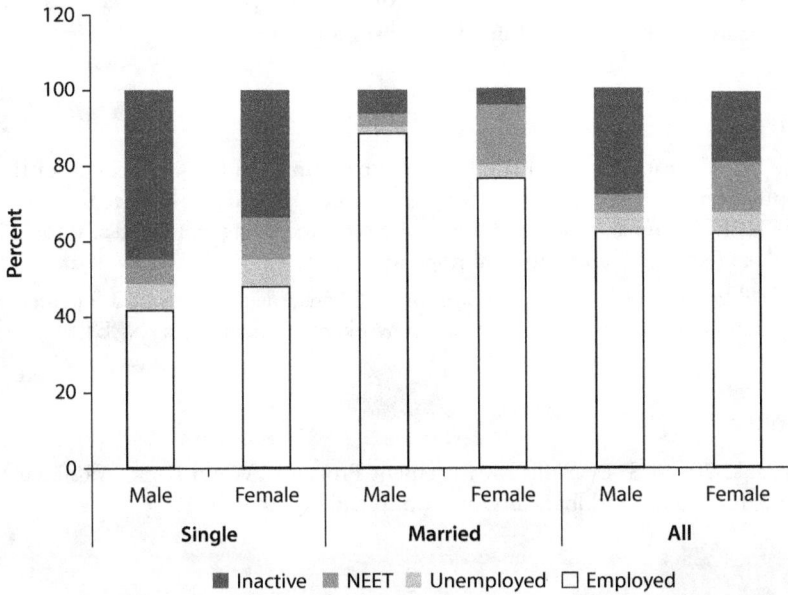

Note: NEET = Not in Education, Employment, or Training.

Figure 5.12 Labor Status, by Gender and Age Group

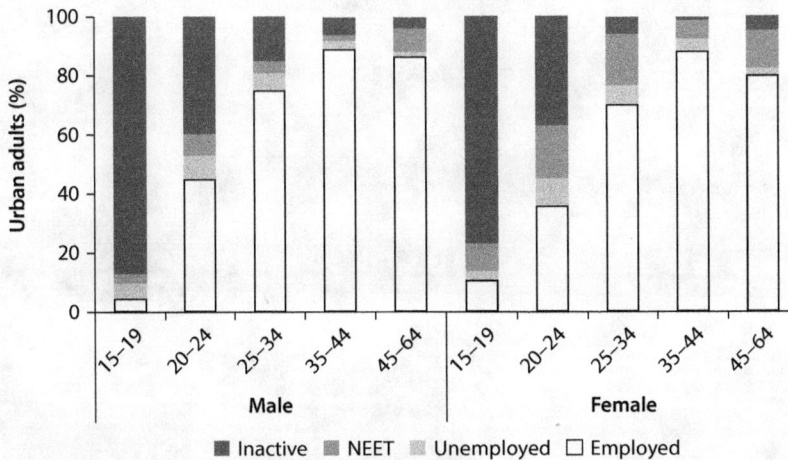

Note: The figure includes people currently studying. NEET = Not in Education, Employment, or Training.

self-employed whereas the other half is almost evenly distributed between formal and informal employment. In contrast, 79 percent of females are self-employed and only 7 percent are formal sector employees.

Notes

1. The inactive category also included a few part-time students (6 percent of the total population) who reported that they were studying and working at the same time. The NEET group also included those who reported being employed as unpaid family workers (3.5 percent of the total population).
2. Unpaid family work is not very common in Ghana, making up only 3.5 percent of the population. In this report, unpaid family workers are classified as NEET.

Reference

World Bank. 2014. "STEP Skills Measurement Program." World Bank, Washington, DC. http://microdata.worldbank.org/index.php/catalog/step/about.

CHAPTER 6

The Use of Cognitive Skills, Job-Specific Skills, and Literacy

Introduction

To the extent that workers' productivity depends on their skills and is reflected by their wages, individuals with more skills should expect higher returns from their labor market participation. Most studies investigate the returns to investments in human capital using the education qualification attained. Only a few recent studies examine the returns to skills (Leuven et al. 2004; Tyler 2004). The data arising from the Skills Toward Employment and Productivity (STEP) survey provide a unique opportunity to analyze skills across a range of dimensions and measure their implications for an individual's well-being and relative opportunity in the labor market.

As mentioned in chapter 3, the STEP survey focuses on three types of skills: (i) cognitive skills (self-reported and direct assessment); (ii) socioemotional skills; and (iii) job-specific skills. The following section will assess the distribution of each category of skill across population subgroups and thereafter proceed to an analysis of the returns to skills.

The Use of Cognitive Skills: Overall Use and Intensity of Use

The use of cognitive skills refers to the overall use of reading, writing, and numeracy skills either in daily life or at work.[1] Almost everybody uses numeracy skills regularly, at all levels of education. Conversely, the regular use of reading and writing skills is positively correlated with education. The large majority of survey respondents who attended tertiary education read and write regularly. This can be compared with the population with a primary education who reported using their reading (64 percent) and writing skills (60 percent) on a regular basis (figure 6.1).

The use of reading and writing skills has increased greatly over time, especially among people with low educational attainment. In fact, the highest disparity in the use of skills by age groups is among people who completed only primary education. In the youngest cohort with only primary education, 89 percent use their writing skills and 90 percent use their reading skills. However, less than half of the oldest age cohort uses them, with only 40 percent using their reading skills and 41 percent using their writing skills (figure 6.2).

The intensity of the use of various skills is linked to the level of proficiency and increase with the level of education attained. Overall, 31 percent

Figure 6.1 The Use of Cognitive Skills, by Level of Education Completed

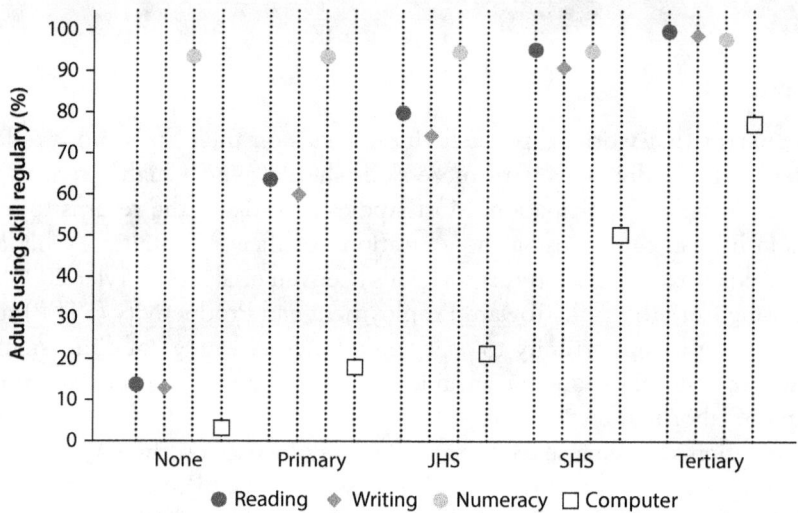

Note: The figure includes those who are currently in school. JHS = junior high school; SHS = senior high school.

Figure 6.2 The Use of Cognitive Skills, by Level of Education Completed and Age

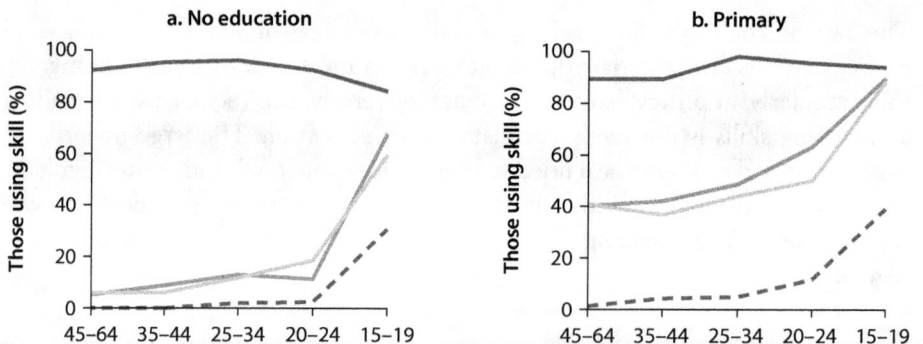

figure continues next page

Figure 6.2 The Use of Cognitive Skills, by Level of Education Completed and Age *(continued)*

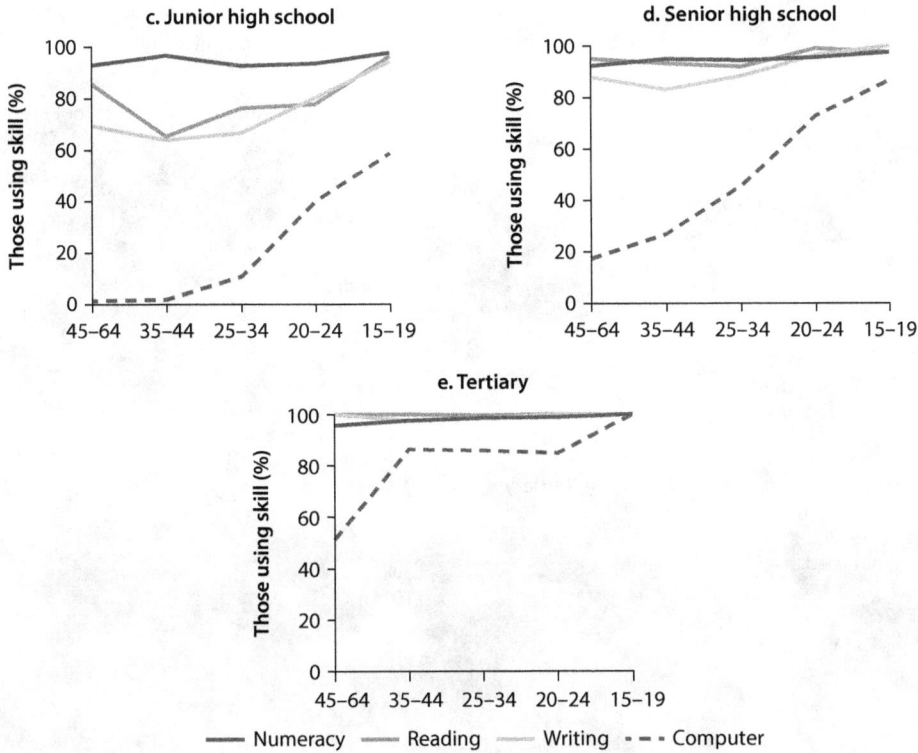

Note: The figure excludes those who are currently in school.

of the population reported not using their reading skills at all. Among the 69 percent using them regularly, half of the population read with low intensity, 24 percent read with medium intensity, and 29 percent read with high intensity. Among those with no formal education, 87 percent do not read at all, and 11 percent read only very short documents, whereas only 1 to 2 percent read intensively (figure 6.3). Reading intensity is higher among graduates of senior high school (SHS) and tertiary education. Nevertheless, there are still 40 percent of SHS and 19 percent of tertiary graduates who do not read or who do so rarely.

With regard to writing skills, about 35 percent of the adult population reported not writing regularly. Furthermore, most people use their writing skills less regularly than their reading skills. As in the case of reading skills, the use of writing skills increases with education. Writing skills significantly improve for those completing primary education and for those completing SHS and tertiary education. Nevertheless, even among those who completed tertiary education, almost half write only with low intensity (figure 6.4).

The use of skills is strongly related to employment status. Formal employment requires an intensive and frequent use of reading skills. More than 84 percent of

Figure 6.3 The Intensity of Use of Reading Skills, by Education Level
percent

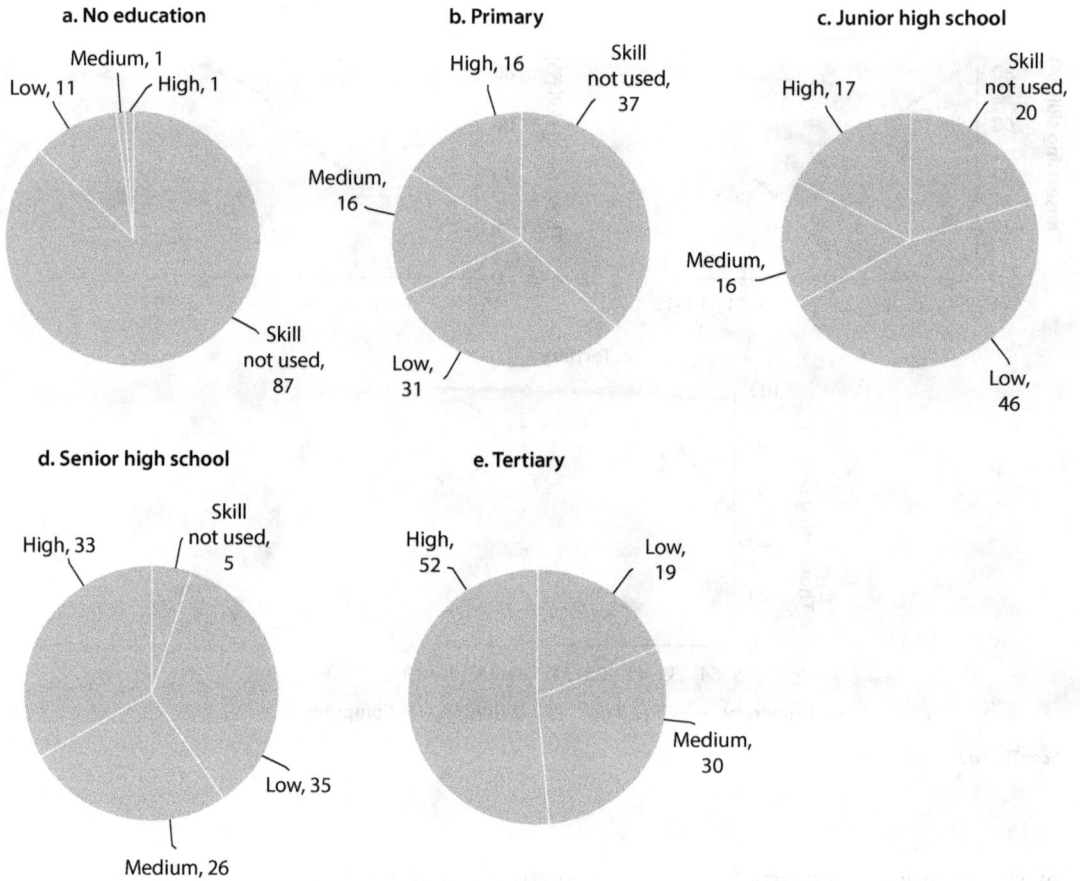

a. No education

Medium, 1
Low, 11
High, 1
Skill not used, 87

b. Primary

High, 16
Skill not used, 37
Medium, 16
Low, 31

c. Junior high school

High, 17
Skill not used, 20
Medium, 16
Low, 46

d. Senior high school

Skill not used, 5
High, 33
Low, 35
Medium, 26

e. Tertiary

High, 52
Low, 19
Medium, 30

Note: The figure includes those currently in school. Percentages in some panels do not add up to 100 percent because figures were rounded up.

formal employees use their reading and writing skills on a daily basis compared with about 41 percent of informal employees and about 21 percent of the self-employed (figure 6.5).

Although the use of numeracy skills is almost universal within all employment groups, computer use is low across the entire workforce. More than one-third of formal wageworkers reported using their computer skills at work, whereas only 11 percent of informal wageworkers and less than 3 percent of the self-employed reported using them (figure 6.5).

Finally, the percentage of workers who use reading and writing skills and computers is significantly higher among those who work in the high-value-added services sector than in any other sectors (figure 6.6).

Figure 6.4 The Intensity of Use of Writing Skills, by Education Level
percent

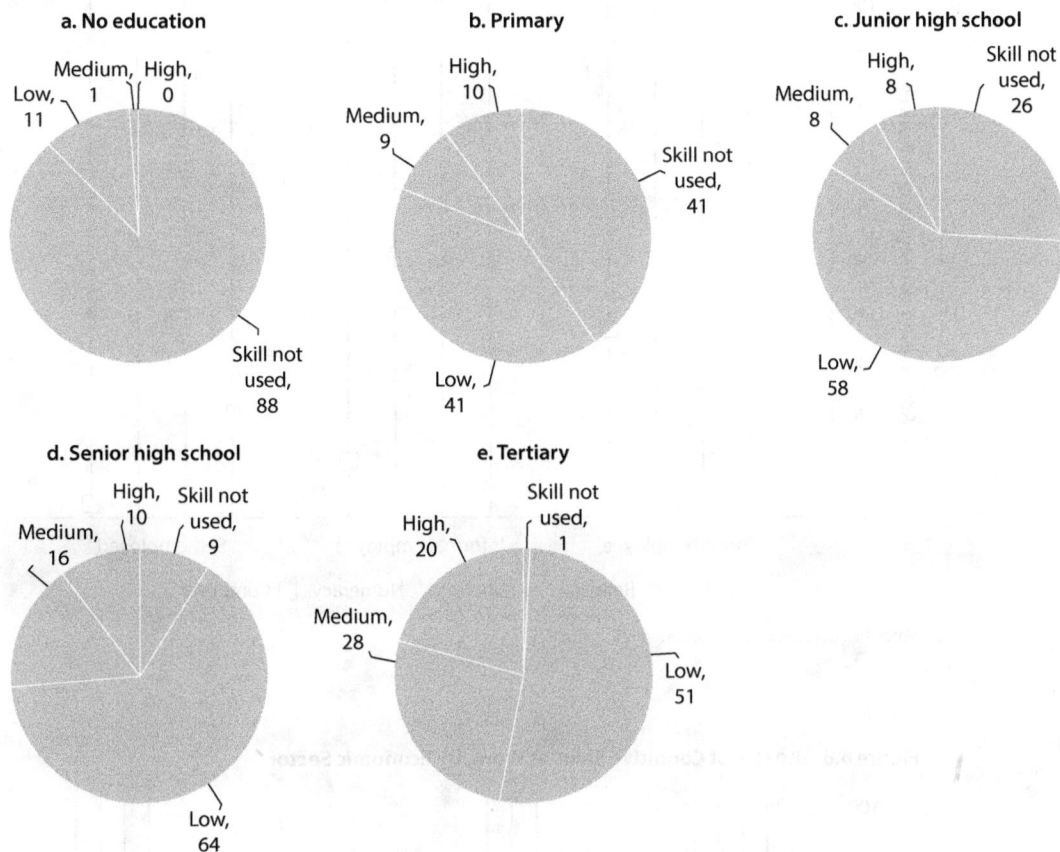

a. No education

Low, 11
Medium, 1
High, 0
Skill not used, 88

b. Primary

Medium, 9
High, 10
Skill not used, 41
Low, 41

c. Junior high school

Medium, 8
High, 8
Skill not used, 26
Low, 58

d. Senior high school

Medium, 16
High, 10
Skill not used, 9
Low, 64

e. Tertiary

High, 20
Skill not used, 1
Medium, 28
Low, 51

Note: The figure includes those currently in school. Percentages in some panels do not add up to 100 percent because figures were rounded up.

Job-Relevant (or Task-Related) Skills

Job-relevant skills are task related and consist of a combination of cognitive and socioemotional skills. The STEP survey includes information on whether employed people perform any of the following tasks at work: repairing and maintaining electronic equipment, operating heavy machinery, making presentations, and supervising others. The survey also asked about the intensity of their computer use, solving and learning from problems, physical tasks, and autonomy and repetitiveness. For each skill, a score ranging from 0 to 3 was computed, with 0 being equivalent to not using the skill, 1 for low use, 2 for medium use, and 3 for high use. The data also include the respondents' self-reported information of the educational attainment required to do their job and the time required to learn how to do it.

Figure 6.5 The Use of Cognitive Skills at Work, by Employment Status

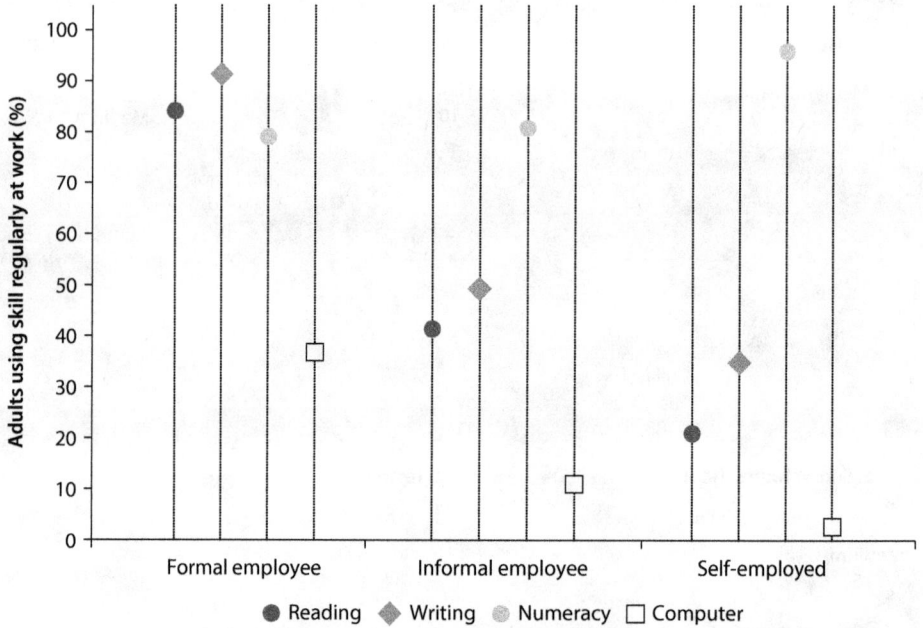

Note: The figure excludes those currently in school.

Figure 6.6 The Use of Cognitive Skills at Work, by Economic Sector

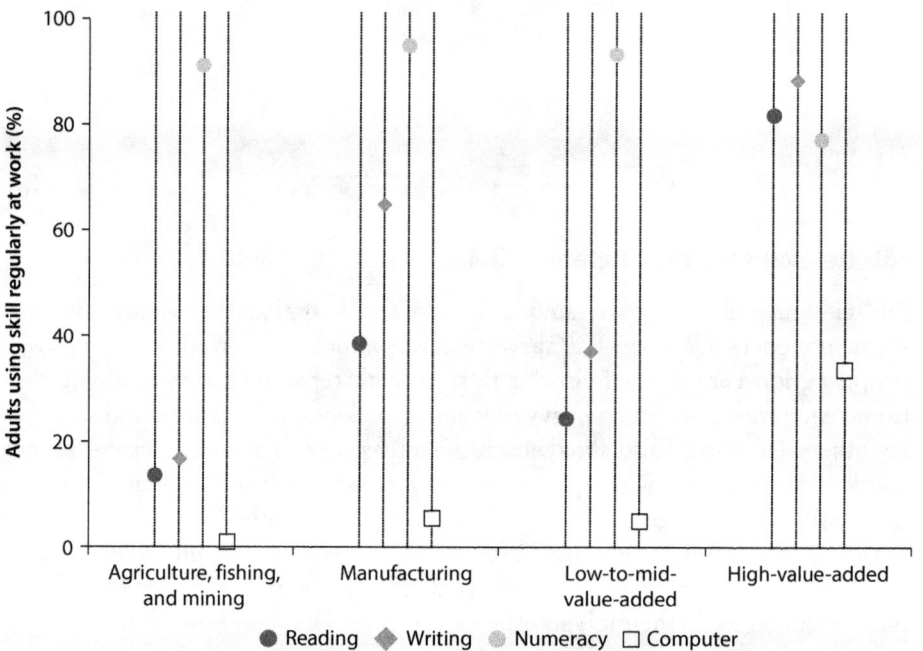

Note: The figure excludes those currently in school.

Working in the formal sector implies regularly learning new things at work and more frequently involves supervising others' work and making presentations. Conversely, work in the informal sector is less cognitively but more physically demanding and is more repetitive. Self-employed workers reported having more autonomy at work and performing more repetitive tasks than wageworkers (figure 6.7).

Figure 6.7 Job-Relevant Skills, by Employment Status

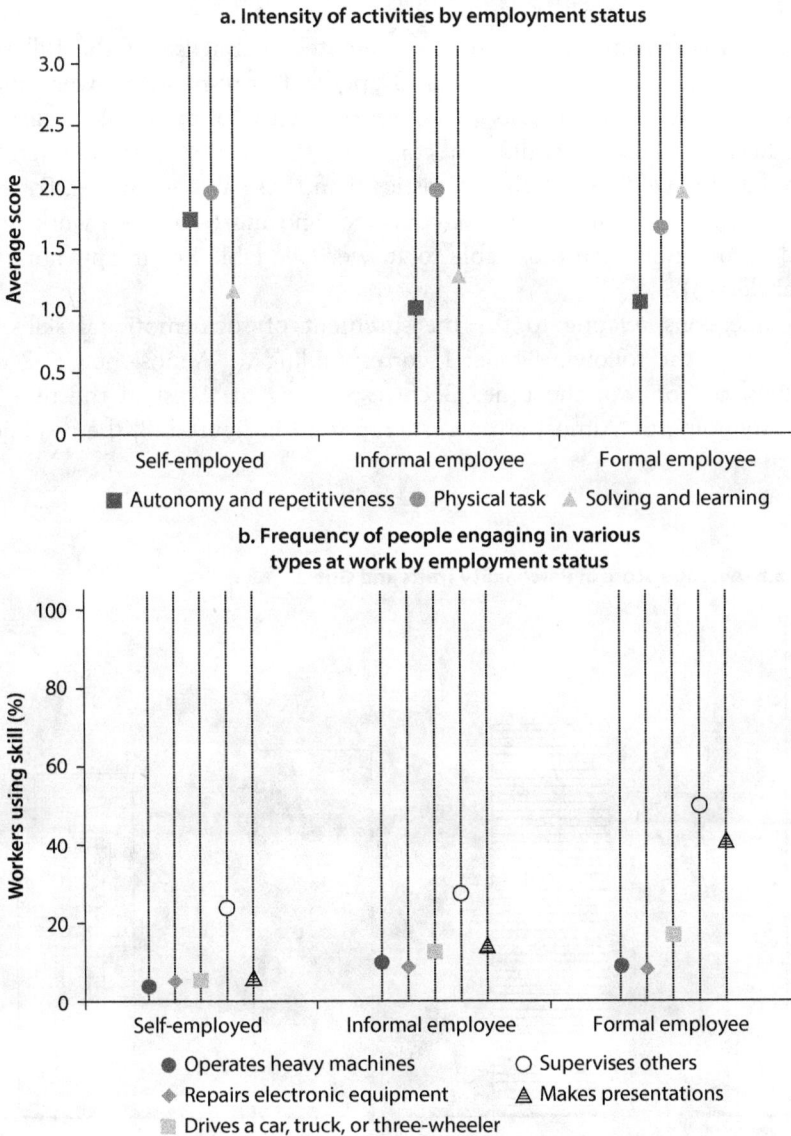

a. Intensity of activities by employment status

■ Autonomy and repetitiveness ● Physical task ▲ Solving and learning

b. Frequency of people engaging in various types at work by employment status

● Operates heavy machines   ○ Supervises others
◆ Repairs electronic equipment △ Makes presentations
▨ Drives a car, truck, or three-wheeler

Note: Excludes those currently in school. In panel a, the intensity of activities by employment status measured as a score ranging from 0 to 3 was computed, with 0 being equivalent to not using the skill, 1 for low use, 2 for medium use, and 3 for high use.

Socioemotional Skills

The survey includes information on socioemotional skills, more specifically on the "Big Five" personality traits (openness, conscientiousness, extraversion, agreeableness, and stability), grit, and hostile bias. Hostile bias is a behavioral characteristic that measures how often the individual believes that others are hostile to him or her. In addition, the survey also asks about risk and time preferences. Risk lovers have a high score, whereas risk-averse people score low. For time preference, those with a high score are more future oriented and those with a low score are more present oriented (more detail about the socioemotional skills can be found in appendix B).

This self-administered section was presented in English to the full survey sample. Because of low literacy, about 37 percent of respondents were not able to answer. Therefore, the results are not representative of the whole urban population because those who did not complete this section were not randomly selected and have different characteristics than those able to answer. For example, nonrespondents are older, less educated, and more likely to work in low-skilled occupations than those able to answer (see table D.5 in appendix D for further details).

All questions relating to the measurement of socioemotional skills were answered on the following scale: 1 corresponding to "Almost never," 2 corresponding to "Some of the time," 3 corresponding to "Most of the time," and 4 corresponding to "Almost always." As reported in figure 6.8, the respondents

Figure 6.8 Average Score of Personality Traits and Grit

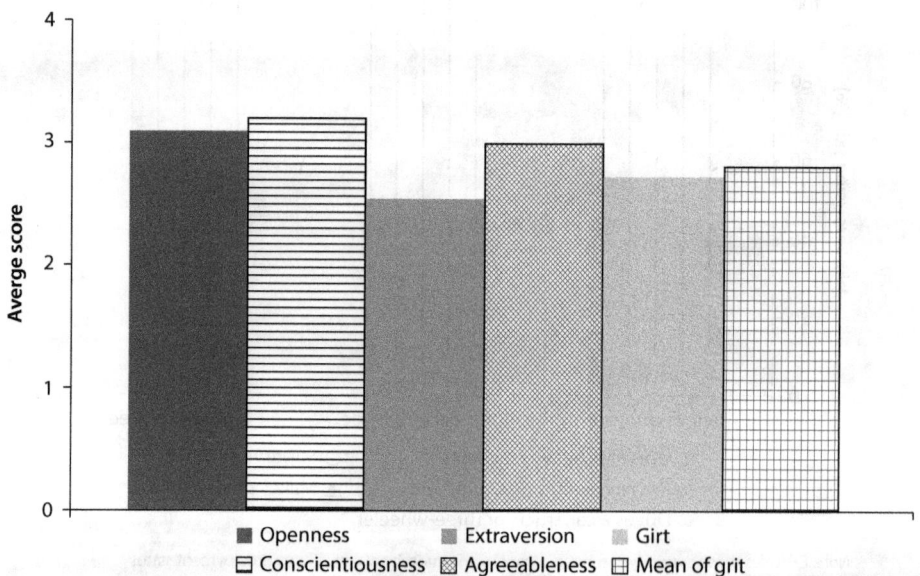

Note: The data include only those answering the socioemotional section.

scored around 3 in nearly all the personality traits, which means that most of the time they identify themselves positively with the Big Five and grit. Among them, extraversion is the trait with the lowest average score (2.5) and conscientiousness the one with the highest average score (3.2). On average, respondents located on the middle to low level in the hostile bias scale. With respect to their preferences, they are on average more likely to be present than future oriented and more likely to be risk averse than risk loving (figure 6.9).

There is a growing literature underscoring the role of socioemotional skills in education and labor market achievement. Figure 6.10 illustrates the estimated coefficients for socioemotional skills as factors associated with the number of school years completed, controlling for sociodemographic characteristics (age, gender, maternal education, socioeconomic status at age 15, and the region of residency). Similarly, in figure 6.11 the same associations are reported for the estimated probability of attending at least SHS. Finally, figure 6.12 illustrates the association between socioemotional skills and the probability of being employed, being self-employed (versus wageworkers), and employment in mid- to high-skilled occupations (versus low-skilled occupations). Overall, the results suggest that socioemotional skills are closely associated with educational attainment (figures 6.10 and 6.11). More specifically, a higher self-reported score relative to the Big Five personality traits is associated with higher educational attainment.

Among the personality traits, conscientiousness has the highest positive correlation, followed by extraversion, openness, and agreeableness. Grit and emotional stability are also positively associated but in smaller magnitude.

Figure 6.9 Average Scores for Hostile Bias and Time and Risk Preferences

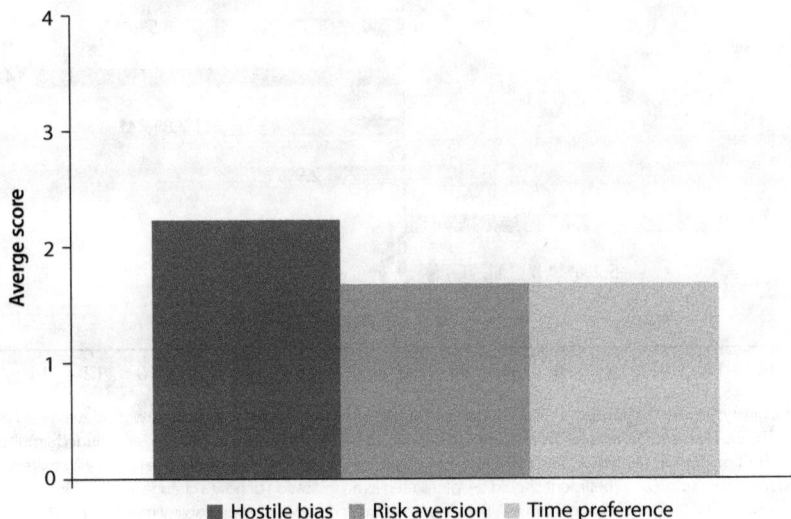

Note: The data include only those answering the socioemotional section.

Figure 6.10 Coefficients of Socioemotional Skills on Years of Education, Controlling for Sociodemographic Characteristics

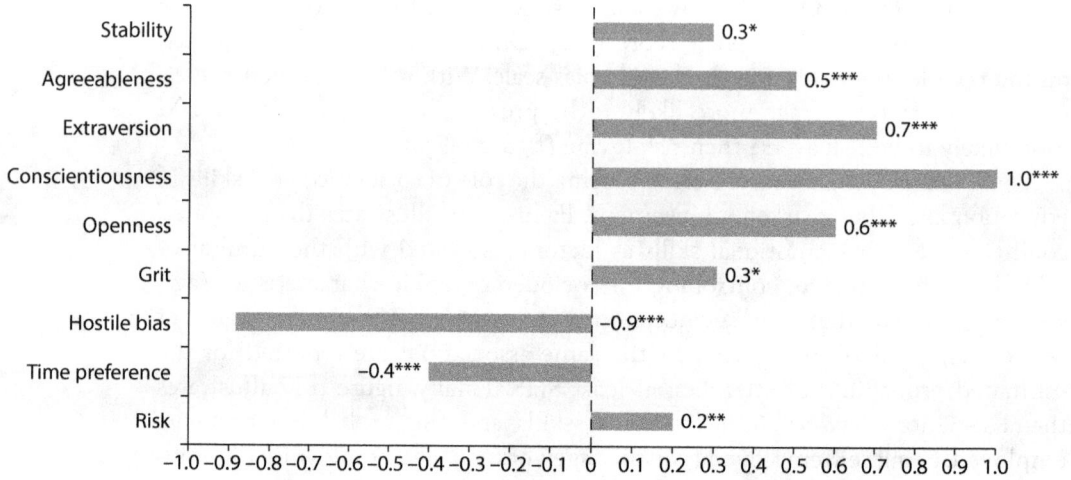

Note: The "Big Five" (stability, agreeableness, extraversion, conscientiousness, and openness) are included simultaneously in the regression model. The rest of the skills are included on their own, with controls. Including each of the Big Five personality traits on their own with controls does not influence the results. Each coefficient should be interpreted as an indication of how a change in one unit of the skills score is related to years of education. *** p<0.01, ** p<0.05, * p<0.1. All models are estimated using ordinary least squares (OLS) controlling for maternal education, region, socioeconomic level at age 15, and gender. See table G.1 in appendix G for full results.
*** *p*<0.01, ** *p*<0.05, * *p*<0.1.

Figure 6.11 Coefficients of Socioemotional Skills on the Probability of Attaining at Least SHS Education, Controlling for Sociodemographic Characteristics

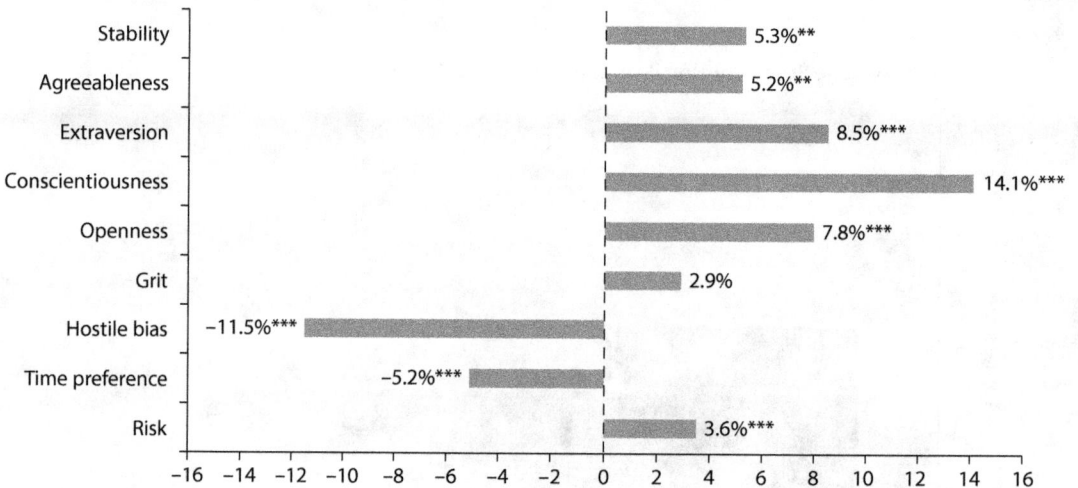

Note: The dependent variable is a binary variable that takes the value of one if the highest educational level is SHS or higher, and zero for all other levels of educational attainment. The Big Five (stability, agreeableness, extraversion, conscientiousness, and openness) are all included simultaneously in the same regression model. The rest of the skills are included on their own with controls. Including each of the Big Five personality traits on their own with controls does not influence the results. Each coefficient should be interpreted as an indication of how a change in one unit of the skills score is related to the probability of attaining SHS education or higher. All models are estimated using linear probability model controlling for maternal education, region, socioeconomic level at age 15 and gender. See table G.2 in appendix G for full results.
*** *p*<0.01, ** *p*<0.05, * *p*<0.1.

The results are in line with the literature that relates better educational outcomes to those with higher levels of the Big Five personality traits and grit. Furthermore, those who are more trustful, more present oriented, and less risk averse have a higher probability of studying one additional year (figure 6.10).

The results are substantially confirmed when analyzing the probability of completing at least SHS education (figure 6.11). In this case, a change in one score unit of conscientiousness is associated with 14 percentage points on the probability of completing SHS or tertiary attainment. As with years of education, higher agreeableness and stability levels, perceiving others as less hostile, being more present oriented, and being a risk lover increase the probability of completing higher levels of education

Finally, we present the results of the association of socioemotional skills and the probability of being employed, being self-employed (versus wageworkers), and working in mid- to high-skill occupations (versus low-skill occupations). Figure 6.12 shows that in most cases the correlation is not statistically significant

Figure 6.12 Coefficients of Socioemotional Skills on the Probability of Selected Labor Market Outcomes

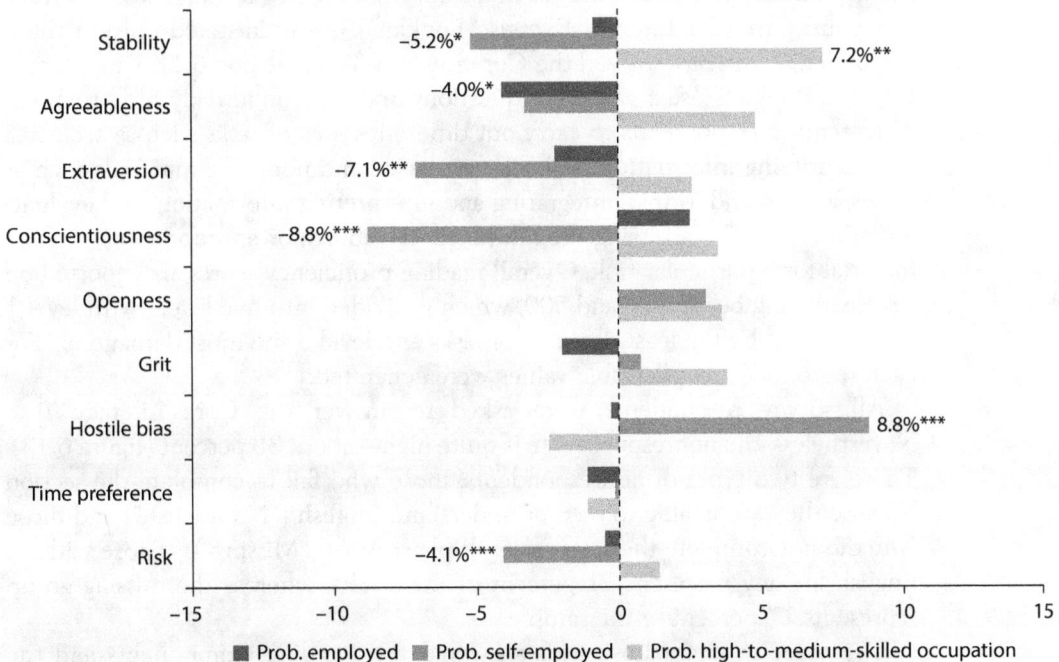

Stability −5.2%* 7.2%**
Agreeableness −4.0%*
Extraversion −7.1%**
Conscientiousness −8.8%***
Openness
Grit
Hostile bias 8.8%***
Time preference
Risk −4.1%***

■ Prob. employed   ■ Prob. self-employed   ▨ Prob. high-to-medium-skilled occupation

Note: The Big Five (stability, agreeableness, extraversion, conscientiousness, and openness) are all included simultaneously in the same regression model. The rest of the skills are included on their own with controls. Including each of the Big Five personality traits on their own with controls does not influence the results. Each coefficient should be interpreted as a measure of how a change in one unit of the score on the skill is related to the probability of being associated with the following labor market outcome: The probability of being employed is relative to those unemployed or inactive. The probability of being self-employed is relative to being a wage earner. The probability of being in high-to-medium-skilled occupations is relative to low-skilled ones. All models are estimated using linear probability model controlling for maternal education, region, socioeconomic level at age 15, gender, and level of education. See tables G.3 through G.5 in appendix G for full results.
*** $p<0.01$, ** $p<0.05$, * $p<0.1$.

(once we controlled for education, one of the control variables included in the model). However, noncognitive skills seem to play a role in determining the quality of the occupation. Individuals with higher levels of the Big Five personality traits and lower levels of hostile bias are less likely to be self-employed (and therefore more likely to be wageworkers). Interestingly, the only socioemotional skill that is significantly associated with having a mid- to high-skill occupation is emotional stability, which relates to the ability to cope with stress. Included in mid- to high-skill occupations are managers, professionals, clerical support workers, and service and sales workers.

Reading Literacy Assessment

The reading literacy assessment consists of three parts, all administered in English. The first part (Reading Components) evaluates foundation reading skills, including word meaning, sentence processing, and passage comprehension. The second part (Core Literacy Test) consists of a core literacy assessment that is intended to sort the least literate adults from those with higher reading skill levels. The Core Literacy Test has a total of eight items, and respondents with three or more correct responses are regarded as having met a minimum reading literacy threshold (see box 6.1 for more information on the Core Literacy Test). The third part (the Literacy Exercise Booklets) is administered only to those respondents who have passed the Core Literacy Test (see box 6.1). The Literacy Exercise Booklets use a variety of questions drafted around daily life situations. They require respondents to carry out different types of tasks such as accessing and identifying information (in both text-based and nonprose materials such as tables, graphs, and forms), integrating and interpreting information, and evaluating information by assessing the relevance, credibility, or appropriateness of the material for a particular task. Overall reading proficiency scores are reported on a scale ranging between 0 and 500, which is divided into five levels, with level 1 characterized by the least demanding tasks and level 5 the most demanding. For each respondent, 10 plausible values were generated.

All survey respondents were asked to answer the Core Literacy Test. Nevertheless, the nonresponse rate is quite high—about 38 percent (figure 6.13). There are two types of nonrespondents: those who fail to complete the section because they are unable to read or understand English ("No English") and those who did not complete the tests for multiple reasons ("Missing").[2] Those with no English literacy represent 21 percent of the adults, whereas the missing group represents 17 percent of the sample.

The three groups (those who answered the Reading Components and the Core Literacy Test, the group with no English literacy, and the missing group) are significantly different; therefore, the findings summarized may not be applicable to the entire urban sample. For example, those who answered are more likely to speak English at work (57 percent versus 18 percent of the missing and those with no English together) and to read and write with higher intensity than those who did not answer the test. Compared to the nonrespondents, they have higher

Box 6.1 What Does It Mean to Pass the Core Literacy Test?

A sizable proportion of adults reported that they read regularly, even though they did not pass the minimum literacy threshold of the Core Literacy Test. One reason could be that the tests are in English whereas many individuals mainly speak a local language. Only 1 percent and 40 percent speak English as their main language at home and at work, respectively (figure B6.1.1). In contrast, Akan is widely used in daily life. Thus, although the literacy assessment captures reading proficiency in English, the self-reported measure could be a better proxy of respondents' capacity to read and write in their daily life in their local language.

Even though only 40 percent of adults speak English at work, 58 percent of the urban adults report being able to speak and to read and write English well enough to work in a job that requires them to do so (figure B6.1.2).

As expected, the vast majority (90 percent) of those with no English and a third of those who failed the Core Literacy Test are unable to write, read, or speak in English at work. In contrast, among those who passed the Core Literacy Test, about 96 percent report being able to write, read, and speak English at work. (figure B6.1.3). Notably, about half of those who failed the Core Literacy Test report being able to use English at work—that is, there is a discrepancy between the self-reported and measured skills.

Poor English language literacy does not seem to prevent people from getting a job (figure B6.1.4). Only 12 percent report that the lack of English kept them from getting a job. However, those who speak English at work tend to have better-quality jobs. They are more likely to be formal employees in high-value-added sectors and in high-skill occupations. They also earn on average 248 GHS per month (or 60 percent) more than those who do not speak English at work.

Figure B6.1.1 Main Language Spoken at Home and Work

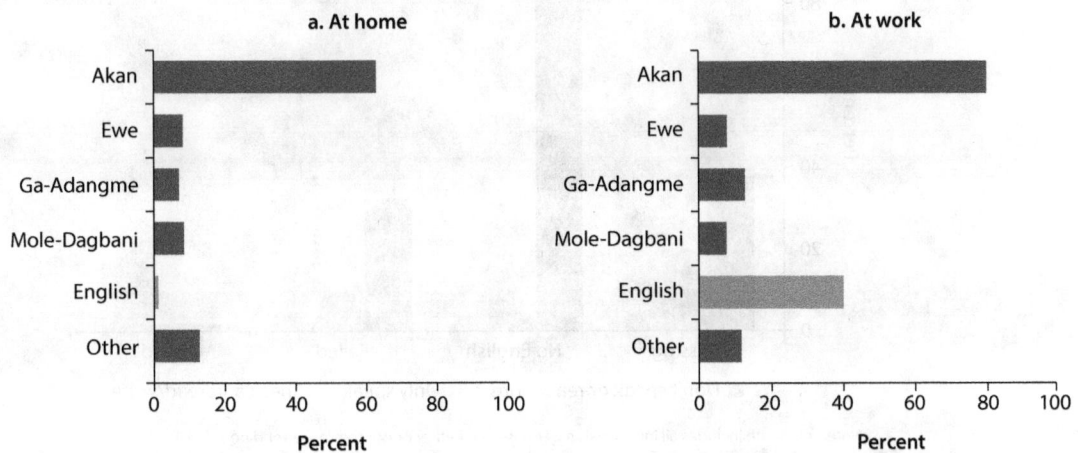

Note: This figure includes all individuals regardless of whether or not they are attending school as well as those who worked at any point during the previous 12 months.

box continues next page

Box 6.1 What Does It Mean to Pass the Core Literacy Test? *(continued)*

Figure B6.1.2 Self-Reported Ability to Speak and Read/Write in English at Work
percent

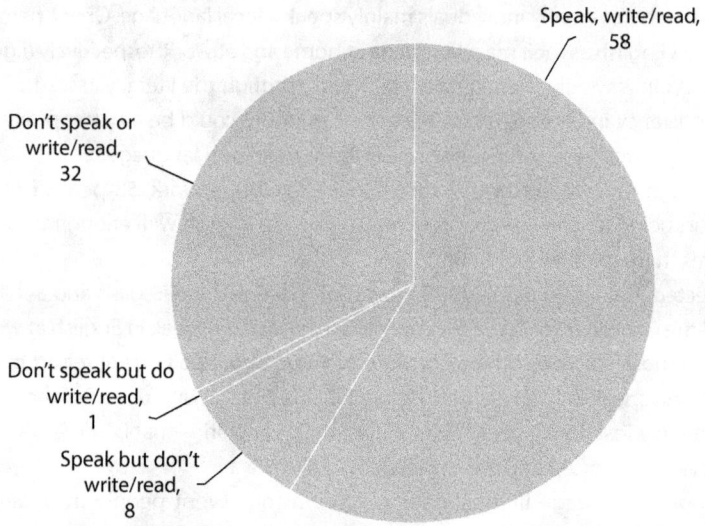

Speak, write/read, 58

Don't speak or write/read, 32

Don't speak but do write/read, 1

Speak but don't write/read, 8

Note: This figure includes individuals regardless of whether or not they are attending school. Proportions may not add up to 100 percent because figures are rounded.

Figure B6.1.3 Performance in the Core Literacy Test According to Self-Reported Ability to Speak and Read/Write in English

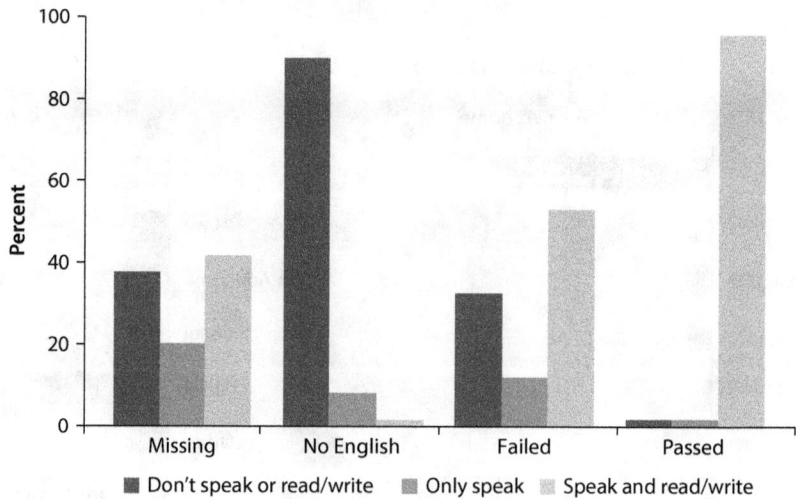

Note: This figure includes all individuals regardless of whether or not they are attending school.

box continues next page

Box 6.1 What Does It Mean to Pass the Core Literacy Test? *(continued)*

Figure B6.1.4 Did the Lack of English Keep You from Getting a Job?
percent

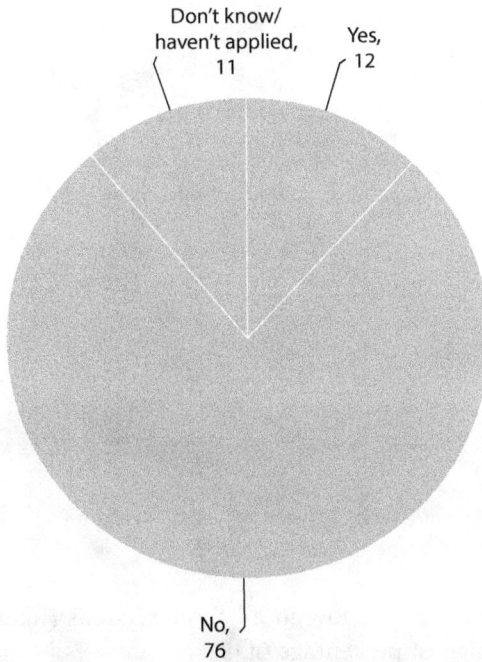

Note: The figure includes all individuals regardless of whether or not they are attending school and those who worked at any point during the previous 12 months. Proportions may not add up to 100 percent because figures are rounded.

education levels, are on average nine years younger, and are more likely to be students, to be wageworkers rather than self-employed, and to work in high-value occupations.

Although one-third of the missing group use English at work, 6 percent of those with no English literacy do. Furthermore, almost three-quarters (72 percent) of those with no English did not complete any formal education, whereas only 18 percent of the missing group has no education and 17 percent completed at least SHS. Also a lower percentage of those with no English reported using their reading and writing skills compared to those in the missing group.

Reading Components

The Reading Components section evaluates the extent to which participants can recognize the printed forms of common objects (*print vocabulary*), comprehend sentences of varying levels of complexity (*sentence processing*), and comprehend the literal meaning of connected text (*basic passage comprehension*).

Figure 6.13 Distribution of Reading Component and Core Literacy Test Respondents
percent

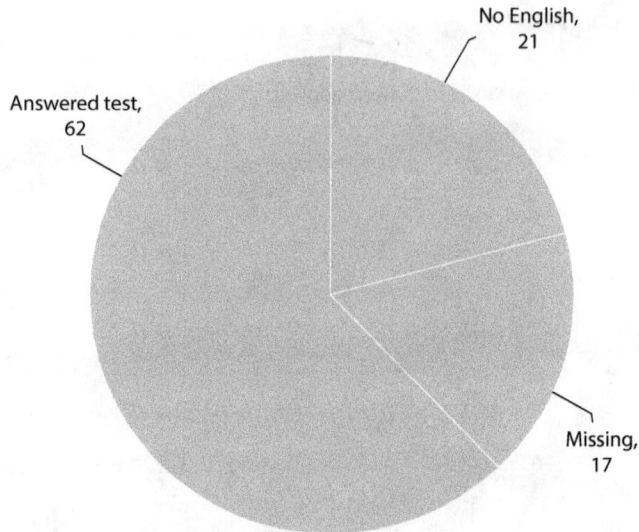

No English, 21

Answered test, 62

Missing, 17

Note: This figure includes only those who are currently in school.

The overall performance is low in all three sections (figure 6.14). Sentence processing has the highest percentage of correct answers (41 percent) at all education levels, age groups, and levels of self-reported use of skills. However, it is also the section with the highest percentage of nonresponse (19 percent) compared to 11 percent in print vocabulary and 9 percent in passage comprehension. In passage comprehension only 38 percent of the items are answered correctly. The lowest performance is in print vocabulary with only 21 percent correct answers.

Respondents reporting to be medium- to high-intensity readers or writers answer a higher percentage of correct answers in both the sentence processing and passage comprehension tests. The only exception is for the print vocabulary component, which does not vary much across groups (figure 6.15, panels a and b).

The percentage of correct answers increased with the education level achieved (figure 6.16, panel a), and younger cohorts performed better than older age groups (figure 6.16, panel b). Those with no formal education answered fewer than 24 percent of the questions in each section correctly. Even though the results improve across all levels of education, there is a more noticeable difference between junior high school (JHS) and SHS graduates. Those with a primary or a JHS education answered less than one-third of the test questions correctly, whereas those with an SHS or a tertiary education answered about 44 percent of the passage questions and 46 percent of the sentence questions correctly. However, even among those with tertiary education, the scores on the print vocabulary section are low, with an average of only 23 percent correct answers—only 4 percentage points

Figure 6.14 Performance on the Reading Component

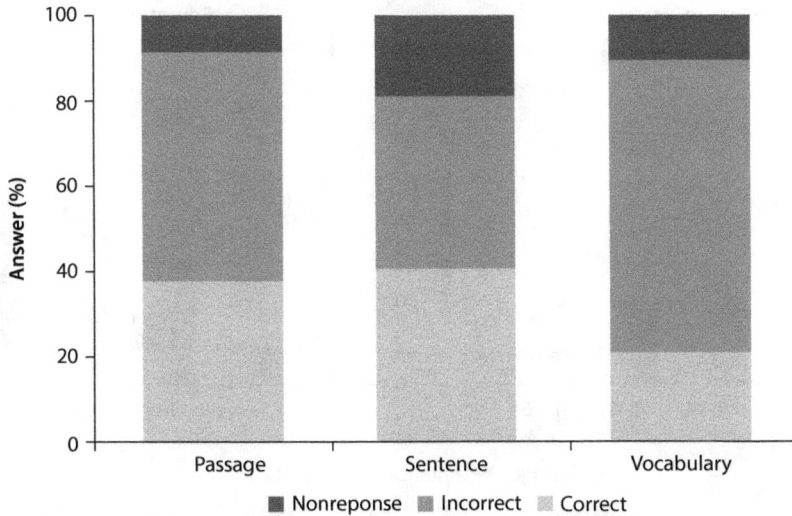

Note: This figure excludes the 38 percent of the sample that did not take these tests and includes people currently attending school. Proportions may not add up to 100 percent because figures are rounded.

Figure 6.15 Performance According to the Self-Reported Use of Reading and Writing Skills

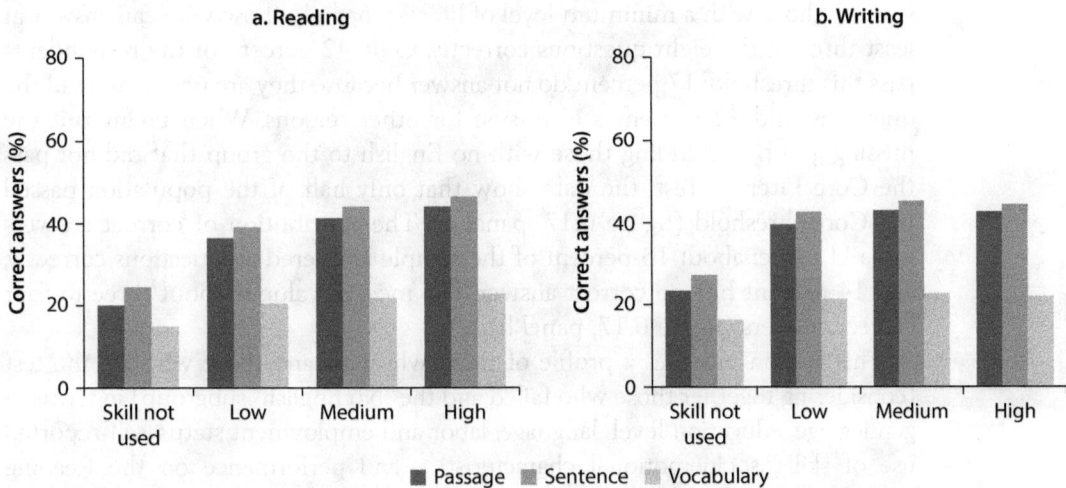

Note: This figure excludes the 17 percent of the sample that did not take these tests. Includes people currently attending school.

higher than those in primary education. Younger generations are more likely to perform better in the sentence and passage comprehension tests than older age groups (figure 6.16, panel b). This might suggest an improvement of the literacy level over time or might simply reflect a greater familiarity of the younger generations with taking assessment tests.

Figure 6.16 Performance According to Age Group and Education Level

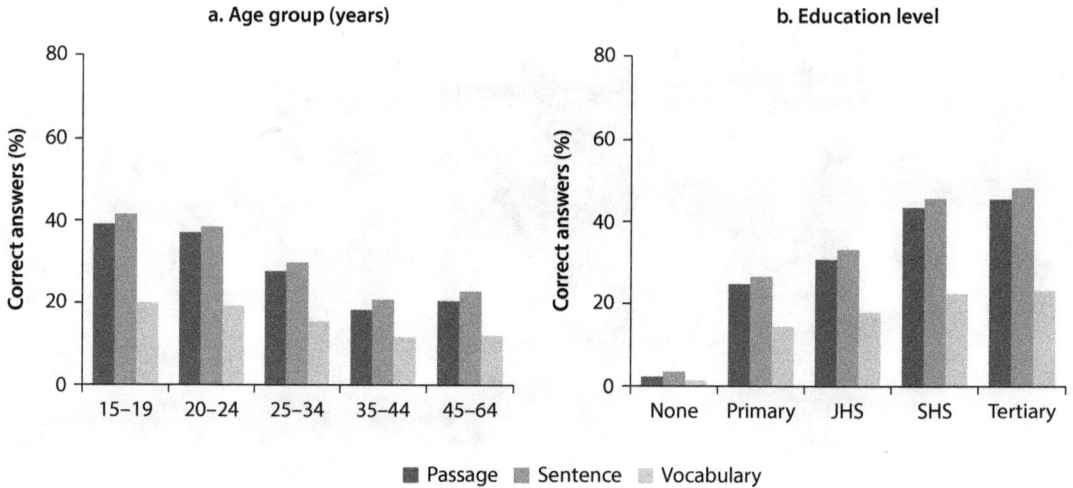

a. Age group (years)

b. Education level

Passage   Sentence   Vocabulary

Note: This figure excludes the 17 percent of the sample that did not take these tests and includes people currently attending school. JHS = junior high school; SHS = senior high school.

Core Literacy Test

The Core Literacy Test contains eight basic literacy questions and is designed to identify those with a minimum level of literacy, namely those who can answer at least three of the eight questions correctly. Only 42 percent of the respondents pass this threshold; 17 percent do not answer because they are unable to read the questions, and 22 percent are missing for other reasons. When taking out the missing group and adding those with no English to the group that did not pass the Core Literacy Test, the data show that only half of the population passed the Core threshold (figure 6.17, panel a). The distribution of correct answers has a U shape: about 15 percent of the sample answered all questions correctly, and 14 percent had no correct answer. The median value is about three to four correct answers (figure 6.17, panel b).

This section provides a profile of those who pass and those who fail the test (considering together those who failed and the "No English" subgroup) in terms of gender, age, education level, language, labor and employment status, self-reported use of skills, socioemotional characteristics, and performance on the Reading Components and Core Literacy Tests. Full results are reported in appendix D.

Young men with at least an SHS education are most likely to pass the test. More than half of those who pass the exam were male and seven years younger than the average. Ninety-three percent of those who failed the test had a JHS education or lower (42 percent have no formal education and 33 percent attended JHS), whereas about 57 percent of those who passed the test had at least an SHS education and about 21 percent have tertiary education. Notably, about 81 percent of those who passed the exam had received early childhood education compared with 47 percent of those who failed.

Figure 6.17 Core Literacy Test Performance
percent

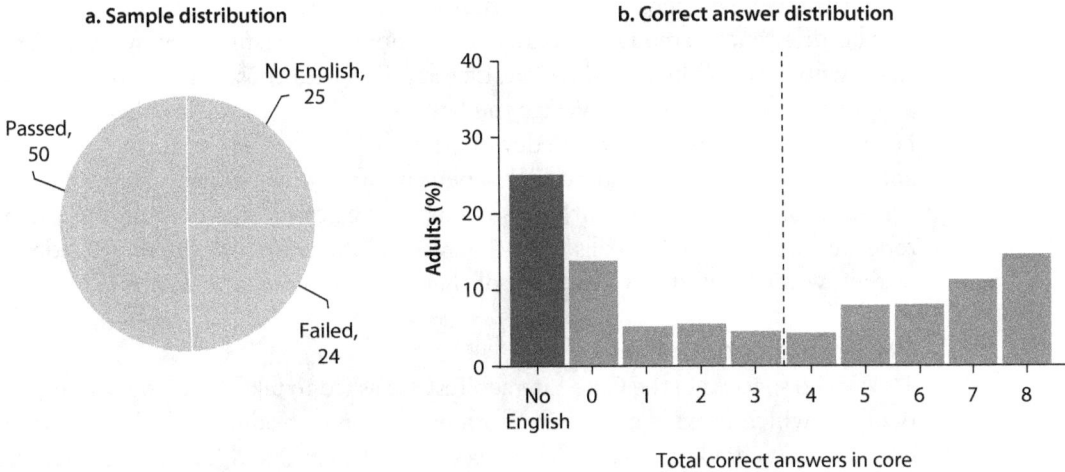

a. Sample distribution

No English, 25

Passed, 50

Failed, 24

b. Correct answer distribution

Total correct answers in core

Note: This figure excludes the 17 percent of the sample that did not take these tests and includes people currently attending school. Proportions may not add up to 100 percent because figures are rounded.

The variables for socioeconomic status (SES) and whether English was the respondent's main language are both highly correlated with the probability of passing the test. About 30 percent of those who failed the test have been poor during their adolescence, and only 15 percent of them passed the Core Literacy Test.

Although English is Ghana's official language, only 1 percent of all respondents reported speaking English at home and 40 percent at work. Because the reading test was in English, it is not surprising that a higher percentage of those who passed the test than of those who failed reported English as the main language at home and at work. Among those who passed the test, 73 percent use English at work compared with 17 percent of those failing the test.

Furthermore, the probability of succeeding is higher for those working in the formal sector and in high-skilled and better-paid occupations. Within the employed group, 81 percent of those who failed the test are self-employed and only 3 percent are formal wageworkers. More than half work in mid-skilled occupations and only 3 percent are in high-skilled jobs. In contrast, 38 percent of those who passed the exam were self-employed and 34 percent were formal wageworkers. One-third worked in high-skilled occupations and earn on average 274 GHS (approximately US$80) more per month than those who failed the test.

Self-reported measures of the use and intensity of use of reading and writing skills is highly correlated with the results of the Core Literacy Test. Nevertheless, a significant number of people who reported using their skills regularly failed the test. Indeed, of those who did not pass the test, about 42 and 38 percent, respectively, reported using their reading and writing skills. The (self-reported) intensity of use of reading and writing skills is a better predictor of the test results. Indeed, 41 percent of those who pass the test are regular (high-intensive) readers compared to only 12 percent of those who fail the test. Similarly, 83 percent of those who fail the test self-report being low-intensity writers, and the percentage of low-intensity writers is lower (63 percent) among those who did not pass the test.

The differences among respondents are more significant when we compare those who successfully pass the Core Literacy Test with those who do not answer any questions correctly. On average the latter have lower education (half of them have not completed any formal education); only 5 percent speak English at work and none of them use it at home. Eighty percent of these respondents are employed and most of them (79 percent) are self-employed. Fewer than one-third of them report using their reading skills (only 9 percent of them are high-intensive readers) or their writing skills (only 2 percent of them are high-intensive writers).

Literacy Exercise Booklets

Those who succeed in the Core Literacy Test are asked to take the Literacy Exercise Booklets, which provide a more in-depth evaluation of reading skills. The Literacy Booklets are scored on a scale that ranges from 0 to 500 and includes six literacy levels from "below level 1" to level 5. The description of the literacy competencies for each one of the levels is provided in table 3.2. The "below level 1" includes those who failed the Core test (half of the original sample) and an imputed score for those who did not answer (about 17 percent of the eligible sample).[3]

The average performance on the Literacy Exercise Booklets is very poor. Most of the population (61 percent) is below level 1, 18 percent reach level 1, 17 percent reach level 2, only 4 percent of the respondents reach level 3 or level 4 (reported together in figure 6.18), and no one is in level 5.

The level achieved is positively correlated with the number of correct answers in the Core Literacy Test. Those with a reading proficiency below level 1 are those who did not reach the minimum threshold set for the Core Literacy Test (three correct answers) (about 33 percent) and the group with no English literacy (34 percent). However, 11 percent of those below level 1 passed the Core test but performed poorly in the subsequent assessment. On the other hand, those in level 3 and 4 answered correctly at least six of the Core test questions. Indeed, 93 percent of them correctly answered seven or more questions in the Core test (figure 6.19).

Like those passing the Core test, those scoring high in the literacy assessment are younger, have higher education (SHS or tertiary), and are more likely to work in the formal sector, to use their reading and writing skills more intensively, and to use English more frequently at work and at home (figure 6.20).

Performance on the Literacy Exercise Booklets is correlated with the self-reported reading intensity as well. For example, among those who passed the Core Literacy Test with three to six correct answers, more of those who self-reported using their reading skills with high intensity reached level 1 than did those who read with low intensity (52 percent versus 43 percent) and level 2 (25 percent versus 14 percent) (figure 6.21). Similarly, among those who completed the whole Core Literacy Test correctly, 27 percent of the high-intensity readers reached levels 3 and 4 on the Literacy Exercise Booklets versus only 7 percent of those who self-reported reading with low intensity.

Figure 6.18 Performance on Literacy Exercise Booklets: Proficiency Levels

percent

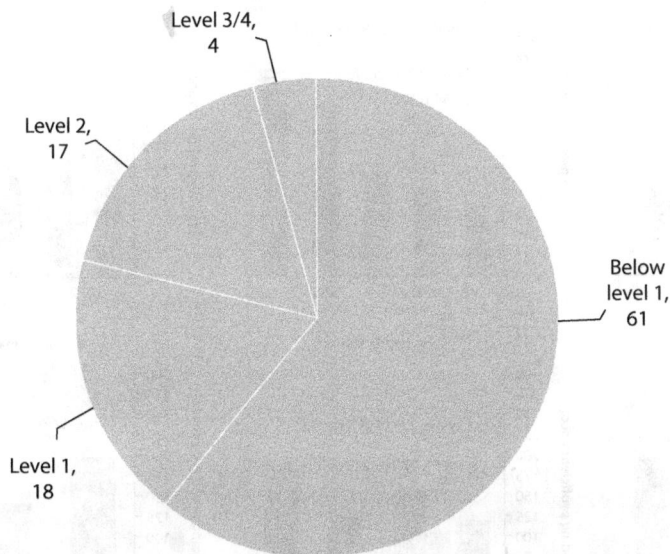

Note: The "below level 1" portion includes those who failed the core test (half of the original sample) and an imputed score for those who did not answer (about 17 percent of the eligible sample).

Figure 6.19 Distribution of Core Literacy Test Results, by Proficiency Levels Achieved on Literacy Exercise Booklets

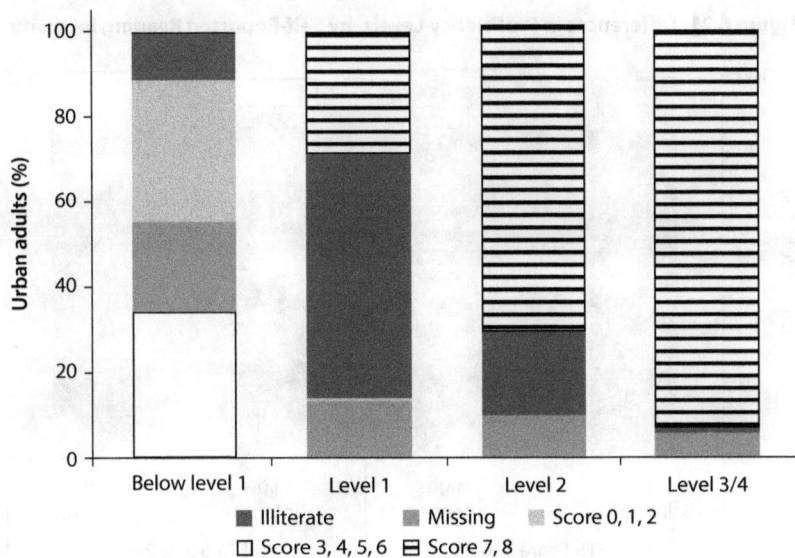

Figure 6.20 Literacy Level According to Gender, Education Level, Age Group, Reading Intensity, Labor Status, and Employment Status

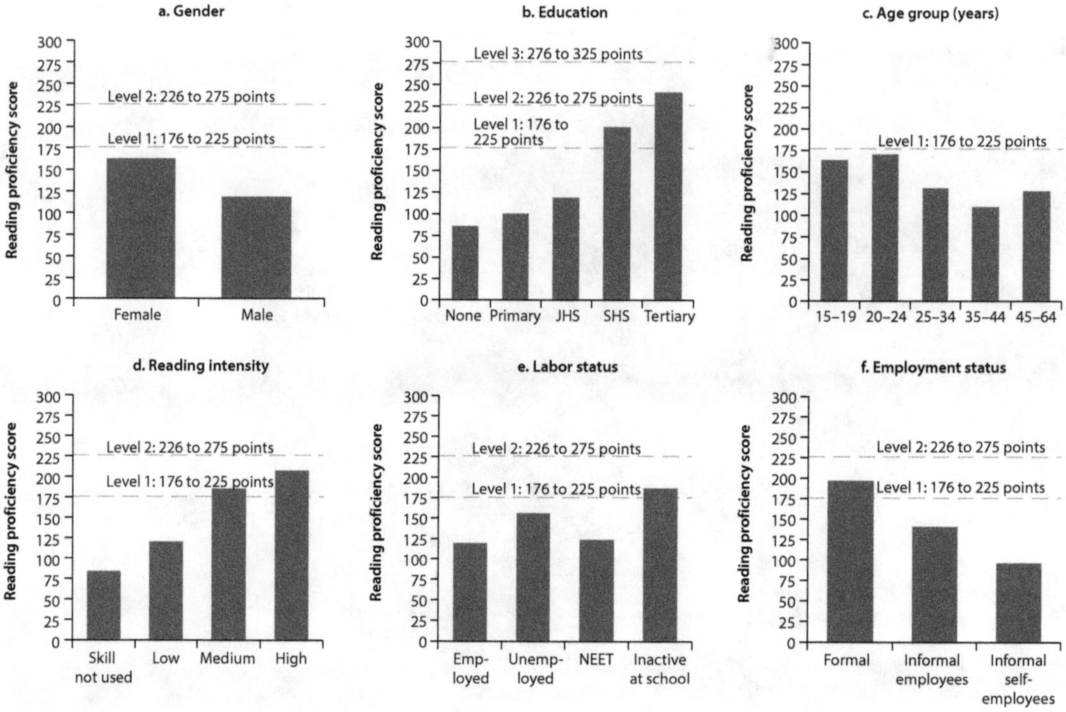

Note: JHS = junior high school; NEET = Not in Education, Employment, or Training; SHS = senior high school.

Figure 6.21 Differences in Proficiency Levels, by Self-Reported Reading Intensity

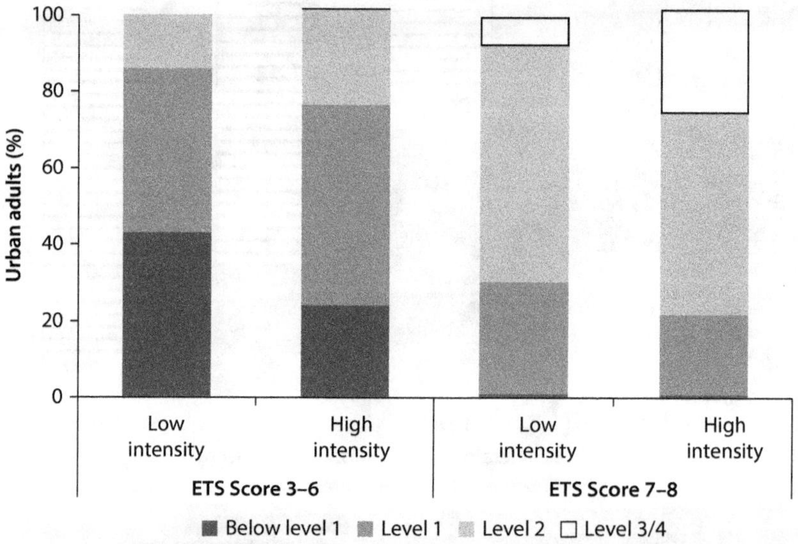

Note: ETS = Educational Testing Service.

Developing Skills beyond Education: Training and Apprenticeships

In Ghana 32 percent of the adult population living in urban areas continue their skills development by participating in skills training courses, by achieving industry- or government-recognized certificates, and through informal apprenticeships. Apprenticeship is the most common: in the 12 months prior the survey, 25 percent of adults participated in an apprenticeship, whereas only 6 percent received a recognized training certificate and less than 7 percent participated in a formal training course of at least 30 hours. It is worth noting that, although apprenticeship is more common for older age cohorts (figure 6.22, panel b) and among those with JHS or lower education, training is more common for those with tertiary education (figure 6.22, panel a).

After completing each level of formal education, students might continue with the next level of formal education or leave the education system and take an apprenticeship instead. As shown in figure 6.23, apprenticeship does not replace formal education. Indeed, most of people who complete an education level either decide to drop out of school or continue in formal education. Among those completing primary education, only 4 percent left the education system for an apprenticeship, 65 percent start JHS, and 10 percent drop out. The percent of those opting for an apprenticeship is the highest among those completing JHS: 13 percent of them choose an apprenticeship while 30 percent continue to SHS.

Formal workers generally have more training outside the formal education system, whereas apprenticeship is more common among the self-employed. Twenty-six percent of formal workers participated in work-related or personal-related skill training courses, 25 percent participated in apprenticeships, and 14 percent achieved an industry- or government-recognized certificate. About 38 percent of the self-employed participate in an apprenticeship (figure 6.24). Apprenticeships are also more common among those working in low-skilled occupations and in the manufacturing sector (figure 6.25). The most common

Figure 6.22 Certificate, Training, and Apprenticeship, by Education Level and Age Group

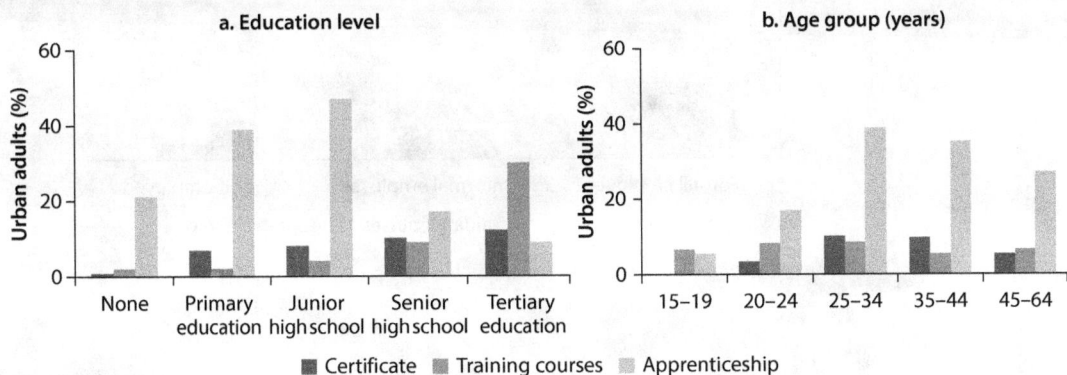

Note: The figure excludes those who are currently at school.

Stepping Up Skills in Urban Ghana • http://dx.doi.org/10.1596/978-1-4648-1012-1

Figure 6.23 Are Students Choosing Apprenticeship Instead of Formal Education?

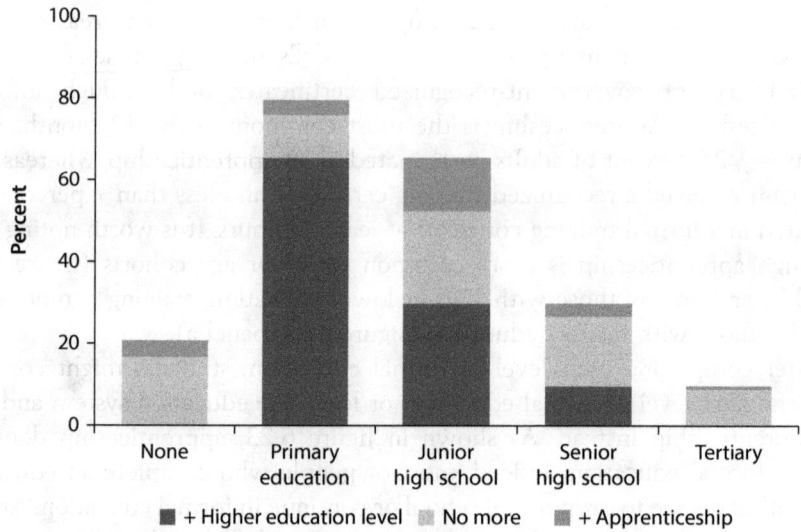

Note: The figure excludes those who are currently at school. The subgroup "+ Higher education level" includes those who, after completing a certain education level, continue with the next level of education. The subgroup "+ Apprenticeship" includes those who complete a certain education level, drop out, and opt for an apprenticeship. The subgroup "No more" includes those who, after completing a certain education level, left school without completing another level of education.

Figure 6.24 Certificate, Training, and Apprenticeship, by Employment Status

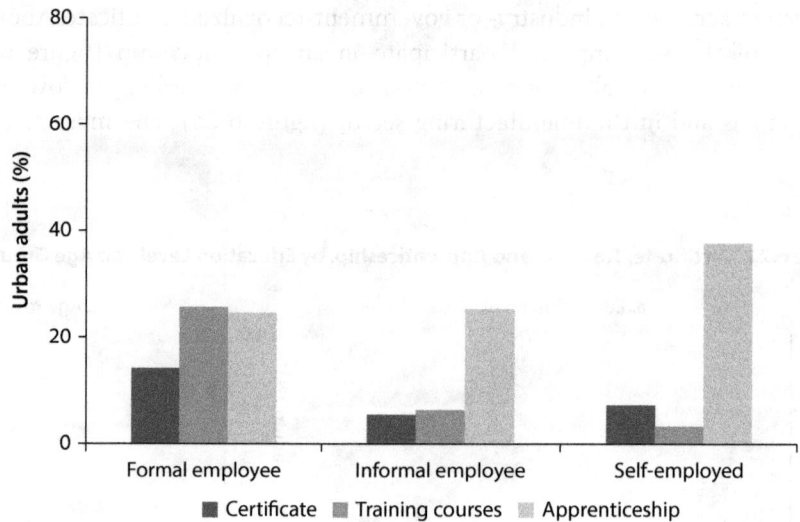

Note: The figure excludes those who are currently at school.

Figure 6.25 Certificate, Training, and Apprenticeship, by Occupation and Economic Sector

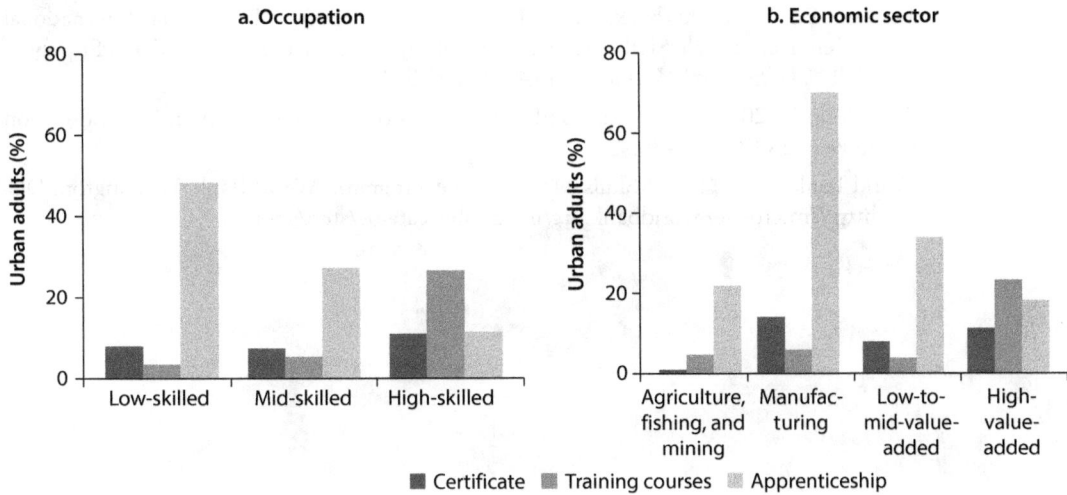

a. Occupation

b. Economic sector

■ Certificate ■ Training courses ░ Apprenticeship

Note: The figure excludes those who are currently at school.

field of apprenticeship is personal service, retail, and related (65 percent), where the category barber, hairdresser, hair stylist, and cosmetologist accounted for close to 40 percent of the apprenticeships.

Notes

1. See appendix B for a definition of skills use and intensity of use variables.
2. This group includes for example those refusing to begin the test booklet (because of time constraints, not wanting to bother, or other general refusal), those who began the booklet but refused to continue, or those who were unable to continue because of an unusual circumstance.
3. The literacy proficiency is modeled using the item response theory in a scale that ranges from 0 to 500. Each point in the 500-point scale has a probability of completing the tested item. The higher the score for a given individual, the more proficient the individual is. The design divides the test into partially linked booklets so that only a portion of the entire battery of items is administered to a single individual. Otherwise, the assessment would be too long if every individual had to take the entire battery of items. In order to estimate the proficiency level, multiple literacy proficiency scores (plausible values) are estimated for each individual on the basis of response to the items as well as some background information. Only those who passed the Core had to respond to this booklet, providing a finer evaluation of reading skills for the most literate respondents. However, imputation allows estimating the reading proficiency level for all respondents.

References

Leuven, E., H. Oosterbeek, and H. van Ophem. 2004. "Explaining International Differences in Male Skill Wage Differentials by Differences in Demand and Supply of Skill." *The Economic Journal* 114 (495): 466–86.

Tyler, John H. 2004. "Basic Skills and the Earnings of Dropouts." Economic of Education Review 23 (3): 221–35.

World Bank. 2014. "STEP Skills Measurement Program." World Bank, Washington, DC. http://microdata.worldbank.org/index.php/catalog/step/about.

CHAPTER 7

The Returns to Education and Skills: Building the Job-Relevant Skills That Employers Demand

Introduction

This section discusses the payoffs of education and skills in term of earnings and job opportunities. This section answers the following questions in detail: To what extent does education explain better labor market opportunities and higher earnings? (And at which educational level does further investment in education not generate a premium?) Do skilled workers have higher earnings? Which skills yield the best labor market opportunities and higher earnings?

The analysis carried out in this section involves descriptive statistics and two multivariate regression models. The first model is a Mincer equation for earnings. The second is an employment participation model. These models look at the correlation between education and/or skills and monthly earnings and employment status, respectively. For the two models we tried different specifications. The first specification reported in the figures and tables below does not include any controls and reports only the "pure" correlation between monthly earnings (or self-employment status) and the education variables (either years of education or education levels where those with no formal education or incomplete primary are used as a reference category). In the second model, we control for a core set of sociodemographic variables including age, gender, work experience, economic sectors, and regional dummies. Then we include a set of controls one at time to see how education returns vary when taking into account (i) the results of the proficiency assessment test (the number of correct answers in the Core Literacy Test and the percentage of correct answers on the Reading Components); (ii) individual personality traits; (iii) the intensity of the use of cognitive skills; (iv) the intensity of the use of job-specific skills (cognitive challenges, physical work, autonomy and repetitiveness, presentation skills, supervision skills, and the use of computer at work); and (v) all of the controls together. All control variables are defined in appendix C and full results are reported in appendixes D and E.[1]

Returns to Education and Skills

Our data show some returns for continued education. An additional year of education increases monthly earnings by 3–7 percent (figure 7.1). Notably, primary education has no distinguishable premium in terms of earnings, considering those with no formal education or incomplete primary education as a base category. We also found that market rewards for primary education and junior high school (JHS) are lower than those for senior high school (SHS) and higher levels of education.[2] For higher education, the premium is between 16 and 63 percent for SHS graduates and between 77 and 156 percent for tertiary graduates compared to workers with no formal education or incomplete primary education. The premium for JHS is much lower (between 10 and 40 percent). Faced with uncertain and binding constraints, people are more likely to drop out of school before SHS. In fact, as mentioned above, the majority of the population (66 percent) leaves the education system before SHS.

Figure 7.1 Returns to Education

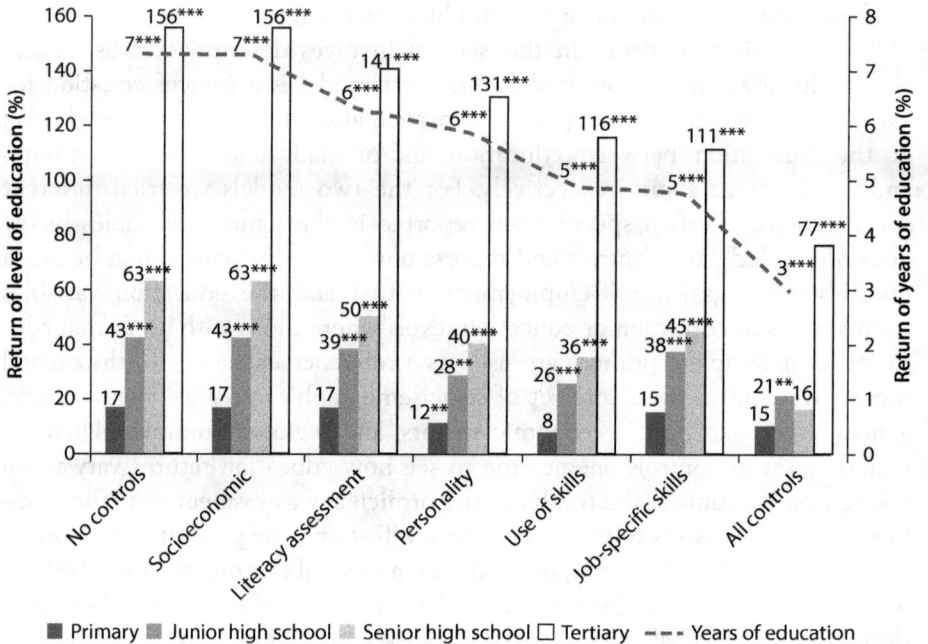

Primary   Junior high school   Senior high school   Tertiary   — — Years of education

Note: All models are estimated using ordinary least squares. The estimated coefficients for each education level (bars) and for the years of education (dotted line) are reported in the figure.
***$p < .01$, **$p < .05$, *$p < 0.1$.

Overall skills are an important determinant of earnings beyond education. In fact the returns of any additional year of education decrease by 2 percentage points after all skills have been controlled for. The best-paid jobs are those that require intensive writing and job-specific skills such as the use of the computer and also involve cognitive challenges and supervision responsibilities. Out of the "Big Five" personality traits (openness, conscientiousness, extraversion, agreeableness, and stability), only the estimated coefficient for conscientiousness is statistically significant (see appendix E). Notably, even after accounting for all skills (cognitive, socioemotional, and job-specific skills), SHS and tertiary education have a significantly higher earnings premium.

The returns to education and skills vary a great deal according to types of employment, with the lowest returns among self-employed and the highest among formal wageworkers. One additional year of education increases the monthly earnings of the self-employed by 1–5 percent, those of informal wageworkers by 4–6 percent, and those of formal wageworkers by 7–10 percent (see figure 7.2 and appendix E).

Earnings differentials are a typical feature of labor market segmentation. More specifically, an earnings gap between informal sector workers and equally qualified formal wage and salaried employees can be interpreted as a measure of the degree of labor market segmentation (Schultz 1961; Becker 1962; and Mincer 1962). In countries such as Ghana, the formal economy is not capable of

Figure 7.2 Returns to Education, by Type of Employment

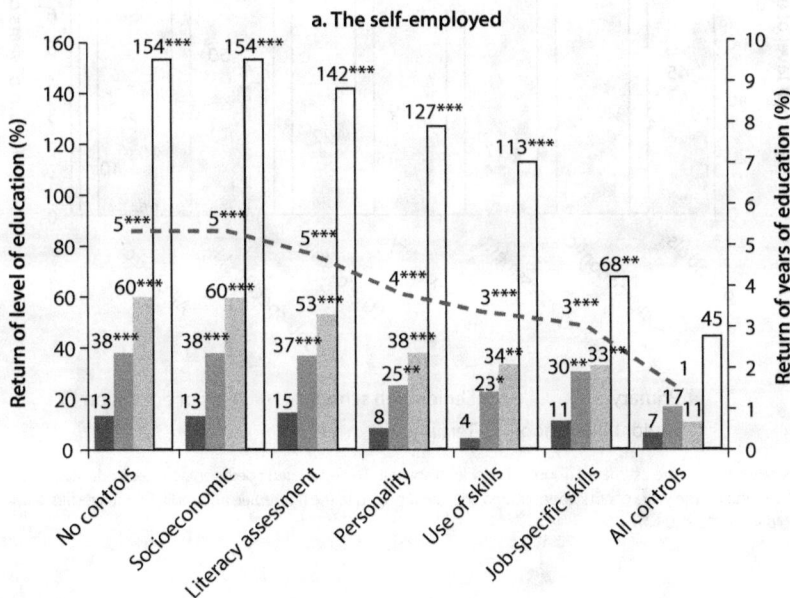

a. The self-employed

figure continues next page

Figure 7.2 Returns to Education *(continued)*

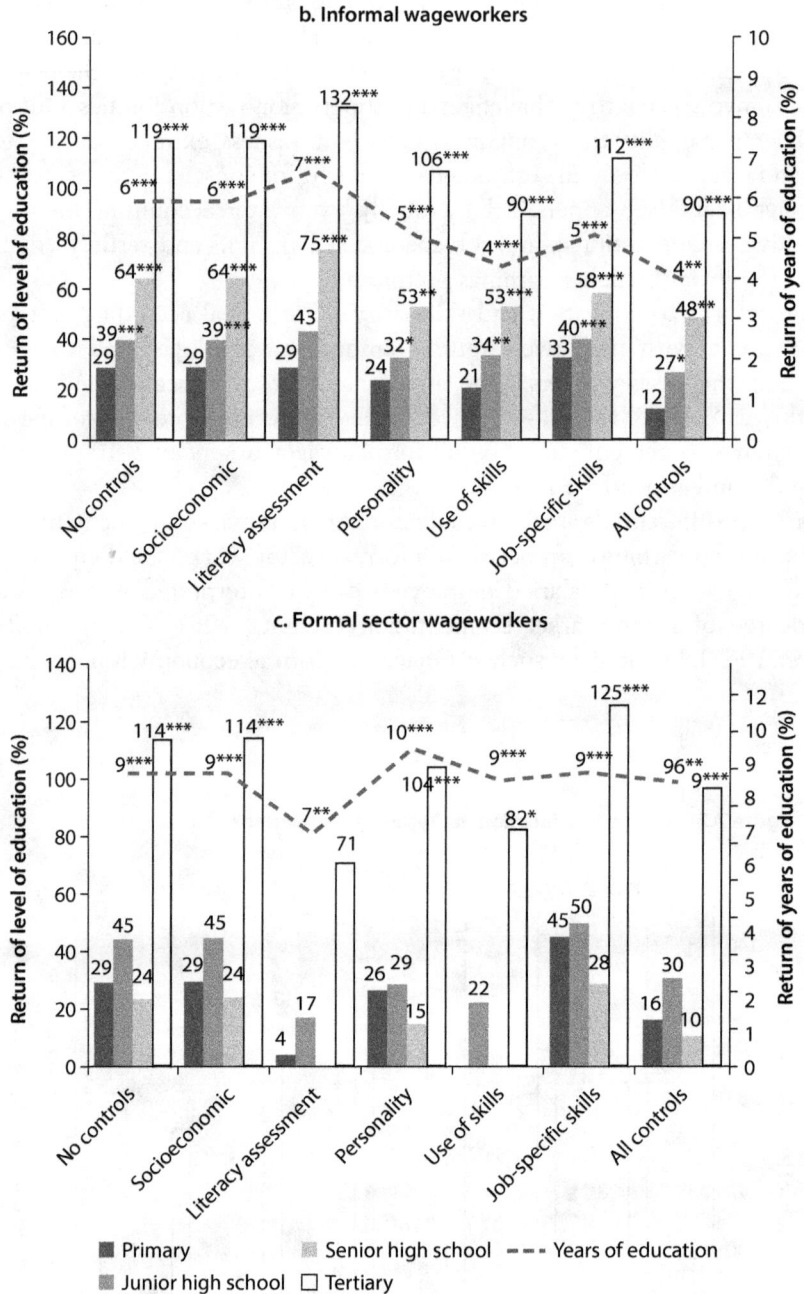

b. Informal wageworkers

c. Formal sector wageworkers

Legend:
- ■ Primary
- ▨ Junior high school
- ▨ Senior high school
- □ Tertiary
- – – – Years of education

Note: All models are estimated using ordinary least squares. The estimated coefficients for each education level (bars) and for the years of education (dotted line) are reported in the figure. See appendix E for full results.
***$p < .01$, **$p < .05$, *$p < 0.1$.

providing enough good, high-wage jobs. The majority of self-employment consists of informal income-earning activities and small businesses pursued by individuals who are unable to secure (formal) wage employment.

The key to accessing the formal wage sector is once again education (figure 7.3). About 44 percent of workers employed in the formal sector have a tertiary education and 32 percent have graduated from SHS, whereas only 24 percent have a JHS education or less. In Ghana the formal sector mainly consists of high-value-added service companies, which require a highly qualified labor force.

Only tertiary education has a significant premium in the formal sector given the selection bias. This means, for example, that individuals with higher ability and motivation are more likely to choose and complete tertiary education and receive higher earnings. Graduates of SHS and JHS and those who have completed primary education all have the same probability as workers with no formal education of being self-employed (figure 7.4). Furthermore, self-employed workers use their numeracy skills more intensively than all other employees and perform fewer repetitive tasks and use the computer less. With respect to socioemotional skills, only grit is positively correlated with being self-employed (see appendix E).

Figure 7.3 Level of Education, by Employment Status

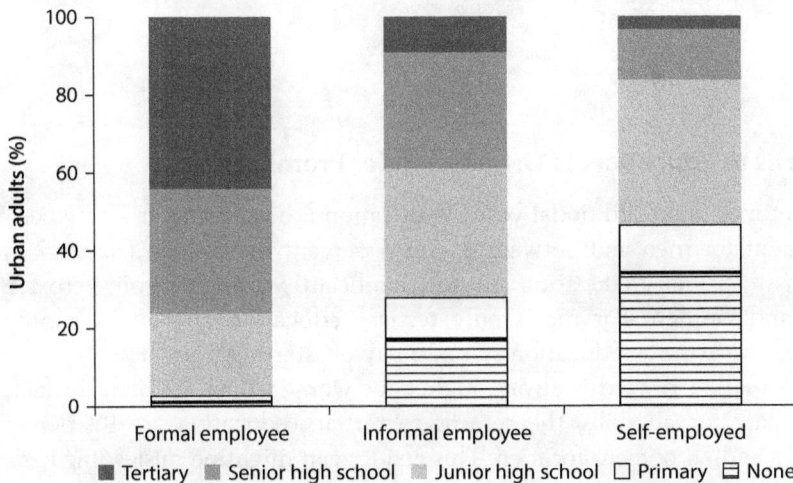

Note: The figure excludes people currently attending school. Proportions may not add up to 100 percent because figures have been rounded.

Figure 7.4 Linear Probability Model of Being Self-Employed

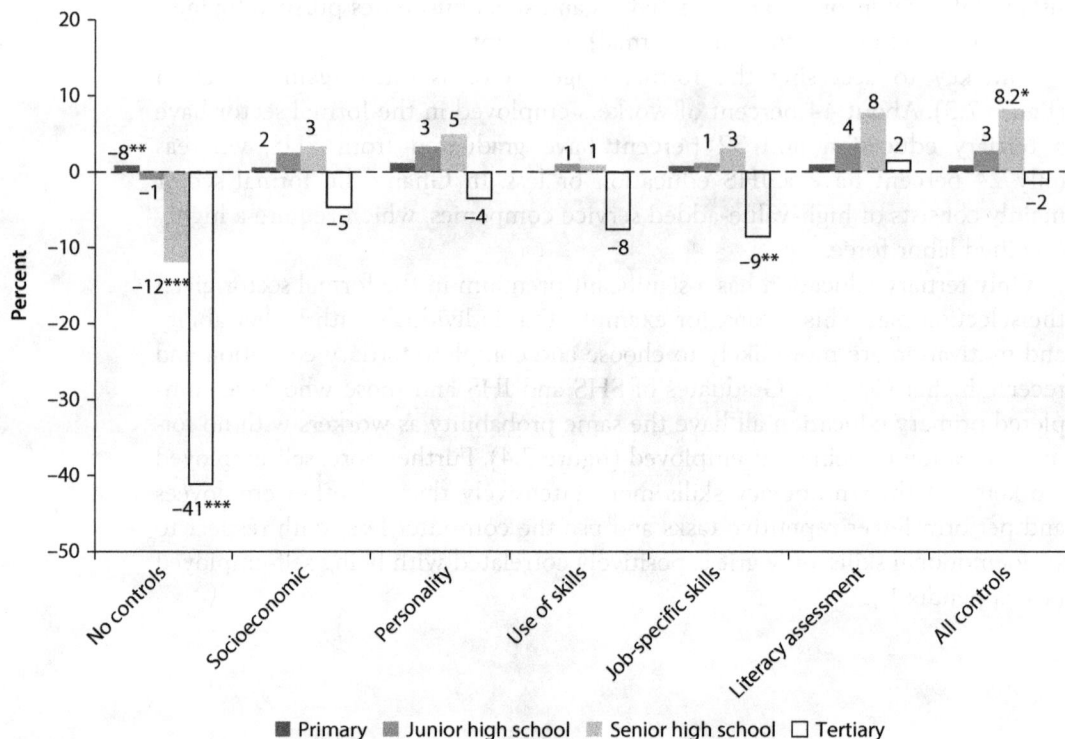

Note: All models are estimated using linear probability model. The estimated coefficients for each education level (bars) are reported in the figure. See appendix E for full results.
***$p < .01$, **$p < .05$, *$p < 0.1$.

Returns to Education: Is There a Gender Premium?

The returns to an additional year of education are very similar—between 3 and 5 percent for men and between 3 and 6 percent for women (figure 7.5). The returns to primary education are not significantly different from zero for both men and women. For males only tertiary education guarantees a premium, whereas for women education starts to pay off starting from JHS.

The market reward is always higher for women than for men. In fact, after controlling for all skills, the returns to tertiary education are 98 percent for females and 73 percent for men. This gender gap might be misleading because it does not take into account that both labor market participation and educational attainments are lower for women.

Figure 7.5 The Returns to Education

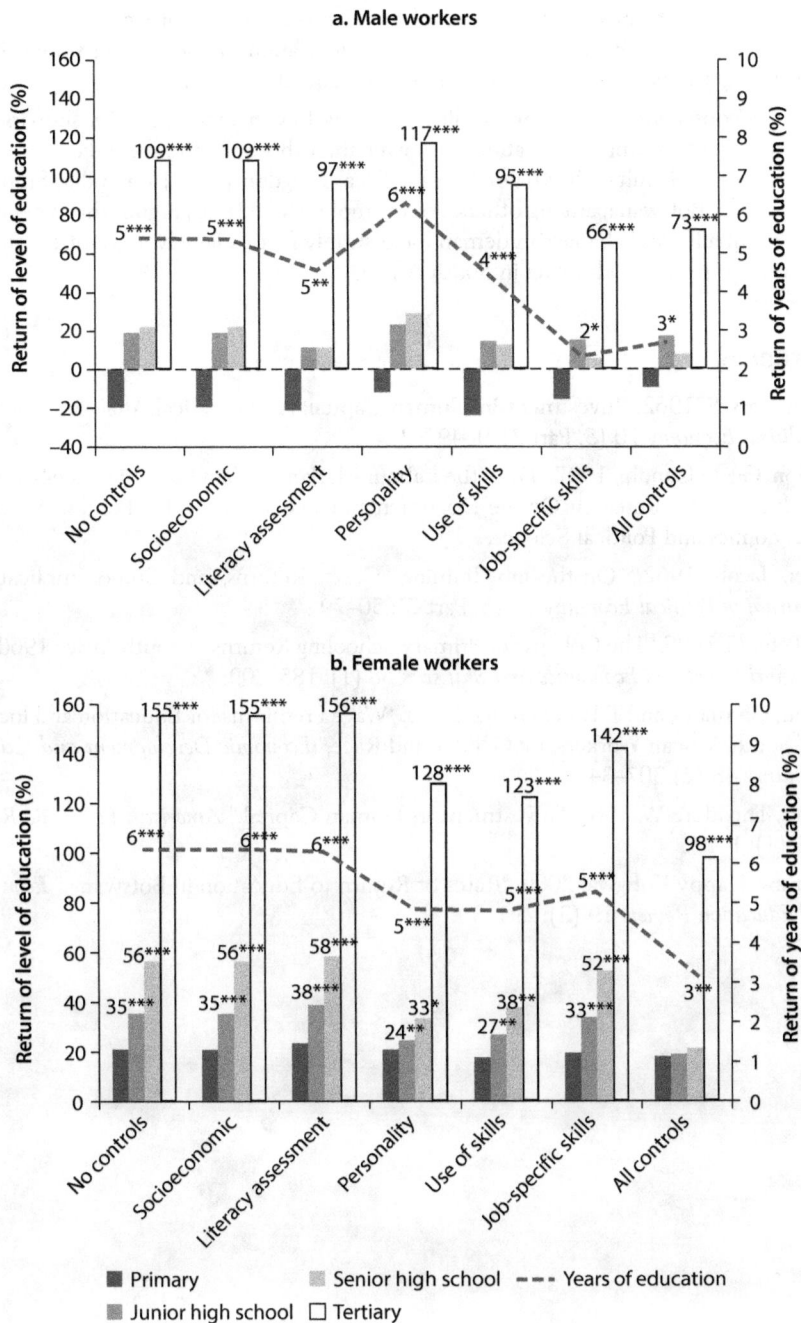

a. Male workers

b. Female workers

■ Primary   ▨ Senior high school   - - - Years of education
▨ Junior high school □ Tertiary

Note: All models are estimated using ordinary least squares. The estimated coefficients for each education level
(bars) and for the years of education (dotted line) are reported in the figure. See appendix E for full results.
***p < .01, **p < .05, *p < 0.1.

Notes

1. We recognize the possible limitations of this estimation procedure in terms of possible multi-collinearity. Furthermore, a causal interpretation of the finding shown in the following sections is not either legitimate or claimed.

2. This is consistent with recent studies for many low-income countries showing that the returns to primary education are lower than those for the secondary level—see Mwabu and Schultz (2000) for South Africa, Kingdon (1997) for India, Siphambe (2000) for Botswana, among others. For example, Moll (1996) argues that a decline in school quality and changes in demand and supply factors largely account for the low returns to primary schooling in South Africa.

References

Becker, Gary S. 1962. "Investment in Human Capital: A Theoretical Analysis." *Journal of Political Economy* 70 (5, Part 2): 9–49.

Kingdon, Geeta Gandhi. 1997. "Does the Labour Market Explain Lower Female Schooling in India?" LSE Research Online Documents of Economics 6715, London School of Economics and Political Science.

Mincer, Jacob. 1962. "On-the-Job Training: Costs, Returns, and Some Implications." *Journal of Political Economy* 70 (5, Part 2): 50–79.

Moll, Peter G. 1996. "The Collapse of Primary Schooling Returns in South Africa 1960–90." *Oxford Bulletin of Economics and Statistics* 58 (1): 185–209.

Mwabu, Germano, and T. Paul Schultz. 2000. "Wage Premiums for Education and location of South African Workers, by Gender and Race." *Economic Development and Cultural Change* 48 (2) 307–34.

Schultz, Theodore W. 1961. "Investment in Human Capital." *American Economic Review* 51 (1): 1–17.

Siphambe, Happy Kufigwa. 2000. "Rates of Return to Education in Botswana." *Economics of Education Review* 19 (3): 291–300.

CHAPTER 8

Mismatch of Skills: A Measurement Issue and Unexploited Potential at Work

Mismatch between Self-Reported Skills and Core Literacy Test Results: Does Language Matter?

Several of the cognitive and job-specific skills captured in the Skills Toward Employment and Productivity (STEP) survey are self-reported. These self-reported measures relate to the intensity of use of these skills at work or outside work. The self-reported reading skill measure can capture a subjective assessment of the mastery and usefulness of the skill, but a key question is how well these assessments fit in with some objective measures such as the Core Literacy Test. If subjective and objective measures reflected a real ability, those reporting that they read frequently should also be able to pass the Core test. However, although 69 percent of adults reported reading regularly, only 42 percent of the population passed the Core test.

This considerable mismatch is due to both the high nonresponse rate for the objective literacy assessment (in contrast to low missing values for the subjective measurements) and the difficulties encountered in the Core test because of the language used. As a consequence, the Core test is more likely to be a measure of the individual's English literacy than of his or her general reading skills. Notably, the self-reported assessment of the use of skills does not specify a particular language, and respondents might indeed take it to mean any of the local languages widely used not only in the rural Ghana but also in urban areas.

There is a considerable mismatch between the self-reported and the assessed reading skills (that is, between those reporting that they read and those passing the Core test). Indeed, about 26 percent of those who reported reading did not pass the Core test. Still, those not passing the Core test and reporting reading are 41 percentage points more likely to speak English at work (74 percent use English at work whereas 33 percent do not) and slightly more likely to speak English at home (close to 2 percentage points).

The mismatch between self-reported and measured literacy is not randomly distributed (see appendix F). Those who failed the Core test and reported being able to read are more likely to be women, to be less educated, to work in low-skilled occupations and less in high-value-added sectors, and to earn about 41 percent less than those who report being able to read and also pass the Core test.

The difference in the intensity of use of reading skills might definitively explain the skills mismatch between self-reported and objective measures of skills. The intensity of use of the skill is a more closely related measure to the Core test. Among those who self-reported reading with low intensity, 66 percent failed the text and 30 percent passed it. Only 14 percent of those who failed indicated reading frequently.

Are There Unexploited Skills in the Workforce?

Among the employed population, a group of individuals reported using their cognitive skills and computer skills in their daily life (that is, using skills outside the realm of a paid job, including a family business) but not at work. This group of people might represent unexploited human capital that the labor market is not able to absorb. In this section, we analyze the profile of those who report using their skills only outside work and those who use their skills at work.

Women—more frequently than men—are likely to be literate but employed in occupations not requiring the use of reading and writing skills. Similarly, there is an unexploited potential among the youngest generations who are able to use computers but work in jobs where this skill is not demanded. Being able to use their computer skills at work would guarantee them a monthly income 38 percent higher than they receive in their current occupations.

Those using a skill only at home are less likely to work at a high-skilled occupation and in a high-value-added sector and are more likely to work at a mid-skilled occupation and a low- to mid-value-added sector. The greatest unexploited potential, as expected, is among those in low-skilled occupations and low-value-added sectors. For example, about 34 percent of the self-employed read at home but never use their reading skills at work. Conversely, only 6 percent of employees in the formal sector have a skills mismatch.

The level of education seems to be closely related to the use of certain skills at work. The level of education of those who read, write, or use computers only at home is lower than for those using their skills at work. The latter are predominantly senior high school (SHS) graduates. The fact that the mismatch of skills occurs more at lower levels of education than SHS might suggest that SHS provides students with the right skills demanded by the labor market and that SHS education provides a clear signal to employers of the cognitive skills potential employees have.

To a certain extent the mismatch of skills used at home but remaining unused at work does reflect the quality of those skills rather than an unexploited potential. Indeed, on average those using their (reading, writing, and computer) skills only at home performed worse on both the Reading Component and the Core test than those who also use them at work.

To sum up, there is a clear connection between the availability of skills and the use of skills at work, whether the skills are cognitive or work related. Moreover, the use of the skills at work appears to explain the difference between objectively measured and self-reported skills. Those who work in low-skilled occupations are more likely to report higher skills than are measured objectively through the literacy assessment.

Conclusions and Looking Forward

In conclusion, the study has provided evidence in a number of areas that are relevant for policy makers, for setting government investment priorities and also for continued diagnostic work. The study demonstrated the positive impact of early childhood education on schooling, on jobs, and on earnings. The country continues to demonstrate progress in education attainment at all levels, but there is also evidence of persistent disparities in attainment by income, gender, and geographical location. There are also continued difficulties with delayed education, dropout, and low completion rate—mostly for the poor, given the high opportunity costs. Importantly, improved education attainment did not bring about comparable improvements in cognitive skills as measured by the adult literacy assessment.

The labor market also shows persistent segregation between employment in higher-value sectors, where employees have higher attainment and education pays off, and employment in sectors such as agriculture, fishing, and mining, where there appears to be an equilibrium of low education and low income. In the first group, employees demonstrate and report higher skills. There is a clear connection between the availability of skills and the use of skills at work, whether the skills are cognitive or work related. Moreover, the use of the skills at work appears to explain the difference between objectively measured and self-reported skills. Those who work in low-skilled occupations are more likely to report higher skills than are measured objectively through the literacy assessment.

These findings offer some priorities and options for policy and investment. For the country, investment and scaled-up access and quality in early childhood education would lead to sustained long-term growth and shared prosperity. For education policy, continued investment into improved literacy and also improved socioemotional and work skills helps build the country's human capital (increasing demand for postbasic, postsecondary education) and improved labor force. Sustainable forms of skills development should incentivize demand and supply of skills through both formal and on-the-job training.

The study also offers options for continued diagnostic work. The household survey data could help carry out more in depth analysis on the return to education and skills (and the role of training), on skills formation (and how cognitive and noncognitive skills correlate), and cross-countries comparison with other similar datasets. Finally, this research could be complemented with a STEP employer survey that focuses on the demand for education and both cognitive and noncognitive skills by both public and private employers in Ghana's key economic sectors.

APPENDIX A

Summary of Statistics

Table A.1 Summary of Statistics from the STEP Survey

	Sample observations	Mean	SD	Min	Max
Female (%)	2,987	58	49	0	100
Age range (years) (%)	2,987	33	13	15	64
15–19	2,987	14	35	0	100
20–24	2,987	18	38	0	100
25–34	2,987	28	45	0	100
35–44	2,987	19	39	0	100
45–64	2,987	21	40	0	100
Education (%)					
No education	2,987	21	40	0	100
Primary education	2,987	14	35	0	100
Junior high school	2,987	36	48	0	100
Senior high school	2,987	20	40	0	100
Tertiary education	2,987	10	29	0	100
Received early childhood education	2,948	64	48	0	100
Socioeconomic status (%)					
Low	2,960	23	42	0	100
Middle	2,960	56	50	0	100
High	2,960	21	41	0	100
Region (%)					
Western	2,987	9	29	0	100
Central	2,987	11	31	0	100
Greater Accra	2,987	26	44	0	100
Volta	2,987	5	22	0	100
Eastern	2,987	6	24	0	100
Ashanti	2,987	22	41	0	100
Brong-Ahafo	2,987	10	31	0	100
Northern	2,987	7	26	0	100
Upper East	2,987	2	15	0	100

table continues next page

Table A.1 Summary of Statistics from the STEP Survey *(continued)*

	Sample observations	*Mean*	*SD*	*Min*	*Max*
Labor status (%)					
Employed	2,981	62	48	0	100
Unemployed	2,981	5	22	0	100
NEET	2,981	10	30	0	100
Inactive	2,981	23	42	0	100
Employment status (%)					
Formal employee	1,973	15	35	0	100
Informal employee	1,973	20	40	0	100
Self-employed	1,973	66	48	0	100
Economic sector (%)					
Agriculture, fishing, and mining	1,973	12	33	0	100
Manufacturing	1,973	10	30	0	100
Low- to mid-value-added	1,973	61	49	0	100
High-value-added	1,973	17	37	0	100
Occupation (%)					
Low-skilled occupation	1,973	39	49	0	100
Mid-skilled occupation	1,973	48	50	0	100
High-skilled occupation	1,973	13	34	0	100
Monthly earnings (in GHS)	1,993	516	1,580	0	34,800
Language spoken at work (%)					
Akan	2,344	80	49	0	100
Ewe	2,344	8	27	0	100
Ga-Adangme	2,344	13	33	0	100
Mole-Dagbani	2,344	8	27	0	100
English	2,344	40	49	0	100
Others	2,344	12	32	0	100
Language spoken at home (%)					
Akan	2,972	63	48	0	100
Ewe	2,972	8	27	0	100
Ga-Adangme	2,972	7	26	0	100
Mole-Dagbani	2,972	8	28	0	100
English	2,972	1	10	0	100
Others	2,972	13	33	0	100

Note: Variables are described in appendix C. NEET = not in employment, education, or training; STEP = Skills Toward Employment and Productivity.

Table A.2 Sampling Procedure Comparison of STEP, GLSS 5, and GLSS 6

		GLSS 5, 2005–06	GLSS 6, 2012–13	STEP, 2011–13
Sampling frame		2000 PHC	2010 PHC	2010 PHC
Target population		All noninstitutionalized persons living in private dwellings	All noninstitutionalized persons living in private dwellings	All noninstitutionalized persons living in private dwellings in urban areas of the country at the time of data collection
Sample design	Sample design	Two-stage stratified	Two-stage stratified	Four-stage (implicit stratified)
	Sample unit	PSU: EA	PSU: EA	PSU: EA
		SSU: household	SSU: household	Second stage sample unit: PSU partition
				Third stage sample unit: household
				Fourth stage sample unit: individual
Sample size	Number of PSUs	580	1,200	201
	Number of household	8,700	18,000	3,015
Observations of urban population		4,074	11,538	2,987

Note: EA = Census Enumeration Area; GLSS = Ghana Living Standards Survey; PHC = Population and Housing Census; PSU = primary sample unit; SSU = secondary sample unit; STEP = Skills Toward Employment and Productivity.

Table A.3 Regional PSU Sample Size Comparison of STEP, GLSS 5, and GLSS 6

	GLSS 5		GLSS 6		STEP	
Region	n	%	n	%	n	%
Western	20	8	51	9	16	8
Central	17	7	55	10	17	8
Greater Accra	73	30	130	24	57	28
Volta	13	5	39	7	12	6
Eastern	22	9	56	10	18	9
Ashanti	53	22	90	17	47	23
Brong-Ahafo	20	8	52	10	16	8
Northern	14	6	35	6	12	6
Upper East	5	2	21	4	4	2
Upper West	3	1	16	3	2	1
Total	240		545		201	

Note: GLSS = Ghana Living Standards Survey; PSU = primary sample unit; STEP = Skills Toward Employment and Productivity.

Skills Definitions, Survey Questions, and Aggregation Strategy

Self-Reported Reading, Writing, and Numeracy Survey Questions

Self-reported reading

"Do you read anything [in daily life/at this work], including very short notes or instructions that are only a few sentences long?"

"Among the things that you normally read [in daily life/at this work], what is the size of the longest document that you read?"

Self-reported writing

"Do you ever have to write anything (else) [in daily life/at work], including very short notes, lists, or instructions that are only a few sentences long?"

"Thinking about all the things you normally write (wrote) [in daily life/at work], what is the longest document that you write (wrote)?"

Aggregation:		Intensity of use	Level
Does not do read/write	=	Does not use	0
Reads/writes documents of 5 pages or less	=	Low	1
Reads/writes documents of 6 to 25 pages	=	Medium	2
Reads/writes documents of more than 25 pages	=	High	3

Self-reported numeracy

"[As a normal part of this work /in daily life], do you do any of the following...?"

Aggregation:		Complexity of use	Level
Does no math	=	Does not use	0
Measures or estimates sizes, weights, distances			
Calculates prices or costs	=	Low	1
Performs any other multiplication or division			
Uses or calculates fractions, decimals or percentages	=	Medium	2
Uses more advanced math such as algebra, geometry, trigonometry	=	High	3

Specific On-the-Job Skills Survey Questions

Computer use

"As a part of your work do you (did you) use a computer?"

"As a part of your life [outside of work as (OCCUPATION)] have you used a computer in the past 3 months?"

Aggregation		Intensity of use	Level
Does not use a computer/use a computer almost never	=	Does not use	0
Uses computer less than three times per week	=	Low	1
Uses computer three times or more per week	=	Medium	2
Uses computer every day	=	High	3

External interpersonal skills

"As part of this work, do you (did you) have any contact with people other than co-workers, for example with customers, clients, students, or the public?"

Using any number from 1 to 10, where 1 is little involvement (…) and 10 means much of the work involves meeting or interacting (…) what number would you use to rate this work?

Aggregation		Intensity of use	Level
Does not have any contacts with clients	=	Does not use	0
Involvement scale ranges from 1 to 4	=	Low	1
Involvement scale ranges from 5 to 7	=	Medium	2
Involvement scale ranges from 8 to 10	=	High	3

Physical tasks

"Using any number from 1 to 10 where 1 is not at all physically demanding (such as sitting at a desk answering a telephone) and 10 is extremely physically demanding (such as carrying heavy loads, construction worker, etc), what number would you use to rate how physically demanding your work is?"

Aggregation		Intensity of use	Level
Not at all physically demanding	=	Does not use	0
Physical demand scale ranges from 2 to 4	=	Low	1
Physical demand scale ranges from 5 to 6	=	Medium	2
Physical demand scale ranges from 7 to 10	=	High	3

Cognitive challenge: average of two indicators

"Some tasks are pretty easy and can be done right away or after getting a little help from others. Other tasks require more thinking to figure out how they should be done. As part of this work as [OCCUPATION], how often do you have to undertake tasks that require at least 30 minutes of thinking?"

Aggregation		Intensity of use	Level
Never	=	Does not use	0
Less than once per month	=	Low	1
Less than once a week but at least once a month OR at least once a week but not every day	=	Medium	2
Every day	=	High	3

"How often does (did) this work involve learning new things?"

Aggregation		Intensity of use	Level
Rarely	=	Does not use	0
At least 2–3 months or at least once a month	=	Low	1
At least once a week	=	Medium	2
Every day	=	High	3

Autonomy and repetitiveness: average of two indicators

"Still thinking of your work as [OCCUPATION] how much freedom do you (did you) have to decide how to do your work in your own way, rather than following a fixed procedure or a supervisor's instructions? Use any number from 1 to 10 where 1 is no freedom and 10 is complete freedom."

Aggregation		Intensity	Level
Decision freedom scale from 1 to 2	=	Close to none	0
Decision freedom scale from 3 to 6	=	Low	1
Decision freedom scale from 7 to 9	=	Medium	2
Decision freedom scale 10	=	High	3

"How often does (did) this work involve carrying out short, repetitive tasks?"

Aggregation		Intensity	Level
Almost all the time	=	Close to none	0
More than half the time	=	Low	1
Less than half the time	=	Medium	2
Almost never	=	High	3

Job learning time: based on three questions

"What minimum level of formal education do you think would be required before someone would be able to carry out this work?

How many years of work experience in other related work do you think would be required before someone with [FILL Q22] would be able to carry out this work?

About how long would it take someone to learn to do this work well if they had [FILL Q22] education and [FILL Q23] years of related work experience?"

Socioemotional Skills Survey Questions

Scale

Almost never	1
Some of the time	2
Most of the time	3
Almost always	4

Openness

- Do you come up with ideas other people haven't thought of before?
- Are you very interested in learning new things?
- Do you enjoy beautiful things, like nature, art, and music?

Conscientiousness

- When doing a task, are you very careful?
- Do you prefer relaxation more than hard work?
- Do you work very well and quickly?

Extraversion

- Are you talkative?
- Do you like to keep your opinions to yourself?
- Are you outgoing and sociable? For example, do you make friends very easily?

Agreeableness

- Do you forgive other people easily?
- Are you very polite to other people?
- Are you generous to other people with your time or money?

Emotional stability (neuroticism)

- Are you relaxed during stressful situations?
- Do you tend to worry?
- Do you get nervous easily?

Grit

- Do you finish whatever you begin?
- Do you work very hard? For example, do you keep working when others stop to take a break?
- Do you enjoy working on things that take a very long time (at least several months) to complete?

Hostile bias

- Do people take advantage of you?
- Are people mean/not nice to you?

Decision making

- Do you think about how the things you do will affect you in the future?
- Do you think carefully before you make an important decision?
- Do you ask for help when you don't understand something?

Definitions of Variables Used in the Analysis

	Definition
Female	A dummy variable equal to 1 if respondent is female, and 0 otherwise.
Age	Age of respondents: a dummy variable for each one of the following age groups: 15–19 years; 20–24 years; 25–34 years; 35–44 years; 45–64 years
Education level	A dummy variable for each one of the following education levels completed: None (equal to 1 if respondent has not completed any formal education level. Takes value 0 if respondent completed at least primary education); primary education (1 for those whose highest level of education completed is primary education); junior high school (1 for those whose highest level of education completed is junior high school); senior high school (1 for those whose highest level of education completed is senior high school); tertiary education (1 for those whose highest level of education completed is tertiary education)
Early childhood education (%)	A dummy variable equal to 1 if the respondent attended early childhood education, and 0 otherwise.
Low socioeconomic status (%)	A dummy variable equal to 1 if the respondent classified him or herself as having belonged to the three first income deciles at age 15 years, and 0 otherwise.
Middle socioeconomic status (%)	A dummy variable equal to 1 if the respondent classified themselves as having belonged to the 4th to 6th income deciles at age 15 years, and 0 otherwise.
High socioeconomic status (%)	A dummy variable equal to 1 if the respondent classified themselves as having belonged to the 7th to 10th income deciles at age 15 years, and 0 otherwise.
Region	A dummy variable equal to 1 if the respondent lives in this region, and 0 otherwise.
Labor status	
Employed (%)	A dummy variable equal to 1 if the respondent is employed and not in education, and 0 otherwise.
Unemployed (%)	A dummy variable equal to 1 if the respondent is unemployed and not in education, and 0 otherwise.
NEET (%)	A dummy variable equal to 1 if the respondent is inactive and not in education, or training or is retired, and 0 otherwise.
Inactive (%)	A dummy variable equal to 1 if the respondent is inactive and not NEET, and 0 otherwise.

table continues next page

	Definition
Employment status only defined for employed population	
Formal employee (%)	A dummy variable equal to 1 if the respondent is a wageworker and does have social security, and 0 otherwise.
Informal employee (%)	A dummy variable equal to 1 if the respondent is a wageworker and does not have social security, and 0 otherwise.
Self-employed (%)	A dummy variable equal to 1 if the respondent is self-employed or an unpaid family worker, and 0 otherwise.
Economic sector defined only for employed population following Economic sector coded to 2 digits, ISIC rev.4	
Agriculture, fishing, and mining (%)	A dummy variable equal to 1 if economic sector is agriculture, fishing, and mining and 0 otherwise.
Manufacturing (%)	A dummy variable equal to 1 if economic sector is manufacturing
Low- to mid-value-added (%)	A dummy variable equal to 1 if economic sector is electricity, gas, steam and air conditioning supply; water supply; sewerage, waste management, and remediation activities; construction; wholesale and retail trade; repair of motor vehicles and motorcycles; transportation and storage; accommodation and food service activities; information and communication; arts, entertainment and recreation; other service activities; activities of households; extraterritorial organizations and bodies, and 0 otherwise.
High-value-added (%)	A dummy variable equal to 1 if economic sector is 64–66 financial and insurance activities; real estate activities; professional, scientific and technical activities; administrative and support service activities; public administration and social security; education; human health and social work activities, and 0 otherwise.
Occupation defined only for employed population	
Low-skilled occupation (%)	A dummy variable equal to 1 if occupation is skilled agricultural, forestry, and fishery worker; craft and related trades worker; plant and machine operator and assembler; elementary occupations and 0 otherwise.
Mid-skilled occupation (%)	A dummy variable equal to 1 if occupation is technician and associate professional; clerical support worker; service and sales worker, and 0 otherwise.
High-skilled occupation (%)	A dummy variable equal to 1 if occupation is manager or professional and 0 otherwise.
Monthly earnings (in GHS)	Considering the main and second occupation
Language	
Language at work	A dummy variable equal to 1 if the respondent speaks this language at work, and 0 otherwise.
Language at home	A dummy variable equal to 1 if the respondent speaks mainly this language at home, and 0 otherwise.

Note: NEET = not in employment, education, or training.

APPENDIX D

Differences in Mean

Table D.1 Difference in Mean of Those Passing the Core Literacy Test Threshold and Those Failing the Core

	Y1: Failed Core test			Y2: Passed Core test			
	Obs	Mean	SD	Obs	Mean	SD	Difference: Y2 – Y1
Female (%)	1,274	70.06	45.82	1,193	43.16	49.55	−26.897***
Socioeconomic status (%)							
Low	1,265	29.92	45.81	1,192	14.69	35.42	−15.233***
Middle	1,265	51.23	50.00	1,192	61.81	48.61	10.576***
High	1,265	18.84	39.12	1,192	23.50	42.42	4.657**
Age range (years) (%)	1,274	35.55	12.73	1,193	28.85	12.27	−6.695***
15–19	1,274	9.15	28.85	1,193	23.23	42.25	14.080***
20–24	1,274	12.51	33.10	1,193	25.69	43.71	13.171***
25–34	1,274	29.25	45.51	1,193	26.25	44.02	−3.002
35–44	1,274	25.28	43.48	1,193	10.79	31.03	−14.491***
45–64	1,274	23.80	42.61	1,193	14.05	34.76	−9.759***
Education (%)							
No education	1,274	42.14	49.40	1,193	0.60	7.75	−41.540***
Primary education	1,274	18.56	38.89	1,193	9.44	29.25	−9.116***
Junior high school	1,274	32.75	46.95	1,193	32.42	46.83	−0.324
Senior high school	1,274	6.25	24.22	1,193	36.81	48.25	30.558***
Tertiary education	1,274	0.30	5.45	1,193	20.72	40.55	20.422***
Received early childhood education	1,260	47.09	49.94	1,184	81.25	39.04	34.162***
Language spoken at work (%)							
Akan	1,077	79.04	40.72	837	77.88	41.53	−1.161
Ewe	1,077	6.60	24.84	837	7.10	25.69	0.495
Ga-Adangme	1,077	9.51	29.35	837	14.81	35.54	5.299***
Mole-Dagbani	1,077	12.10	32.62	837	3.09	17.31	−9.006***
English	1,077	16.72	37.33	837	73.28	44.28	56.559***
Others	1,077	16.30	36.96	837	7.82	26.87	−8.480***
Language spoken at home (%)							
Akan	1,274	58.43	49.30	1,193	65.35	47.60	6.925***
Ewe	1,274	5.98	23.72	1,193	9.03	28.67	3.048**
Ga-Adangme	1,274	3.55	18.50	1,193	9.75	29.68	6.204***

table continues next page

Table D.1 Difference in Mean of Those Passing the Core Literacy Test Threshold and Those Failing the Core *(continued)*

	Y1: Failed Core test			Y2: Passed Core test			
	Obs	Mean	SD	Obs	Mean	SD	Difference: Y2 – Y1
Mole-Dagbani	1,274	12.86	33.48	1,193	5.42	22.65	−7.438***
English	1,274	0.23	4.79	1,193	1.98	13.92	1.745***
Others	1,274	18.96	39.21	1,193	8.47	27.86	−10.483***
Labor status (%)							
Employed	1,274	73.31	44.25	1,193	45.84	49.85	−27.472***
Unemployed	1,274	4.05	19.72	1,193	6.39	24.46	2.337*
NEET	1,274	11.97	32.47	1,193	7.74	26.74	−4.226***
Inactive	1,274	10.67	30.89	1,193	40.03	49.02	29.362***
Employment status (%)							
Formal employee	964	3.29	17.85	611	33.81	47.34	30.517***
Informal employee	964	15.62	36.32	611	28.03	44.95	12.404***
Self-employed	964	81.09	39.18	611	38.17	48.62	−42.922***
Occupation (%)							
Low-skilled occupation	964	44.74	49.75	611	25.04	43.36	−19.695***
Mid-skilled occupation	964	52.75	49.95	611	41.42	49.30	−11.326***
High-skilled occupation	964	2.52	15.67	611	33.54	47.25	31.021***
Economic sector (%)							
Agriculture, fishing, and mining	964	17.20	37.76	611	5.22	22.26	−11.981***
Manufacturing	964	10.04	30.07	611	8.82	28.39	−1.220
Low-to mid-value-added	964	68.61	46.43	611	47.40	49.97	−21.208***
High-value-added	964	4.15	19.94	611	38.55	48.71	34.409***
Earnings							
Monthly earnings	928	388.33	1,213.30	674	662.31	2,046.88	273.980**
Socioemotional skills							
Extraversion (score)	437	2.43	0.60	1,175	2.58	0.60	0.149***
Missing extraversion	1,274	67.27	46.94	1,193	1.53	12.26	−65.742***
Conscientiousness (score)	431	2.93	0.64	1,175	3.31	0.53	0.375***
Missing conscientiousness	1,274	67.37	46.90	1,193	1.53	12.26	−65.844***
Openness (score)	432	2.82	0.63	1,175	3.22	0.52	0.395***
Missing openness	1,274	67.45	46.88	1,193	1.53	12.26	−65.920***
Emotional stability (score)	426	2.65	0.59	1,173	2.75	0.55	0.097**
Missing stability	1,274	67.93	46.69	1,193	1.87	13.56	−66.052***
Agreeableness (score)	430	2.79	0.69	1,175	3.15	0.58	0.363***
Missing agreeableness	1,274	67.47	46.87	1,193	1.53	12.26	−65.944***
Self-reported skills							
Reading							
Use reading skill	1,274	41.71	49.33	1,193	96.66	17.97	54.957***
Read with low intensity	546	68.68	46.42	1,131	30.46	46.04	−38.220***
Read with medium intensity	546	19.12	39.36	1,131	28.23	45.03	9.111***
Read with high intensity	546	12.20	32.76	1,131	41.31	49.26	29.109***

table continues next page

Table D.1 Difference in Mean of Those Passing the Core Literacy Test Threshold and Those Failing the Core
(continued)

	Y1: Failed Core test			Y2: Passed Core test			Difference: Y2 – Y1
	Obs	Mean	SD	Obs	Mean	SD	
Writing							
Use writing skill	1,274	38.02	48.56	1,193	93.31	25.00	55.294***
Write with low intensity	506	82.98	37.62	1,096	63.43	48.18	−19.545***
Write with medium intensity	506	9.95	29.96	1,096	19.82	39.89	9.873***
Write with high intensity	506	7.07	25.66	1,096	16.74	37.35	9.672***
Numeracy							
Use numeracy skill	1,274	93.71	24.28	1,193	95.82	20.01	2.110*
Numeracy with low intensity	1,201	44.55	49.72	1,134	11.94	32.44	−32.616***
Numeracy with medium intensity	1,201	53.01	49.93	1,134	62.01	48.56	9.007***
Numeracy with high intensity	1,201	2.44	15.43	1,134	26.05	43.91	23.610***
Computer							
Use computer skill	1,274	6.63	24.90	1,193	56.37	49.61	49.736***
Computer with low intensity	70	45.36	50.14	643	32.73	46.96	−12.623
Computer with medium intensity	70	12.67	33.50	643	18.12	38.55	5.456
Computer with high intensity	70	41.97	49.71	643	49.14	50.03	7.168
Literacy assessment							
Reading proficiency	1,274	77.11		1,193	221.68		144.571***

Note: NEET = not in employment, education, or training; Obs = number of observations.
***$p < .01$, **$p < .05$, *$p < 0.1$.

Table D.2 Difference in Mean of Those Passing the Core Literacy Test Threshold and Those English Illiterate

	Y1: English illiterate			Y2: Passed Core test			Difference: Y2 – Y1
	Obs	Mean	SD	Obs	Mean	SD	
Female (%)	659	75.12	43.27	1,193	43.16	49.55	−31.956***
Socioeconomic status (%)							
Low	656	36.07	48.06	1,192	14.69	35.42	−21.379***
Middle	656	48.08	50.00	1,192	61.81	48.61	13.723***
High	656	15.84	36.54	1,192	23.50	42.42	7.656***
Age range (years) (%)	659	39.33	12.18	1,193	28.85	12.27	−10.474***
15–19	659	2.43	15.41	1,193	23.23	42.25	20.804***
20–24	659	7.48	26.33	1,193	25.69	43.71	18.201***
25–34	659	28.61	45.23	1,193	26.25	44.02	−2.358
35–44	659	30.33	46.00	1,193	10.79	31.03	−19.541***
45–64	659	31.15	46.35	1,193	14.05	34.76	−17.106***
Education (%)							
No education	659	72.14	44.87	1,193	0.60	7.75	−71.534***
Primary education	659	13.41	34.10	1,193	9.44	29.25	−3.967**
Junior high school	659	13.85	34.57	1,193	32.42	46.83	18.572***
Senior high school	659	0.60	7.74	1,193	36.81	48.25	36.209***
Tertiary education	659	0.00	0.00	1,193	20.72	40.55	20.720***
Received early childhood education	651	30.96	46.27	1,184	81.25	39.04	50.288***

table continues next page

Table D.2 Difference in Mean of Those Passing the Core Literacy Test Threshold and Those English Illiterate (continued)

	Y1: English illiterate			Y2: Passed Core test			
	Obs	Mean	SD	Obs	Mean	SD	Difference: Y2 − Y1
Language spoken at work (%)							
Akan	570	70.99	45.42	837	77.88	41.53	6.890**
Ewe	570	6.82	25.22	837	7.10	25.69	0.279
Ga-Adangme	570	10.90	31.19	837	14.81	35.54	3.916*
Mole-Dagbani	570	17.46	38.00	837	3.09	17.31	−14.373***
English	570	5.77	23.34	837	73.28	44.28	67.508***
Others	570	21.33	41.00	837	7.82	26.87	−13.508***
Language spoken at home (%)							
Akan	659	45.85	49.87	1,193	65.35	47.60	19.500***
Ewe	659	6.68	24.98	1,193	9.03	28.67	2.355*
Ga-Adangme	659	3.70	18.89	1,193	9.75	29.68	6.049***
Mole-Dagbani	659	18.43	38.80	1,193	5.42	22.65	−13.013***
English	659	0.07	2.68	1,193	1.98	13.92	1.903***
Others	659	25.27	43.49	1,193	8.47	27.86	−16.795***
Labor status (%)							
Employed	659	81.53	38.84	1,193	45.84	49.85	−35.690***
Unemployed	659	3.67	18.81	1,193	6.39	24.46	2.716*
NEET	659	12.64	33.25	1,193	7.74	26.74	−4.896**
Inactive	659	2.17	14.57	1,193	40.03	49.02	37.869***
Employment status (%)							
Formal employee	539	0.76	8.68	611	33.81	47.34	33.049***
Informal employee	539	13.93	34.66	611	28.03	44.95	14.095***
Self-employed	539	85.31	35.43	611	38.17	48.62	−47.143***
Occupation (%)							
Low-skilled occupation	539	45.81	49.87	611	25.04	43.36	−20.771***
Mid-skilled occupation	539	51.91	50.01	611	41.42	49.30	−10.490***
High-skilled occupation	539	2.28	14.93	611	33.54	47.25	31.261***
Economic sector (%)							
Agriculture, fishing, and mining	539	20.89	40.69	611	5.22	22.26	−15.666***
Manufacturing	539	9.43	29.26	611	8.82	28.39	−0.609
Low- to mid-value-added	539	67.81	46.76	611	47.40	49.97	−20.410***
High-value-added	539	1.87	13.56	611	38.55	48.71	36.685***
Earnings							
Monthly earnings	519	409.79	1,442.84	674	662.31	2,046.88	252.526*
Socioemotional skills							
Extraversion (score)	28	2.38	0.51	1,175	2.58	0.60	0.203**
Missing extraversion	659	96.43	18.57	1,193	1.53	12.26	−94.905***
Conscientiousness (score)	27	3.12	0.56	1,175	3.31	0.53	0.187*
Missing conscientiousness	659	96.53	18.31	1,193	1.53	12.26	−95.008***
Openness (score)	26	2.55	0.70	1,175	3.22	0.52	0.664***
Missing openness	659	96.59	18.16	1,193	1.53	12.26	−95.065***

table continues next page

Table D.2 Difference in Mean of Those Passing the Core Literacy Test Threshold and Those English Illiterate
(continued)

	Y1: English illiterate			Y2: Passed Core test			
	Obs	Mean	SD	Obs	Mean	SD	Difference: Y2 – Y1
Emotional stability (score)	25	2.85	0.72	1,173	2.75	0.55	−0.100
Missing stability	659	96.83	17.54	1,193	1.87	13.56	−94.956***
Agreeableness (score)	26	2.55	0.69	1,175	3.15	0.58	0.605***
Missing agreeableness	659	96.62	18.10	1,193	1.53	12.26	−95.089***
Self-reported skills							
Reading							
Use reading skill	659	13.19	33.87	1,193	96.66	17.97	83.471***
Read with low intensity	98	81.36	39.15	1,131	30.46	46.04	−50.899***
Read with medium intensity	98	13.57	34.43	1,131	28.23	45.03	14.663***
Read with high intensity	98	5.07	22.06	1,131	41.31	49.26	36.236***
Writing							
Use writing skill	659	11.83	32.32	1,193	93.31	25.00	81.481***
Write with low intensity	90	89.48	30.85	1,096	63.43	48.18	−26.051***
Write with medium intensity	90	10.52	30.85	1,096	19.82	39.89	9.307**
Write with high intensity	90	0.00	0.00	1,096	16.74	37.35	16.744***
Numeracy							
Use numeracy skill	659	91.56	27.82	1,193	95.82	20.01	4.263**
Numeracy with low intensity	611	53.60	49.91	1,134	11.94	32.44	−41.665***
Numeracy with medium intensity	611	46.16	49.89	1,134	62.01	48.56	15.853***
Numeracy with high intensity	611	0.24	4.85	1,134	26.05	43.91	25.813***
Computer							
Use computer skill	659	0.59	7.65	1,193	56.37	49.61	55.783***
Computer with low intensity	3	50.79	61.23	643	32.73	46.96	−18.053
Computer with medium intensity	3	0.00	0.00	643	18.12	38.55	18.124***
Computer with high intensity	3	49.21	61.23	643	49.14	50.03	−0.071
Literacy assessment							
Reading proficiency	659		104.82	1,193		221.68	116.864***

Note: NEET = not in employment, education, or training; Obs = number of observations.
*** $p < 0.01$, ** $p < 0.05$, * $p < 0.1$.

Table D.3 Difference in Mean of Those Answering Core Literacy Test and Those Who Did Not Answer It

	Y1: Did not answer Core			Y2: Answered Core			
	Obs	Mean	SD	Obs	Mean	SD	Difference: Y2 – Y1
Female (%)	1,179	70.37	45.68	1,808	50.26	50.01	−20.110***
Socioeconomic status (%)							
Low	1,159	30.85	46.21	1,801	17.60	38.09	−13.248***
Middle	1,159	50.72	50.02	1,801	59.42	49.12	8.693***
High SES	1,159	18.43	38.79	1,801	22.99	42.09	4.555**
Age range (years) (%)	1,179	38.27	12.32	1,808	29.78	12.29	−8.493***
15–19	1,179	3.76	19.04	1,808	20.88	40.66	17.117***
20–24	1,179	9.13	28.81	1,808	23.06	42.14	13.938***

table continues next page

Table D.3 Difference in Mean of Those Answering Core Literacy Test and Those Who Did Not Answer It (continued)

	Y1: Did not answer Core			Y2: Answered Core			
	Obs	Mean	SD	Obs	Mean	SD	Difference: Y2 − Y1
25–34	1,179	29.40	45.58	1,808	27.45	44.64	−1.954
35–44	1,179	27.77	44.81	1,808	13.83	34.53	−13.942***
45–64	1,179	29.94	45.82	1,808	14.78	35.50	−15.159***
Education (%)							
No education	1,179	47.55	49.96	1,808	4.14	19.94	−43.401***
Primary education	1,179	13.58	34.28	1,808	14.14	34.86	0.559
JHS education	1,179	30.74	46.16	1,808	38.85	48.76	8.111***
SHS education	1,179	5.93	23.63	1,808	28.72	45.26	22.784***
Tertiary education	1,179	2.20	14.67	1,808	14.14	34.86	11.947***
Received ECE	1,155	44.52	49.72	1,793	75.50	43.02	30.983***
Language spoken at work (%)							
Akan	1,000	77.15	42.01	1,344	81.67	38.70	4.527**
Ewe	1,000	9.20	28.92	1,344	6.82	25.22	−2.382
Ga-Adangme	1,000	13.43	34.11	1,344	12.24	32.79	−1.188
Mole-Dagbani	1,000	12.19	32.73	1,344	4.25	20.17	−7.945***
English	1,000	17.70	38.19	1,344	56.54	49.59	38.836***
Others	1,000	15.38	36.09	1,344	8.92	28.52	−6.457***
Language spoken at home (%)							
Akan	1,164	55.04	49.77	1,808	67.30	46.93	12.255***
Ewe	1,164	8.74	28.25	1,808	7.80	26.83	−0.935
Ga-Adangme	1,164	5.88	23.53	1,808	7.67	26.62	1.794
Mole-Dagbani	1,164	12.37	32.93	1,808	5.98	23.72	−6.382***
English	1,164	0.48	6.92	1,808	1.46	11.99	0.977***
Others	1,164	17.50	38.01	1,808	9.79	29.72	−7.709***
Labor status (%)							
Employed	1,173	79.48	40.40	1,808	52.07	49.97	−27.410***
Unemployed	1,173	3.72	18.93	1,808	5.75	23.28	2.029*
NEET	1,173	11.32	31.70	1,808	8.90	28.48	−2.423
Inactive	1,173	5.48	22.77	1,808	33.28	47.14	27.803***
Employment status (%)							
Formal employee	937	5.80	23.39	1,036	22.70	41.91	16.901***
Informal employee	937	15.41	36.13	1,036	23.86	42.64	8.443***
Self-employed	937	78.79	40.90	1,036	53.44	49.91	−25.344***
Occupation (%)							
Low-skilled occupation	937	46.89	49.93	1,036	32.50	46.86	−14.391***
Mid-skilled occupation	937	48.98	50.02	1,036	46.47	49.90	−2.507
High-skilled occupation	937	4.13	19.90	1,036	21.03	40.77	16.898***
Economic sector (%)							
Agriculture, fishing, and mining	937	16.26	36.92	1,036	8.17	27.41	−8.085***
Manufacturing	937	10.83	31.09	1,036	9.64	29.53	−1.185
Low- to mid-value-added	937	66.05	47.38	1,036	56.46	49.60	−9.591***
High-value-added	937	6.87	25.31	1,036	25.73	43.74	18.861***

table continues next page

Table D.3 Difference in Mean of Those Answering Core Literacy Test and Those Who Did Not Answer It *(continued)*

	Y1: Did not answer Core			Y2: Answered Core			
	Obs	Mean	SD	Obs	Mean	SD	Difference: Y2 – Y1
Earnings							
Monthly earnings	910	477.44	1,421.51	1,083	549.53	1,702.99	72.094
Socioemotional skills							
Extraversion (score)	336	2.50	0.65	1,584	2.55	0.60	0.044
Missing extraversion	1,179	72.99	44.42	1,808	13.26	33.92	−59.736***
Conscientiousness (score)	333	3.11	0.59	1,579	3.22	0.58	0.103**
Missing conscientiousness	1,179	73.33	44.24	1,808	13.29	33.95	−60.045***
Openness (score)	327	2.90	0.67	1,581	3.13	0.57	0.228***
Missing openness	1,179	73.58	44.11	1,808	13.32	33.99	−60.264***
Emotional stability (score)	320	2.71	0.58	1,574	2.72	0.56	0.010
Missing stability	1,179	74.03	43.87	1,808	13.79	34.49	−60.237***
Agreeableness (score)	323	2.90	0.67	1,579	3.07	0.62	0.168***
Missing agreeableness	1,179	73.85	43.96	1,808	13.33	34.00	−60.526***
Self-reported skills							
Reading							
Use reading skill	1,172	37.08	48.32	1,808	88.24	32.22	51.163***
Read with low intensity	444	73.13	44.38	1,579	39.89	48.98	−33.245***
Read with medium intensity	444	15.66	36.38	1,579	26.11	43.94	10.452***
Read with high intensity	444	11.21	31.58	1,579	34.00	47.39	22.792***
Writing							
Use writing skill	1,172	34.27	47.48	1,808	84.00	36.67	49.732***
Write with low intensity	415	86.94	33.74	1,512	68.08	46.63	−18.858***
Write with medium intensity	415	8.39	27.76	1,512	17.30	37.84	8.906***
Write with high intensity	415	4.67	21.13	1,512	14.62	35.35	9.952***
Numeracy							
Use numeracy skill	1,172	92.27	26.73	1,808	95.85	19.94	3.588***
Numeracy with low intensity	1,093	44.80	49.75	1,724	19.71	39.79	−25.084***
Numeracy with medium intensity	1,093	53.33	49.91	1,724	61.26	48.73	7.923***
Numeracy with high intensity	1,093	1.87	13.55	1,724	19.03	39.27	17.161***
Computer							
Use computer skill	1,168	5.20	22.22	1,808	42.14	49.39	36.936***
Computer with low intensity	67	39.31	49.21	710	33.90	47.37	−5.418
Computer with medium intensity	67	17.97	38.69	710	17.65	38.15	−0.326
Computer with high intensity	67	42.71	49.84	710	48.46	50.01	5.744
Literacy assessment							
Reading Proficiency	1,179		90.66	1,808		165.16	74.498***

Note: NEET = not in employment, education, or training; Obs = number of observations.
*** $p < 0.01$, ** $p < 0.05$, * $p < 0.1$.

Table D.4 Difference in Mean of Those Missing and Those English Illiterate

	Y1: Missing			Y2: English illiterate			
	Obs	Mean	SD	Obs	Mean	SD	Difference: Y2 – Y1
Female (%)	520	64.61	47.86	659	75.12	43.27	10.505***
Socioeconomic status (%)							
Low	503	24.30	42.93	656	36.07	48.06	11.774***
Middle	503	54.03	49.89	656	48.08	50.00	−5.946
High	503	21.67	41.24	656	15.84	36.54	−5.828**
Age range (years) (%)	520	36.99	12.37	659	39.33	12.18	2.340**
15–19	520	5.38	22.59	659	2.43	15.41	−2.953**
20–24	520	11.12	31.47	659	7.48	26.33	−3.634*
25–34	520	30.36	46.03	659	28.61	45.23	−1.752
35–44	520	24.68	43.16	659	30.33	46.00	5.648*
45–64	520	28.46	45.17	659	31.15	46.35	2.691
Education (%)							
No education	520	17.72	38.22	659	72.14	44.87	54.422***
Primary education	520	13.80	34.52	659	13.41	34.10	−0.390
Junior high school	520	51.23	50.03	659	13.85	34.57	−37.375***
Senior high school	520	12.40	32.98	659	0.60	7.74	−11.793***
Tertiary education	520	4.86	21.53	659	0.00	0.00	−4.863***
Received early childhood education	504	61.33	48.75	651	30.96	46.27	−30.369***
Language spoken at work (%)							
Akan	430	85.02	35.73	570	70.99	45.42	−14.033***
Ewe	430	12.25	32.83	570	6.82	25.22	−5.437**
Ga-Adangme	430	16.67	37.31	570	10.90	31.19	−5.771**
Mole-Dagbani	430	5.44	22.71	570	17.46	38.00	12.020***
English	430	32.98	47.07	570	5.77	23.34	−27.205***
Others	430	7.76	26.79	570	21.33	41.00	13.571***
Language spoken at home (%)							
Akan	505	66.54	47.23	659	45.85	49.87	−20.685***
Ewe	505	11.32	31.71	659	6.68	24.98	−4.640**
Ga-Adangme	505	8.60	28.06	659	3.70	18.89	−4.898***
Mole-Dagbani	505	4.78	21.35	659	18.43	38.80	13.652***
English	505	0.99	9.92	659	0.07	2.68	−0.921*
Others	505	7.78	26.81	659	25.27	43.49	17.492***
Labor status (%)							
Employed	514	76.97	42.15	659	81.53	38.84	4.561
Unemployed	514	3.78	19.09	659	3.67	18.81	−0.111
NEET	514	9.71	29.64	659	12.64	33.25	2.925
Inactive	514	9.54	29.41	659	2.17	14.57	−7.375***
Employment status (%)							
Formal employee	398	12.34	32.93	539	0.76	8.68	−11.580***
Informal employee	398	17.34	37.91	539	13.93	34.66	−3.407
Self-employed	398	70.32	45.74	539	85.31	35.43	14.987***
Occupation (%)							
Low-skilled occupation	398	48.29	50.03	539	45.81	49.87	−2.480

table continues next page

Table D.4 Difference in Mean of Those Missing and Those English Illiterate *(continued)*

	Y1: Missing			Y2: English illiterate			
	Obs	Mean	SD	Obs	Mean	SD	Difference: Y2 – Y1
Mid-skilled occupation	398	45.18	49.83	539	51.91	50.01	6.732
High-skilled occupation	398	6.53	24.73	539	2.28	14.93	−4.252**
Economic sector (%)							
Agriculture, fishing, and mining	398	10.25	30.37	539	20.89	40.69	10.634***
Manufacturing	398	12.63	33.26	539	9.43	29.26	−3.197
Low- to mid-value-added	398	63.77	48.13	539	67.81	46.76	4.044
High-value-added	398	13.35	34.06	539	1.87	13.56	−11.482***
Earnings							
Monthly earnings	391	564.52	1,390.53	519	409.79	1,442.84	−154.735
Socioemotional skills							
Extraversion (score)	308	2.51	0.66	28	2.38	0.51	−0.134
Missing extraversion	520	44.56	49.75	659	96.43	18.57	51.874***
Conscientiousness (score)	306	3.11	0.59	27	3.12	0.56	0.008
Missing conscientiousness	520	45.19	49.82	659	96.53	18.31	51.343***
Openness (score)	301	2.93	0.66	26	2.55	0.70	−0.374**
Missing openness	520	45.67	49.86	659	96.59	18.16	50.919***
Emotional stability (score)	295	2.70	0.57	25	2.85	0.72	0.145
Missing stability	520	46.37	49.92	659	96.83	17.54	50.462***
Agreeableness (score)	297	2.93	0.66	26	2.55	0.69	−0.382***
Missing agreeableness	520	46.24	49.91	659	96.62	18.10	50.374***
Self-reported skills							
Reading							
Use reading skill	513	66.38	47.29	659	13.19	33.87	−53.189***
Read with low intensity	346	71.12	45.39	98	81.36	39.15	10.234*
Read with medium intensity	346	16.17	36.87	98	13.57	34.43	−2.599
Read with high intensity	346	12.71	33.35	98	5.07	22.06	−7.635*
Writing							
Use writing skill	513	61.79	48.64	659	11.83	32.32	−49.965***
Write with low intensity	325	86.35	34.39	90	89.48	30.85	3.138
Write with medium intensity	325	7.90	27.01	90	10.52	30.85	2.618
Write with high intensity	325	5.76	23.33	90	0.00	0.00	−5.756***
Numeracy							
Use numeracy skill	513	93.13	25.32	659	91.56	27.82	−1.569
Numeracy with low intensity	482	34.18	47.48	611	53.60	49.91	19.426***
Numeracy with medium intensity	482	61.98	48.59	611	46.16	49.89	−15.821***
Numeracy with high intensity	482	3.84	19.24	611	0.24	4.85	−3.605***
Computer							
Use computer skill	509	10.92	31.22	659	0.59	7.65	−10.332***
Computer with low intensity	64	38.87	49.13	3	50.79	61.23	11.913
Computer with medium intensity	64	18.66	39.27	3	0.00	0.00	−18.664***
Computer with high intensity	64	42.46	49.82	3	49.21	61.23	6.750
Literacy assessment							
Reading Proficiency	520		73.49	659		104.82	31.3294***

Note: NEET = not in employment, education, or training; Obs = number of observations.
*** $p < 0.01$, ** $p < 0.05$, * $p < 0.1$.

Table D.5 Difference in Mean of Those Answering the Socioemotional Section and Those Who Did Not

	Y1: Did not answer socioemotional section			Y2: Answered socioemotional section			
	Obs	Mean	SD	Obs	Mean	SD	Difference: Y2 – Y1
Female (%)	1,045	73.60	44.10	1,930	49.32	50.01	−24.281***
Socioeconomic status (%)							
Low	1,038	35.69	47.93	1,922	15.44	36.15	−20.245***
Middle	1,038	48.58	50.00	1,922	60.27	48.95	11.692***
High	1,038	15.73	36.43	1,922	24.29	42.89	8.553***
Age range (years) (%)	1,045	37.79	12.02	1,930	30.41	12.75	−7.378***
15–19	1,045	3.91	19.40	1,930	20.12	40.10	16.206***
20–24	1,045	9.21	28.93	1,930	22.45	41.74	13.245***
25–34	1,045	30.09	45.89	1,930	27.05	44.43	−3.046
35–44	1,045	28.49	45.16	1,930	13.98	34.68	−14.514***
45–64	1,045	28.30	45.07	1,930	16.41	37.04	−11.891***
Education (%)							
No education	1,045	54.16	49.85	1,930	2.33	15.07	−51.833***
Primary education	1,045	16.41	37.06	1,930	12.66	33.26	−3.755**
JHS education	1,045	27.35	44.60	1,930	40.34	49.07	12.986***
SHS education	1,045	2.05	14.18	1,930	29.87	45.78	27.819***
Tertiary education	1,045	0.03	1.63	1,930	14.81	35.53	14.783***
Received ECE	1,029	41.24	49.25	1,907	76.03	42.70	34.783***
Language spoken at work (%)							
Akan	907	80.06	39.98	1,436	79.52	40.37	−0.544
Ewe	907	6.17	24.08	1,436	8.97	28.59	2.799**
Ga-Adangme	907	9.16	28.86	1,436	15.20	35.91	6.037***
Mole-Dagbani	907	11.22	31.57	1,436	5.18	22.18	−6.032***
English	907	10.17	30.25	1,436	60.39	48.93	50.213***
Others	907	14.96	35.68	1,436	9.44	29.24	−5.518***
Language spoken at home (%)							
Akan	1,045	60.78	48.85	1,927	63.73	48.09	2.952
Ewe	1,045	5.61	23.02	1,927	9.54	29.39	3.936***
Ga-Adangme	1,045	3.92	19.41	1,927	8.68	28.16	4.765***
Mole-Dagbani	1,045	11.84	32.32	1,927	6.49	24.65	−5.347***
English	1,045	0.04	2.06	1,927	1.66	12.79	1.621***
Others	1,045	17.81	38.28	1,927	9.89	29.85	−7.928***
Labor status (%)							
Employed	1,045	79.95	40.05	1,930	52.85	49.93	−27.108***
Unemployed	1,045	3.64	18.73	1,930	5.73	23.25	2.092**
NEET	1,045	11.72	32.18	1,930	8.76	28.28	−2.960**
Inactive	1,045	4.69	21.15	1,930	32.67	46.91	27.976***
Employment status (%)							
Formal employee	838	1.88	13.60	1,131	25.00	43.32	23.119***
Informal employee	838	14.64	35.37	1,131	24.00	42.73	9.362***
Self-employed	838	83.48	37.16	1,131	51.00	50.01	−32.481***
Occupation (%)							
Low-skilled occupation	838	48.34	50.00	1,131	32.17	46.73	−16.174***

table continues next page

Table D.5 Difference in Mean of Those Answering the Socioemotional Section and Those Who Did Not (continued)

| | Y1: Did not answer socioemotional section | | | Y2: Answered socioemotional section | | | |
	Obs	Mean	SD	Obs	Mean	SD	Difference: Y2 – Y1
Mid-skilled occupation	838	49.56	50.03	1,131	46.11	49.87	−3.458
High-skilled occupation	838	2.09	14.32	1,131	21.72	41.26	19.633***
Economic sector (%)							
Agriculture, fishing, and mining	838	19.71	39.80	1,131	5.72	23.23	−13.985***
Manufacturing	838	9.70	29.61	1,131	10.68	30.90	0.984
Low- to mid-value-added	838	67.58	46.83	1,131	55.75	49.69	−11.831***
High-value-added	838	3.01	17.10	1,131	27.84	44.84	24.832***
Earnings							
Monthly earnings	804	402.45	1,217.70	1,184	602.31	1,803.02	199.860**
Self-reported skills							
Reading							
Don't use read skill	1,040	72.62	44.61	1,901	8.85	28.41	−63.768***
Read with low intensity	1,040	21.96	41.42	1,901	37.50	48.43	15.542***
Read with medium intensity	1,040	3.59	18.60	1,901	23.44	42.37	19.854***
Read with high intensity	1,040	1.84	13.44	1,901	30.21	45.93	28.372***
Writing							
Don't use writing skill	1,043	75.34	43.13	1,911	12.94	33.57	−62.401***
Write with low intensity	1,043	22.34	41.67	1,911	60.03	49.00	37.688***
Write with medium intensity	1,043	1.71	12.99	1,911	14.65	35.37	12.938***
Write with high intensity	1,043	0.61	7.77	1,911	12.38	32.95	11.776***
Numeracy							
Don't use numeracy skill	1,045	6.93	25.41	1,930	4.74	21.25	−2.195*
Numeracy with low intensity	1,045	43.97	49.66	1,930	18.28	38.66	−25.699***
Numeracy with medium intensity	1,045	48.68	50.01	1,930	58.73	49.24	10.055***
Numeracy with high intensity	1,045	0.42	6.44	1,930	18.26	38.64	17.840***
Computer							
Don't use computer skill	1,044	98.23	13.18	1,897	58.63	49.26	−39.600***
Computer with low intensity	1,044	0.60	7.75	1,897	14.17	34.88	13.562***
Computer with medium intensity	1,044	0.00	0.00	1,897	7.48	26.32	7.482***
Computer with high intensity	1,044	1.16	10.73	1,897	19.72	39.80	18.555***
Literacy assessment							
Reading Component (average)							
Sentence missing (%)	1,045	77.44	41.82	1,930	15.99	36.66	−61.450***
Sentence correct answers (%)	218	19.77	18.41	1,590	43.60	12.33	23.827***
Passage correct answers (%)	218	14.50	17.11	1,590	41.20	12.38	26.704***
Vocabulary correct answers (%)	218	13.67	8.46	1,590	21.90	3.81	8.230***
Core							
Score Core Test	218	0.59	1.31	1,590	4.95	2.71	4.357***
Passed Core Test	847	2.15	14.50	1,620	75.00	43.31	72.856***
Literacy assessment							
Reading Proficiency	1,045		77.54	1,930		169.10	91.556***

Note: NEET = not in employment, education, or training; Obs = number of observations.
*** $p < 0.01$, ** $p < 0.05$, * $p < 0.1$.

APPENDIX E

Returns to Education and Skills

Table E.1 Returns to Years of Education (Mincer Equation), Controlling for Skills

	No controls	Socioeconomic	Literacy assessment	Personality	Use of skills	Job-specific skills	All controls
Years of education	0.1019***	0.1019***	0.0898***	0.0956***	0.0802***	0.0843***	0.0632***
	(0.0111)	(0.0111)	(0.0180)	(0.0135)	(0.0135)	(0.0126)	(0.0168)
Socioemotional skills (relative to score 2 or lower)							
Extraversion>2				0.0017			0.0228
				(0.1460)			(0.1387)
Conscientiousness>2				0.4564**			0.2193
				(0.1915)			(0.2118)
Openness>2				0.1216			0.0110
				(0.1955)			(0.1820)
Stability>2				0.0430			0.0589
				(0.2930)			(0.2870)
Agreeableness>2				−0.0304			0.0138
				(0.1988)			(0.1958)
Grit>2				0.0479			0.0085
				(0.1503)			(0.1711)
Cognitive skills (relative to skill not used)							
Reading							
Read with low intensity					−0.2853		−0.2766*
					(0.1742)		(0.1655)
Read with medium intensity					−0.3427*		−0.4154**
					(0.2007)		(0.2037)
Read with high intensity					−0.4598**		−0.5218**
					(0.2241)		(0.2185)

table continues next page

Table E.1 **Returns to Years of Education (Mincer Equation), Controlling for Skills** *(continued)*

	No controls	Socioeconomic	Literacy assessment	Personality	Use of skills	Job-specific skills	All controls
Writing							
Write with low intensity					0.4973***		0.4204**
					(0.1578)		(0.1746)
Write with medium intensity					0.8394***		0.8296***
					(0.1913)		(0.2183)
Write with high intensity					0.8989***		0.8828***
					(0.2746)		(0.3125)
Numeracy							
Numeracy with low intensity					0.0310		−0.0623
					(0.1996)		(0.1991)
Numeracy with medium intensity					0.3047**		0.1953
					(0.1510)		(0.1636)
Numeracy with high intensity					0.3670		0.2565
					(0.2665)		(0.2658)
Job-specific skills							
Cognitive challenge							
Low think and learn						−0.0004	−0.0649
						(0.1358)	(0.1252)
Medium think and learn						0.1657	0.1059
						(0.1380)	(0.1359)
High think and learn						0.0314	0.0003
						(0.1851)	(0.1615)
Physical							
Low physical demand						−0.1321	−0.0895
						(0.1782)	(0.1969)
Medium physical demand						−0.0698	−0.0717
						(0.1842)	(0.1907)
High physical demand						0.0529	0.1037
						(0.1730)	(0.1801)
Autonomy and repetitiveness							
Low autonomy and repetitive						0.0838	0.0747
						(0.1580)	(0.1274)
Medium autonomy and repetitive						0.1405	0.1079
						(0.2023)	(0.1703)
High autonomy and repetitive						−0.0986	−0.0269
						(0.2574)	(0.2419)
Make presentations						−0.0138	−0.1471
						(0.2261)	(0.2226)
Supervise others						0.2121	0.2407**
						(0.1297)	(0.1131)

table continues next page

Table E.1 Returns to Years of Education (Mincer Equation), Controlling for Skills (continued)

	No controls	Socioeconomic	Literacy assessment	Personality	Use of skills	Job-specific skills	All controls
Computer use at work (relative to no use)							
Computer work with low intensity						0.0272 (0.2801)	−0.0526 (0.2717)
Computer work with medium intensity						0.4043 (0.2760)	0.3359 (0.2886)
Computer work with high intensity						0.3084 (0.2124)	0.2992 (0.1873)
Reading proficiency							
Sentence correct answers (%)			−0.0040 (0.0058)				−0.0063 (0.0054)
Passage correct answers (%)			0.0116* (0.0067)				0.0096 (0.0063)
Vocabulary correct answers (%)			−0.0044 (0.0141)				0.0072 (0.0137)
Passed Core test			−0.0220 (0.2915)				−0.0915 (0.2664)
Failed Core test			−0.0846 (0.2127)				−0.1091 (0.1990)
Number of observations	675	675	675	675	675	675	675
R^2	0.228	0.228	0.239	0.235	0.283	0.265	0.329

Note: All models estimated using ordinary least squares. Excluding self-employed. Robust standard errors are in parentheses. Controls include experience, experience squared, gender, economic sector and dummies for region. For all skills dummies of nonresponse (missing) were created and included in the regression, but they are not displayed in the table. Dependent variable is monthly earning considering main and second occupation. *** $p < 0.01$, ** $p < 0.05$, * $p < 0.1$.

Table E.2 Returns to Education Level (Mincer Equation), Controlling for Skills

	No controls	Socioeconomic	Literacy assessment	Personality	Use of skills	Job-specific skills	All controls
Education level (relative to none)							
Primary education (%)	0.3186* (0.1834)	0.3186* (0.1834)	0.2609 (0.1989)	0.2408 (0.1937)	0.1857 (0.1683)	0.3176* (0.1829)	0.1388 (0.1872)
Junior high school (%)	0.5921*** (0.1548)	0.5921*** (0.1548)	0.4815*** (0.1640)	0.4413*** (0.1537)	0.4197*** (0.1487)	0.5858*** (0.1558)	0.3525** (0.1523)
Senior high school (%)	0.7882*** (0.2160)	0.7882*** (0.2160)	0.5513* (0.2978)	0.5791** (0.2353)	0.5097** (0.2057)	0.6962*** (0.2132)	0.2917 (0.2465)
Tertiary education (%)	1.7174*** (0.1681)	1.7174*** (0.1681)	1.4883*** (0.2584)	1.4939*** (0.2040)	1.3415*** (0.2050)	1.5899*** (0.2082)	1.1183*** (0.2618)

table continues next page

Table E.2 **Returns to Education Level (Mincer Equation), Controlling for Skills** *(continued)*

	No controls	Socioeconomic	Literacy assessment	Personality	Use of skills	Job-specific skills	All controls
Socioemotional skills (relative to score 2 or lower)							
Extraversion>2				−0.0158			0.0338
				(0.1370)			(0.1327)
Conscientiousness>2				0.4631**			0.2422
				(0.1987)			(0.2141)
Openness>2				0.0709			−0.0060
				(0.1968)			(0.1836)
Stability>2				0.0593			0.0872
				(0.3046)			(0.2903)
Agreeableness>2				−0.0460			0.0049
				(0.1975)			(0.2018)
Grit>2				0.0008			−0.0430
				(0.1480)			(0.1547)
Cognitive skills (relative to skill not used)							
Reading							
Read with low intensity				−0.2164			−0.2617*
				(0.1581)			(0.1561)
Read with medium intensity				−0.2754			−0.3666*
				(0.1824)			(0.1906)
Read with high intensity				−0.3958**			−0.4742**
				(0.2013)			(0.2002)
Writing							
Write with low intensity				0.5616***			0.4663***
				(0.1515)			(0.1691)
Write with medium intensity				0.8029***			0.7854***
				(0.1921)			(0.2151)
Write with high intensity				0.9096***			0.8858***
				(0.2677)			(0.2894)
Numeracy							
Numeracy with low intensity				0.0125			−0.0881
				(0.1921)			(0.1912)
Numeracy with medium intensity				0.2467			0.1257
				(0.1598)			(0.1702)
Numeracy with high intensity				0.1919			0.1478
				(0.2668)			(0.2586)
Job-specific skills (relative to score 0)							
Cognitive challenge							
Low think and learn						0.0172	−0.0554
						(0.1349)	(0.1217)
Medium think and learn						0.1504	0.0822
						(0.1377)	(0.1345)

table continues next page

Table E.2 Returns to Education Level (Mincer Equation), Controlling for Skills *(continued)*

	No controls	*Socioeconomic*	*Literacy assessment*	*Personality*	*Use of skills*	*Job-specific skills*	*All controls*
High think and learn						−0.0431	−0.0686
						(0.1782)	(0.1563)
Physical							
Low physical demand						−0.0731	−0.0208
						(0.1816)	(0.1943)
Medium physical demand						0.0414	0.0441
						(0.1878)	(0.1879)
High physical demand						0.1540	0.2231
						(0.1677)	(0.1737)
Autonomy and repetitiveness							
Low autonomy and repetitive						0.0327	0.0274
						(0.1379)	(0.1149)
Medium autonomy and repetitive						0.0177	−0.0071
						(0.1740)	(0.1538)
High autonomy and repetitive						−0.1011	−0.0259
						(0.2393)	(0.2214)
Make presentations						−0.0298	−0.1428
						(0.2309)	(0.2146)
Supervise others						0.2123*	0.2320**
						(0.1259)	(0.1084)
Computer use at work (relative to no use)							
Computer use with low intensity						0.0029	−0.0624
						(0.2832)	(0.2744)
Computer use with medium intensity						0.2490	0.1699
						(0.2935)	(0.3049)
Computer use with high intensity						0.1793	0.1872
						(0.1855)	(0.1708)
Reading proficiency							
Sentence correct answers (%)			−0.0072				−0.0088
			(0.0057)				(0.0055)
Passage correct answers (%)			0.0137**				0.0117*
			(0.0064)				(0.0061)
Vocabulary correct answers (%)			0.0012				0.0099
			(0.0136)				(0.0133)
Passed Core test			−0.0134				−0.0607
			(0.2965)				(0.2764)
Failed Core test			−0.0098				−0.0526
			(0.2288)				(0.2163)
Number of observations	675	675	675	675	675	675	675
R^2	0.270	0.270	0.286	0.281	0.320	0.298	0.364

Note: All models estimated using ordinary least squares. Excluding self-employed. Robust standard errors are in parentheses. Controls include experience, experience squared, gender, economic sector and dummies for region. For all skills dummies of nonresponse (missing) were created and included in the regression, but they are not displayed in the table. Dependent variable is monthly earning considering main and second occupation.
*** $p < 0.01$, ** $p < 0.05$, * $p < 0.1$.

Table E.3 Returns to Years of Education (Mincer Equation) for Informal Wageworkers, Controlling for Skills

	No controls	Socioeconomic	Literacy assessment	Use of skills	Job-specific skills	All controls
Years of education	0.0591***	0.0667***	0.0513***	0.0431***	0.0508***	0.0392***
	(0.0132)	(0.0163)	(0.0157)	(0.0142)	(0.0132)	(0.0153)
Socioemotional skills (relative to score 2 or lower)						
Extraversion>2			0.2324*			0.2113**
			(0.1401)			(0.1384)
Conscientiousness>2			0.3148			0.1219
			(0.2440)			(0.2126)
Openness>2			0.0927			0.1104
			(0.2083)			(0.2005)
Stability>2			0.1037			0.0595
			(0.2398)			(0.2302)
Agreeableness>2			0.0063			0.0704
			(0.2609)			(0.2514)
Grit>2			(−0.1268)			(−0.2334)
			(0.1511)			(0.1461)
Cognitive skills (relative to skill not used)						
Reading						
Read with low intensity				−0.3320**		−0.2426
				(0.1696)		(0.1685)
Read with medium intensity				−0.3557**		−0.2863
				(0.2048)		(0.2059)
Read with high intensity				−0.3564*		−0.3573
				(0.2127)		(0.2050)
Writing						
Write with low intensity				0.5207***		0.4269***
				(0.1568)		(0.1701)
Write with medium intensity				0.6020***		0.5452***
				(0.2254)		(0.2230)
Write with high intensity				1.2538***		1.2017***
				(0.3060)		(0.3337)
Numeracy						
Numeracy with low intensity				−0.0310		−0.2354*
				(0.1867)		(0.1883)
Numeracy with medium intensity				0.0421		−0.1644
				(0.1753)		(0.1915)
Numeracy with high intensity				−0.1045		−0.1206
				(0.2778)		(0.2866)
Job-specific skills (relative to score 0)						
Cognitive challenge						
Low think and learn					−0.0847	−0.1587
					(0.1224)	(0.1164)
Medium think and learn					0.0201	−0.0215
					(0.1491)	(0.1535)
High think and learn					0.1683	0.1503
					(0.1781)	(0.1705)

table continues next page

Table E.3 Returns to Years of Education (Mincer Equation) for Informal Wageworkers, Controlling for Skills (continued)

	No controls	Socioeconomic	Literacy assessment	Use of skills	Job-specific skills	All controls
Physical						
Low physical demand					0.0114	0.0691
					(0.1843)	(0.2108)
Medium physical demand					0.1611	0.1819
					(0.2098)	(0.2256)
High physical demand					0.4199	0.4646
					(0.1748)	(0.2112)
Autonomy and repetitiveness						
Low autonomy and repetitive					−0.0737	−0.0447
					(0.1043)	(0.1072)
Medium autonomy and repetitive					−0.1788	−0.1817
					(0.1860)	(0.1923)
High autonomy and repetitive					−0.3558	−0.1763
					(0.1866)	(0.2018)
Make presentations					−0.1404	−0.1978*
					(0.2063)	(0.1868)
Supervise others					0.3356*	0.3211**
					(0.1327)	(0.1298)
Computer use at work (relative to no use)						
Computer use with low intensity					0.4667	0.3215
					(0.3951)	(0.3338)
Computer use with medium intensity					0.2478	−0.1337
					(0.3652)	(0.5208)
Computer use with high intensity					0.1323**	0.0676*
					(0.2700)	(0.2438)
Reading proficiency						
Sentence correct answers (%)		(−0.0037)				(−0.0100)
		(0.0068)				(0.0068)
Passage correct answers (%)		(0.0101)				(0.0112)
		(0.0073)				(0.0078)
Vocabulary correct answers (%)		(−0.0090)				(0.0029)
		(0.0161)				(0.0157)
Passed Core test		(−0.2260)				(−0.2427)
		(0.3442)				(0.3458)
Failed Core test		−0.0133				0.0380
		(0.2371)				(0.2401)
Number of observations	387	387	387	387	387	387
R^2	0.098	0.108	0.125	0.186	0.192	0.300

Note: All models estimated using ordinary least squares. Robust standard errors are in parentheses. Controls include experience, experience squared, gender, economic sector, and dummies for region. For all skills dummies of nonresponse (missing) were created and included in the regression, but they are not displayed in the table. Dependent variable is monthly earning considering main and second occupation.
*** $p < 0.01$, ** $p < 0.05$, * $p < 0.1$.

Table E.4 Returns to Education Level (Mincer Equation) for Informal Wageworkers, Controlling for Skills

	No controls	Socioeconomic	Literacy assessment	Use of skills	Job-specific skills	All controls
Education level (relative to none)						
Primary education (%)	0.2856	0.2883	0.2390	0.2093	0.3256*	0.1215
	(0.1899)	(0.1945)	(0.2090)	(0.1734)	(0.1895)	(0.2034)
Junior high school (%)	0.3940***	0.4268***	0.3244*	0.3360**	0.3970***	0.2673*
	(0.1469)	(0.1499)	(0.1716)	(0.1590)	(0.1436)	(0.1585)
Senior high school (%)	0.6408***	0.7543***	0.5273**	0.5258***	0.5829***	0.4845**
	(0.1699)	(0.2173)	(0.2092)	(0.1920)	(0.1789)	(0.2154)
Tertiary education (%)	1.1907***	1.3209***	1.0638***	0.8967***	1.1197***	0.9016***
	(0.3063)	(0.3383)	(0.3128)	(0.2973)	(0.2869)	(0.2699)
Socioemotional skills (relative to score 2 or lower)						
Extraversion>2			0.2066			0.1925
			(0.1347)			(0.1365)
Conscientiousness>2			0.3094			0.1052
			(0.2498)			(0.2156)
Openness>2			0.0463			0.0944
			(0.2094)			(0.2016)
Stability>2			0.1368			0.0888
			(0.2640)			(0.2385)
Agreeableness>2			−0.0205			0.0504
			(0.2606)			(0.2586)
Grit>2			−0.1343			−0.2493*
			(0.1531)			(0.1469)
Cognitive skills (relative to skill not used)						
Reading						
Read with low intensity				−0.3387**		−0.2445
				(0.1611)		(0.1637)
Read with medium intensity				−0.3869*		−0.2993
				(0.2032)		(0.2064)
Read with high intensity				−0.4016*		−0.3925*
				(0.2137)		(0.2040)
Writing						
Write with low intensity				0.5317***		0.4376***
				(0.1556)		(0.1669)
Write with medium intensity				0.6135***		0.5278**
				(0.2270)		(0.2191)
Write with high intensity				1.1775***		1.1263***
				(0.3292)		(0.3317)
Numeracy						
Numeracy with low intensity				−0.0352		−0.2713
				(0.1904)		(0.1874)

table continues next page

Table E.4 Returns to Education Level (Mincer Equation) for Informal Wageworkers, Controlling for Skills *(continued)*

	No controls	Socioeconomic	Literacy assessment	Use of skills	Job-specific skills	All controls
Numeracy with medium intensity				0.0155		−0.2245
				(0.1785)		(0.1911)
Numeracy with high intensity				−0.1288		−0.1731
				(0.2807)		(0.2806)
Job-specific skills (relative to score 0)						
Cognitive challenge						
Low think and learn					−0.0825	−0.1535
					(0.1193)	(0.1146)
Medium think and learn					0.0005	−0.0370
					(0.1493)	(0.1548)
High think and learn					0.1528	0.1491
					(0.1736)	(0.1663)
Physical						
Low physical demand					0.0552	0.1066
					(0.1880)	(0.2030)
Medium physical demand					0.2426	0.2305
					(0.2072)	(0.2161)
High physical demand					0.4886***	0.5131**
					(0.1771)	(0.2024)
Autonomy and repetitiveness						
Low autonomy and repetitive					−0.0889	−0.0595
					(0.1035)	(0.1039)
Medium autonomy and repetitive					−0.1960	−0.1992
					(0.1909)	(0.1969)
High autonomy and repetitive					−0.3438*	−0.1597
					(0.1905)	(0.2027)
Make presentations					−0.1499	−0.2023
					(0.2114)	(0.1891)
Supervise others					0.3106**	0.3119**
					(0.1278)	(0.1301)
Computer use at work (relative to no use)						
Computer use with low intensity					0.3657	0.2876
					(0.3604)	(0.3321)
Computer use with medium intensity					0.1611	−0.2094
					(0.4063)	(0.5478)
Computer use with high intensity					0.0307	−0.0090
					(0.2671)	(0.2430)
Reading proficiency						
Sentence correct answers (%)		−0.0038				−0.0104
		(0.0068)				(0.0069)

table continues next page

Table E.4 Returns to Education Level (Mincer Equation) for Informal Wageworkers, Controlling for Skills *(continued)*

	No controls	Socioeconomic	Literacy assessment	Use of skills	Job-specific skills	All controls
Passage correct answers (%)		0.0086				0.0110
		(0.0072)				(0.0079)
Vocabulary correct answers (%)		−0.0046				0.0051
		(0.0159)				(0.0158)
Passed Core test		−0.2775				−0.2738
		(0.3481)				(0.3502)
Failed Core test		0.0203				0.0681
		(0.2392)				(0.2489)
Number of observations	387	387	387	387	387	387
R^2	0.116	0.126	0.142	0.194	0.207	0.310

Note: All models estimated using ordinary least squares. Robust standard errors are in parentheses. Controls include experience, experience squared, gender, economic sector and dummies for region. For all skills dummies of non-response (missing) were created and included in the regression, but they are not displayed in the table. Dependent variable is monthly earning considering main and second occupation. JHS = junior high school; SHS = senior high school.
*** $p < 0.01$, ** $p < 0.05$, * $p < 0.1$.

Table E.5 Returns to Years of Education (Mincer Equation) for Formal Wageworkers, Controlling for Skills

	No controls	Socioeconomic	Literacy assessment	Use of skills	Job-specific skills	All controls
Years of education	0.0944***	0.0749**	0.1025***	0.0918***	0.0946***	0.0914***
	(0.0273)	(0.0359)	(0.0268)	(0.0319)	(0.0353)	(0.0320)
Socioemotional skills (relative to score 2 or lower)						
Extraversion>2			−0.3074*			−0.3692*
			(0.1859)			(0.2155)
Conscientiousness>2			0.6214*			0.3945
			(0.3329)			(0.4364)
Openness>2			−0.1851			−0.1046
			(0.2369)			(0.2385)
Stability>2			−0.1854			−0.0490
			(0.4990)			(0.4707)
Agreeableness>2			−0.2409			−0.3834
			(0.2402)			(0.2700)
Grit>2			0.3177			0.3255
			(0.2913)			(0.2965)
Cognitive skills (relative to skill not used)						
Reading						
Read with low intensity				−0.0587		−0.2557
				(0.3558)		(0.3472)

table continues next page

Table E.5 Returns to Years of Education (Mincer Equation) for Formal Wageworkers, Controlling for Skills *(continued)*

	No controls	Socioeconomic	Literacy assessment	Use of skills	Job-specific skills	All controls
Read with medium intensity				−0.1809		−0.4497
				(0.3793)		(0.4015)
Read with high intensity				−0.3465		−0.5582
				(0.3646)		(0.3905)
Writing						
Write with low intensity				0.2104		−0.0757
				(0.2699)		(0.3083)
Write with medium intensity				0.4048		0.1047
				(0.2860)		(0.3381)
Write with high intensity				0.3263		0.1177
				(0.3529)		(0.3707)
Numeracy						
Numeracy with low intensity				−0.0341		0.0043
				(0.3980)		(0.3314)
Numeracy with medium intensity				0.5189**		0.3861
				(0.2194)		(0.2554)
Numeracy with high intensity				0.3131		0.2708
				(0.3604)		(0.3435)
Job-specific skills (relative to score 0)						
Cognitive challenge						
Low think and learn					0.1443	0.2795
					(0.2725)	(0.2631)
Medium think and learn					0.2753	0.4169*
					(0.2501)	(0.2508)
High think and learn					−0.2385	0.0778
					(0.3188)	(0.2652)
Physical						
Low physical demand					0.0282	−0.1511
					(0.2477)	(0.2695)
Medium physical demand					−0.0172	−0.2942
					(0.2335)	(0.2392)
High physical demand					−0.1174	−0.2737
					(0.2795)	(0.2728)
Autonomy and repetitiveness						
Low autonomy and repetitive					0.2523	0.2650
					(0.2804)	(0.2098)
Medium autonomy and repetitive					0.2755	0.2476
					(0.3134)	(0.2647)

table continues next page

Table E.5 Returns to Years of Education (Mincer Equation) for Formal Wageworkers, Controlling for Skills *(continued)*

	No controls	Socioeconomic	Literacy assessment	Use of skills	Job-specific skills	All controls
High autonomy and repetitive					0.7046	0.9453**
					(0.4544)	(0.4556)
Make presentations					−0.0052	−0.0519
					(0.3045)	(0.2646)
Supervise others					0.0980	0.1014
					(0.1961)	(0.1496)
Computer use at work (relative to no use)						
Computer use with low intensity					−0.2233	−0.1649
					(0.3276)	(0.3313)
Computer use with medium intensity					0.4662**	0.5208**
					(0.1962)	(0.2286)
Computer use with high intensity					0.1477	0.0986
					(0.2220)	(0.2147)
Reading proficiency						
Sentence correct answers (%)		−0.0115				−0.0108
		(0.0079)				(0.0084)
Passage correct answers (%)		0.0107				0.0048
		(0.0089)				(0.0099)
Vocabulary correct answers (%)		0.0043				0.0181
		(0.0175)				(0.0193)
Passed Core test		0.4454				0.2707
		(0.4625)				(0.4119)
Failed Core test		0.0791				−0.1837
		(0.4179)				(0.3463)
Number of observations	288	288	288	288	288	288
R^2	0.093	0.134	0.125	0.158	0.170	0.277

Note: All models estimated using ordinary least squares. Robust standard errors are in parentheses. Controls include experience, experience squared, gender, economic sector, and dummies for region. For all skills dummies of nonresponse (missing) were created and included in the regression, but they are not displayed in the table. Dependent variable is monthly earning considering main and second occupation.
*** $p < 0.01$, ** $p < 0.05$, * $p < 0.1$.

Table E.6 Returns to Education Level (Mincer Equation) for Formal Wageworkers, Controlling for Skills

	No controls	Socioeconomic	Literacy assessment	Use of skills	Job-specific skills	All controls
Education level (relative to none)						
Primary education (%)	0.2928	0.0374	0.2616	−0.0484	0.4489	0.1584
	(0.4344)	(0.6760)	(0.4813)	(0.4963)	(0.5645)	(0.6628)
JHS education (%)	0.4450	0.1683	0.2855	0.2182	0.4958	0.3042
	(0.3439)	(0.3831)	(0.3214)	(0.3345)	(0.3275)	(0.3958)
SHS education (%)	0.2360	−0.1607	0.1456	−0.0278	0.2834	0.1042
	(0.4336)	(0.5481)	(0.4459)	(0.4512)	(0.3710)	(0.4470)
Tertiary education (%)	1.1384***	0.7088	1.0394***	0.8243*	1.2545***	0.9646**
	(0.3398)	(0.4805)	(0.3549)	(0.4251)	(0.3818)	(0.4473)
Socioemotional skills (relative to score 2 or lower)						
Extraversion>2			−0.2490			−0.2514
			(0.1744)			(0.1946)
Conscientiousness>2			0.4825*			0.2224
			(0.2737)			(0.3698)
Openness>2			−0.3270			−0.2816
			(0.2264)			(0.2647)
Stability>2			−0.1719			−0.0512
			(0.4698)			(0.4299)
Agreeableness>2			−0.1443			−0.2504
			(0.2345)			(0.2619)
Grit>2			0.2738			0.2488
			(0.2522)			(0.2557)
Cognitive Skills (relative to skill not used)						
Reading						
Read with low intensity				0.1837		−0.1505
				(0.3971)		(0.3778)
Read with medium intensity				0.1256		−0.2512
				(0.4144)		(0.4191)
Read with high intensity				−0.0101		−0.3388
				(0.3943)		(0.4239)
Writing						
Write with low intensity				0.2481		0.0166
				(0.2696)		(0.2880)
Write with medium intensity				0.3944		0.1636
				(0.2878)		(0.3235)
Write with high intensity				0.4449		0.2797
				(0.3438)		(0.3437)
Numeracy						
Numeracy with low intensity				0.0016		0.0034
				(0.3639)		(0.3262)

table continues next page

Table E.6 Returns to Education Level (Mincer Equation) for Formal Wageworkers, Controlling for Skills *(continued)*

	No controls	Socioeconomic	Literacy assessment	Use of skills	Job-specific skills	All controls
Numeracy with medium intensity				0.5156**		0.3465
				(0.2395)		(0.2675)
Numeracy with high intensity				0.2631		0.2520
				(0.3622)		(0.3446)
Job-specific skills (relative to score 0)						
Cognitive challenge						
Low think and learn					0.2136	0.2547
					(0.2573)	(0.2456)
Medium think and learn					0.2371	0.3076
					(0.2395)	(0.2403)
High think and learn					−0.3254	−0.0825
					(0.2974)	(0.2671)
Physical						
Low physical demand					0.1116	−0.0010
					(0.2456)	(0.2631)
Medium physical demand					0.1269	−0.1099
					(0.2557)	(0.2496)
High physical demand					0.0359	−0.0434
					(0.2729)	(0.2704)
Autonomy and repetitiveness						
Low autonomy and repetitive					0.1599	0.1615
					(0.2377)	(0.1891)
Medium autonomy and repetitive					0.0943	0.0690
					(0.2618)	(0.2359)
High autonomy and repetitive					0.5873	0.7399*
					(0.3939)	(0.3807)
Make presentations					0.0141	−0.0667
					(0.2859)	(0.2522)
Supervise others					0.1955	0.1946
					(0.1844)	(0.1543)
Computer use at work (relative to no use)						
Computer use with low intensity					−0.1210	−0.1003
					(0.3586)	(0.3482)
Computer use with medium intensity					0.2826	0.3083
					(0.1787)	(0.1962)
Computer use with high intensity					0.0900	0.0659
					(0.1963)	(0.1986)
Reading proficiency						
Sentence correct answers (%)		−0.0129				−0.0117
		(0.0086)				(0.0081)

table continues next page

Table E.6 Returns to Education Level (Mincer Equation) for Formal Wageworkers, Controlling for Skills *(continued)*

	No controls	Socioeconomic	Literacy assessment	Use of skills	Job-specific skills	All controls
Passage correct answers (%)		0.0183*				0.0103
		(0.0101)				(0.0096)
Vocabulary correct answers (%)		−0.0015				0.0138
		(0.0165)				(0.0178)
Passed Core test		0.3477				0.2030
		(0.4756)				(0.4121)
Failed Core test		0.0700				−0.1231
		(0.4205)				(0.3474)
Number of observations	288	288	288	288	288	288
R^2	0.157	0.208	0.182	0.216	0.236	0.322

Note: All models estimated using ordinary least squares. Robust standard errors are in parentheses. Controls include experience, experience squared, gender, economic sector, and dummies for region. For all skills dummies of nonresponse (missing) were created and included in the regression, but they are not displayed in the table. Dependent variable is monthly earning considering main and second occupation.
*** $p < 0.01$, ** $p < 0.05$, * $p < 0.1$.

Table E.7 Returns to Years of Education (Mincer Equation) for Male Workers, Controlling for Skills

	No controls	Socioeconomic	Literacy assessment	Use of skills	Job-specific skills	All controls
Years of education	0.0821***	0.0686***	0.0944***	0.0806***	0.0662***	0.0624***
	(0.0156)	(0.0258)	(0.0174)	(0.0173)	(0.0172)	(0.0220)
Socioemotional skills (relative to score 2 or lower)						
Extraversion>2			−0.0059			0.0422
			(0.1703)			(0.1637)
Conscientiousness>2			0.4383*			−0.0224
			(0.2357)			(0.3114)
Openness>2			−0.0065			−0.0437
			(0.1801)			(0.1831)
Stability>2			−0.1271			−0.2001
			(0.3880)			(0.3785)
Agreeableness>2			−0.2579			−0.2465
			(0.1941)			(0.2005)
Grit>2			0.1604			0.1718
			(0.2199)			(0.2288)
Cognitive skills (relative to skill not used)						
Reading						
Read with low intensity				−0.3859*		−0.3590
				(0.2260)		(0.2206)

table continues next page

Table E.7 Returns to Years of Education (Mincer Equation) for Male Workers, Controlling for Skills *(continued)*

	No controls	Socioeconomic	Literacy assessment	Use of skills	Job-specific skills	All controls
Read with medium intensity				−0.5224**		−0.5639**
				(0.2427)		(0.2752)
Read with high intensity				−0.6218**		−0.5933**
				(0.2819)		(0.2924)
Writing						
Write with low intensity				0.4664**		0.5645**
				(0.2058)		(0.2307)
Write with medium intensity				0.6412**		0.7750**
				(0.2591)		(0.3042)
Write with high intensity				0.8619**		0.9770**
				(0.3523)		(0.3977)
Numeracy						
Numeracy with low intensity				0.2629		0.2190
				(0.2687)		(0.2606)
Numeracy with medium intensity				0.4744**		0.3842*
				(0.1892)		(0.2289)
Numeracy with high intensity				0.4698		0.2906
				(0.3668)		(0.3631)
Job-specific skills (relative to score 0)						
Cognitive challenge						
Low think and learn					−0.0341	−0.0369
					(0.1921)	(0.1693)
Medium think and learn					0.1034	0.1151
					(0.1757)	(0.1699)
High think and learn					−0.1847	−0.1343
					(0.2354)	(0.2000)
Physical						
Low physical demand					−0.1036	−0.1291
					(0.2332)	(0.2360)
Medium physical demand					−0.0518	−0.1612
					(0.2431)	(0.2422)
High physical demand					−0.0943	−0.1206
					(0.2201)	(0.2239)
Autonomy and repetitiveness						
Low autonomy and repetitive					0.1612	0.1707
					(0.2188)	(0.1815)
Medium autonomy and repetitive					0.2790	0.2713
					(0.2492)	(0.2115)
High autonomy and repetitive					0.0510	0.1784
					(0.3501)	(0.3418)

table continues next page

Table E.7 **Returns to Years of Education (Mincer Equation) for Male Workers, Controlling for Skills** *(continued)*

	No controls	Socioeconomic	Literacy assessment	Use of skills	Job-specific skills	All controls
Make presentations					−0.0657	−0.1311
					(0.2940)	(0.2691)
Supervise others					0.2440	0.2224*
					(0.1547)	(0.1307)
Computer use at work (relative to no use)						
Computer use with low intensity					0.1596	0.1160
					(0.3874)	(0.3717)
Computer use with medium intensity					0.5847**	0.4686
					(0.2976)	(0.3126)
Computer use with high intensity					0.3244	0.3399
					(0.2750)	(0.2454)
Reading proficiency						
Sentence correct answers (%)		−0.0068				−0.0074
		(0.0064)				(0.0064)
Passage correct answers (%)		0.0091				0.0070
		(0.0075)				(0.0074)
Vocabulary correct answers (%)		0.0064				0.0197
		(0.0168)				(0.0156)
Passed Core test		0.0079				−0.0787
		(0.3671)				(0.3641)
Failed Core test		−0.0972				−0.2103
		(0.2759)				(0.2484)
Number of observations	429	429	429	429	429	429
R^2	0.142	0.154	0.157	0.195	0.194	0.271

Note: All models estimated using ordinary least squares. Robust standard errors are in parentheses. Controls include experience, experience squared, gender, economic sector, and dummies for region. For all skills dummies of nonresponse (missing *)* were created and included in the regression, but they are not displayed in the table. Dependent variable is monthly earning considering main and second occupation.
*** $p < 0.01$, ** $p < 0.05$, * $p < 0.1$.

Table E.8 **Returns to Education Level (Mincer Equation) for Male Workers, Controlling for Skills**

	No controls	Socioeconomic	Literacy assessment	Use of skills	Job-specific skills	All controls
Education level (relative to none)						
Primary education (%)	0.0169	−0.0538	0.0343	−0.0514	0.0684	0.0198
	(0.2009)	(0.2217)	(0.2200)	(0.2000)	(0.2066)	(0.2194)
Junior high school (%)	0.3425**	0.1980	0.3531**	0.3072*	0.3531**	0.2752
	(0.1645)	(0.1802)	(0.1716)	(0.1788)	(0.1687)	(0.1900)
Senior high school (%)	0.3803	0.1119	0.4190	0.3132	0.3598	0.1930
	(0.2696)	(0.3837)	(0.2924)	(0.2594)	(0.2601)	(0.3096)

table continues next page

Table E.8 Returns to Education Level (Mincer Equation) for Male Workers, Controlling for Skills *(continued)*

	No controls	Socioeconomic	Literacy assessment	Use of skills	Job–specific skills	All controls
Tertiary education (%)	1.3544***	1.1057***	1.3990***	1.3153***	1.3461***	1.1786***
	(0.1928)	(0.3225)	(0.2354)	(0.2526)	(0.2648)	(0.3298)
Socioemotional skills (relative to score 2 or lower)						
Extraversion>2			0.0021			0.0786
			(0.1588)			(0.1556)
Conscientiousness>2			0.3845*			−0.0435
			(0.2291)			(0.2742)
Openness>2			−0.0416			−0.0800
			(0.1734)			(0.1782)
Stability>2			−0.1689			−0.2126
			(0.3825)			(0.3580)
Agreeableness>2			−0.2124			−0.2296
			(0.1873)			(0.1970)
Grit>2			0.0783			0.0887
			(0.2118)			(0.2013)
Cognitive skills (relative to skill not used)						
Reading						
Read with low intensity				−0.2334		−0.2992
				(0.2209)		(0.2153)
Read with medium intensity				−0.3417		−0.4566*
				(0.2295)		(0.2540)
Read with high intensity				−0.4847*		−0.5189*
				(0.2579)		(0.2686)
Writing						
Write with low intensity				0.4947**		0.5589**
				(0.2058)		(0.2312)
Write with medium intensity				0.5499**		0.6607**
				(0.2516)		(0.2985)
Write with high intensity				0.8401**		0.9446**
				(0.3374)		(0.3696)
Numeracy						
Numeracy with low intensity				0.2834		0.2168
				(0.2392)		(0.2483)
Numeracy with medium intensity				0.4737**		0.3465
				(0.2014)		(0.2385)
Numeracy with high intensity				0.2603		0.1549
				(0.3515)		(0.3530)

table continues next page

Table E.8 Returns to Education Level (Mincer Equation) for Male Workers, Controlling for Skills *(continued)*

	No controls	Socioeconomic	Literacy assessment	Use of skills	Job–specific skills	All controls
Job-specific skills (relative to score 0)						
Cognitive challenge						
Low think and learn					−0.0205	−0.0157
					(0.1968)	(0.1684)
Medium think and learn					0.1175	0.1261
					(0.1746)	(0.1655)
High think and learn					−0.2634	−0.1828
					(0.2307)	(0.1932)
Physical						
Low physical demand					0.0281	0.0124
					(0.2289)	(0.2245)
Medium physical demand					0.1739	0.0532
					(0.2480)	(0.2398)
High physical demand					0.1060	0.0863
					(0.2077)	(0.2173)
Autonomy and repetitiveness						
Low autonomy and repetitive					0.1165	0.1432
					(0.1886)	(0.1605)
Medium autonomy and repetitive					0.1580	0.1665
					(0.2116)	(0.1890)
High autonomy and repetitive					0.0369	0.1470
					(0.3103)	(0.2957)
Make presentations					−0.0655	−0.0975
					(0.2923)	(0.2533)
Supervise others					0.2130	0.1847
					(0.1505)	(0.1231)
Computer use at work (relative to no use)						
Computer use with low intensity					0.0905	0.0623
					(0.3887)	(0.3746)
Computer use with medium intensity					0.3364	0.2039
					(0.3220)	(0.3327)
Computer use with high intensity					0.1473	0.1806
					(0.2261)	(0.2148)
Reading proficiency						
Sentence correct answers (%)		−0.0112				−0.0097
		(0.0069)				(0.0067)
Passage correct answers (%)		0.0149*				0.0106
		(0.0078)				(0.0074)

table continues next page

Stepping Up Skills in Urban Ghana • http://dx.doi.org/10.1596/978-1-4648-1012-1

Table E.8 Returns to Education Level (Mincer Equation) for Male Workers, Controlling for Skills *(continued)*

	No controls	Socioeconomic	Literacy assessment	Use of skills	Job–specific skills	All controls
Vocabulary correct answers (%)		0.0092 (0.0155)				0.0208 (0.0148)
Passed Core test		−0.0174 (0.3760)				−0.1081 (0.3545)
Failed Core test		−0.0572 (0.2890)				−0.1977 (0.2551)
Number of observations	429	429	429	429	429	429
R^2	0.205	0.228	0.214	0.256	0.243	0.319

Note: All models estimated using ordinary least squares. Robust standard errors are in parentheses. Controls include experience, experience squared, gender, economic sector, and dummies for region. For all skills dummies of nonresponse (missing) were created and included in the regression, but they are not displayed in the table. Dependent variable is monthly earning considering main and second occupation. JHS = junior high school; SHS = senior high school.
*** $p < 0.01$, ** $p < 0.05$, * $p < 0.1$

Table E.9 Returns to Years of Education (Mincer Equation) for Female Workers, Controlling for Skills

	No controls	Socioeconomic	Literacy assessment	Use of skills	Job-specific skills	All controls
Years of education	0.1248*** (0.0122)	0.1260*** (0.0173)	0.1092*** (0.0183)	0.0939*** (0.0180)	0.1103*** (0.0170)	0.0886*** (0.0204)
Socioemotional skills (relative to score 2 or lower)						
Extraversion>2			0.0796 (0.1718)			0.0980 (0.1541)
Conscientiousness>2			−0.0219 (0.3320)			−0.2704 (0.3749)
Openness>2			−0.0474 (0.3065)			−0.4414 (0.3278)
Stability>2			0.3484 (0.3328)			0.5365* (0.3052)
Agreeableness>2			0.6757* (0.3852)			0.7056* (0.3919)
Grit>2			−0.1010 (0.1875)			−0.3204* (0.1941)
Cognitive skills (relative to skill not used)						
Reading						
Read with low intensity				−0.0896 (0.2482)		−0.1866 (0.2422)
Read with medium intensity				−0.0275 (0.3582)		−0.0439 (0.3606)
Read with high intensity				−0.1740 (0.3050)		−0.2822 (0.2868)

table continues next page

Table E.9 Returns to Years of Education (Mincer Equation) for Female Workers, Controlling for Skills (continued)

	No controls	Socioeconomic	Literacy assessment	Use of skills	Job-specific skills	All controls
Writing						
Write with low intensity				0.2225		0.1639
				(0.2531)		(0.2464)
Write with medium intensity				0.8702***		0.8462***
				(0.2724)		(0.2701)
Write with high intensity				0.5741		0.4050
				(0.3906)		(0.3540)
Numeracy						
Numeracy with low intensity				−0.2961		−0.3563*
				(0.1958)		(0.1955)
Numeracy with medium intensity				−0.0280		−0.0250
				(0.1865)		(0.1906)
Numeracy with high intensity				0.1788		0.2868
				(0.2565)		(0.2959)
Job-specific skills (relative to score 0)						
Cognitive challenge						
Low think and learn					−0.0188	−0.0368
					(0.1904)	(0.1543)
Medium think and learn					0.1362	0.0164
					(0.1929)	(0.1665)
High think and learn					0.2075	0.1928
					(0.2390)	(0.2169)
Physical						
Low physical demand					−0.1409	−0.1024
					(0.2323)	(0.2868)
Medium physical demand					−0.2135	−0.1550
					(0.2664)	(0.2870)
High physical demand					0.1024	0.1532
					(0.2267)	(0.2643)
Autonomy and repetitiveness						
Low autonomy and repetitive					−0.0378	0.0739
					(0.1500)	(0.1250)
Medium autonomy and repetitive					−0.1028	−0.1493
					(0.2240)	(0.2157)
High autonomy and repetitive					−0.3109	−0.1523
					(0.2452)	(0.3167)
Make presentations					0.1021	−0.0914
					(0.2217)	(0.1969)
Supervise others					0.0606	0.2123
					(0.2088)	(0.1690)

table continues next page

Table E.9 Returns to Years of Education (Mincer Equation) for Female Workers, Controlling for Skills *(continued)*

	No controls	Socioeconomic	Literacy assessment	Use of skills	Job-specific skills	All controls
Computer use at work (relative to no use)						
Computer use with low intensity					−0.1790	−0.3520
					(0.3608)	(0.4408)
Computer use with medium intensity					−0.5476	−0.6718
					(0.4123)	(0.4293)
Computer use with high intensity					0.2913	0.3859*
					(0.2810)	(0.2111)
Reading proficiency						
Sentence correct answers (%)		−0.0073				−0.0126
		(0.0098)				(0.0084)
Passage correct answers (%)		0.0110				0.0120
		(0.0102)				(0.0104)
Vocabulary correct answers (%)		−0.0088				−0.0052
		(0.0202)				(0.0190)
Passed Core test		−0.0018				0.0561
		(0.4059)				(0.3695)
Failed Core test		−0.0935				0.0858
		(0.3014)				(0.3175)
Number of observations	246	246	246	246	246	246
R^2	0.401	0.413	0.445	0.462	0.439	0.559

Note: All models estimated using ordinary least squares. Robust standard errors are in parentheses. Controls include experience, experience squared, gender, economic sector, and dummies for region. For all skills dummies of nonresponse (missing) were created and included in the regression, but they are not displayed in the table. Dependent variable is monthly earning considering main and second occupation.
*** $p < 0.01$, ** $p < 0.05$, * $p < 0.1$.

Table E.10 Returns to Education Level (Mincer Equation) for Female Workers, Controlling for Skills

	No controls	Socioeconomic	Literacy assessment	Use of skills	Job-specific skills	All controls
Education Level (relative to none)						
Primary education (%)	0.2825	0.2438	0.1458	0.3042	0.2806	0.0419
	(0.2219)	(0.2306)	(0.2219)	(0.2485)	(0.2328)	(0.2410)
Junior high school (%)	0.5477***	0.5532**	0.4536**	0.4565**	0.5437***	0.4290*
	(0.2013)	(0.2158)	(0.2198)	(0.2105)	(0.2003)	(0.2272)
Senior high school (%)	1.0766***	1.1053***	0.9449***	0.8253***	1.0569***	0.7940***
	(0.2110)	(0.2679)	(0.2714)	(0.2605)	(0.2487)	(0.3078)
Tertiary education (%)	1.9808***	2.0489***	1.8514***	1.6017***	1.9526***	1.6394***
	(0.2128)	(0.2928)	(0.2755)	(0.2955)	(0.2808)	(0.3437)

table continues next page

Table E.10 Returns to Education Level (Mincer Equation) for Female Workers, Controlling for Skills *(continued)*

	No controls	Socioeconomic	Literacy assessment	Use of skills	Job-specific skills	All controls
Socioemotional skills (relative to score 2 or lower)						
Extraversion>2			0.0386			0.1002
			(0.1643)			(0.1574)
Conscientiousness>2			−0.2087			−0.4056
			(0.3219)			(0.3695)
Openness>2			−0.2421			−0.4383
			(0.2903)			(0.3224)
Stability>2			0.4671			0.6062*
			(0.3625)			(0.3330)
Agreeableness>2			0.5900			0.6056
			(0.3774)			(0.3996)
Grit>2			−0.0939			−0.3274*
			(0.1880)			(0.1909)
Cognitive skills (relative to skill not used)						
Reading						
Read with low intensity				−0.1334		−0.2002
				(0.1876)		(0.2046)
Read with medium intensity				−0.1886		−0.2094
				(0.3042)		(0.3423)
Read with high intensity				−0.2695		−0.3422
				(0.2808)		(0.2672)
Writing						
Write with low intensity				0.3236		0.2774
				(0.2136)		(0.2065)
Write with medium intensity				0.8419***		0.8777***
				(0.2622)		(0.2356)
Write with high intensity				0.5962		0.4322
				(0.4008)		(0.3281)
Numeracy						
Numeracy with low intensity				−0.3490*		−0.4421**
				(0.1895)		(0.1827)
Numeracy with medium intensity				−0.1930		−0.1827
				(0.1857)		(0.1776)
Numeracy with high intensity				−0.0451		0.1409
				(0.2632)		(0.2830)

table continues next page

Table E.10 Returns to Education Level (Mincer Equation) for Female Workers, Controlling for Skills *(continued)*

	No controls	Socioeconomic	Literacy assessment	Use of skills	Job-specific skills	All controls
Job-specific skills (relative to score 0)						
Cognitive challenge						
Low think and learn					−0.0642	−0.0479
					(0.1707)	(0.1434)
Medium think and learn					−0.0388	−0.0624
					(0.1736)	(0.1660)
High think and learn					0.0030	0.0947
					(0.2210)	(0.2173)
Physical						
Low physical demand					−0.0583	−0.1043
					(0.2353)	(0.2800)
Medium physical demand					−0.1113	−0.1502
					(0.2470)	(0.2757)
High physical demand					0.1334	0.1088
					(0.2232)	(0.2528)
Autonomy and repetitiveness						
Low autonomy and repetitive					−0.0761	0.0210
					(0.1450)	(0.1274)
Medium autonomy and repetitive					−0.2425	−0.2699
					(0.2162)	(0.2214)
High autonomy and repetitive					−0.2488	−0.1428
					(0.2571)	(0.3168)
Make presentations					0.0234	−0.1881
					(0.2496)	(0.2210)
Supervise others					0.0740	0.2096
					(0.1935)	(0.1548)
Computer use at work (relative to no use)						
Computer use with low intensity					−0.2007	−0.3515
					(0.3747)	(0.4651)
Computer use with medium intensity					−0.6498	−0.9862*
					(0.6101)	(0.5453)
Computer use with high intensity					0.1299	0.3077
					(0.2855)	(0.2136)
Reading proficiency						
Sentence correct answers (%)		−0.0082				−0.0148*
		(0.0091)				(0.0082)
Passage correct answers (%)		0.0077				0.0119
		(0.0095)				(0.0096)
Vocabulary correct answers (%)		−0.0047				−0.0075
		(0.0211)				(0.0191)

table continues next page

Table E.10 Returns to Education Level (Mincer Equation) for Female Workers, Controlling for Skills *(continued)*

	No controls	Socioeconomic	Literacy assessment	Use of skills	Job-specific skills	All controls
Passed Core test		0.0648				0.1867
		(0.4226)				(0.3835)
Failed Core test		0.2063				0.3686
		(0.3268)				(0.3355)
Number of observations	246	246	246	246	246	246
R^2	0.457	0.462	0.500	0.496	0.481	0.590

Note: All models estimated using ordinary least squares. Robust standard errors are in parentheses. Controls include experience, experience squared, gender, economic sector, and dummies for region. For all skills dummies of nonresponse (missing) were created and included in the regression, but they are not displayed in the table. Dependent variable is monthly earning considering main and second occupation.

*** $p < 0.01$, ** $p < 0.05$, * $p < 0.1$.

Table E.11 Linear Probability Model of Self-Employment, Controlling for Skills

	No controls	Socioeconomic	Literacy assessment	Use of skills	Job-specific skills	All controls
Education Level (relative to none)						
Primary education (%)	−0.0803**	0.0051	0.0135	−0.0003	0.0064	0.0187
	(0.0381)	(0.0347)	(0.0350)	(0.0350)	(0.0334)	(0.0338)
Junior high school (%)	−0.1164***	0.0073	0.0244	−0.0002	−0.0036	0.0232
	(0.0264)	(0.0266)	(0.0302)	(0.0310)	(0.0243)	(0.0298)
Senior high school (%)	−0.3106***	−0.0411	−0.0114	−0.0560	−0.0345	0.0074
	(0.0333)	(0.0345)	(0.0406)	(0.0398)	(0.0318)	(0.0393)
Tertiary education (%)	−0.6318***	−0.2107***	−0.1804***	−0.2207***	−0.2283***	−0.1812***
	(0.0328)	(0.0387)	(0.0452)	(0.0468)	(0.0409)	(0.0488)
Socioemotional Skills (relative to score 2 or lower)						
Extraversion score >2			−0.0148			0.0003
			(0.0277)			(0.0254)
Conscientiousness >2			−0.0233			0.0023
			(0.0653)			(0.0571)
Openness>2			0.0070			0.0102
			(0.0453)			(0.0408)
Stability>2			−0.0277			−0.0396
			(0.0367)			(0.0348)
Agreeableness>2			0.0101			−0.0100
			(0.0406)			(0.0395)

table continues next page

Table E.11 Linear Probability Model of Self-Employment, Controlling for Skills *(continued)*

	No controls	Socioeconomic	Literacy assessment	Use of skills	Job-specific skills	All controls
Cognitive skills (relative to skill not used)						
Reading						
Read with low intensity				−0.0150		0.0078
				(0.0316)		(0.0296)
Read with medium intensity				−0.0033		0.0119
				(0.0403)		(0.0375)
Read with high intensity				−0.0039		0.0300
				(0.0426)		(0.0388)
Writing						
Write with low intensity				0.0395		0.0521*
				(0.0290)		(0.0268)
Write with medium intensity				0.0104		0.0139
				(0.0430)		(0.0401)
Write with high intensity				−0.0137		−0.0030
				(0.0561)		(0.0528)
Numeracy						
Numeracy with low intensity				0.1551***		0.1147***
				(0.0424)		(0.0409)
Numeracy with medium intensity				0.1625***		0.1134***
				(0.0412)		(0.0398)
Numeracy with high intensity				0.1508**		0.1005*
				(0.0625)		(0.0591)
Cognitive challenge						
Low think and learn					0.0471**	0.0483**
					(0.0220)	(0.0222)
Medium think and learn					0.0598**	0.0603**
					(0.0247)	(0.0247)
High think and learn					0.1071***	0.1085***
					(0.0304)	(0.0307)
Physical						
Low physical demand					0.0146	0.0156
					(0.0388)	(0.0380)
Medium physical demand					0.0260	0.0236
					(0.0394)	(0.0386)
High physical demand					−0.0080	−0.0118
					(0.0396)	(0.0387)
Autonomy and repetitiveness						
Low autonomy and repetitive					0.2061***	0.2105***
					(0.0314)	(0.0307)
Medium autonomy and repetitive					0.4185***	0.4231***
					(0.0323)	(0.0314)

table continues next page

Table E.11 Linear Probability Model of Self-Employment, Controlling for Skills *(continued)*

	No controls	Socioeconomic	Literacy assessment	Use of skills	Job-specific skills	All controls
High autonomy and repetitive					0.4370***	0.4398***
					(0.0391)	(0.0383)
Make presentations					0.0048	0.0131
					(0.0318)	(0.0320)
Supervise others					0.0060	0.0043
					(0.0218)	(0.0221)
Computer use at work (relative to no use)						
Computer use with low intensity					−0.1850**	−0.1853**
					(0.0741)	(0.0738)
Computer use with medium intensity					0.0994	0.1025
					(0.1026)	(0.1007)
Computer use with high intensity					−0.0567	−0.0664*
					(0.0401)	(0.0383)
Number of observations	1,963	1,963	1,963	1,963	1,963	1,963
R^2	0.159	0.390	0.392	0.399	0.477	0.487

Note: All models estimated using ordinary least squares. Robust standard errors are in parentheses. Controls include gender, economic sector, and dummies for region. For all skills dummies of nonresponse (missing) were created and included in the regression, but they are not displayed in the table. Dependent variable is monthly earning considering main and second occupation. Y = 1 if self-employed and 0 if wage employed.
*** $p < 0.01$, ** $p < 0.05$, * $p < 0.1$.

Mismatch of Skills and Unexploited Potential Tables

Table F.1 Difference in Mean of Self-Reported Readers Who Passed and Who Failed the Reading Assessment Core Literacy Test

	Y1: Read and passed Core			Y2: Read and failed Core			
	Obs	Mean	SD	Obs	Mean	SD	Difference: Y2–Y1
Female (%)	1,150	42.59	49.47	457	62.56	48.45	19.970***
Low SES (%)	1,149	14.16	34.88	452	19.62	39.76	5.463**
Middle SES (%)	1,149	62.36	48.47	452	52.76	49.98	−9.605***
High SES (%)	1,149	23.48	42.40	452	27.62	44.76	4.142
Age range (years) (%)	1,150	28.86	12.32	457	30.98	12.16	2.119**
15–19 years	1,150	23.64	42.51	457	17.68	38.20	−5.957**
20–24 years	1,150	25.29	43.49	457	16.59	37.24	−8.701***
25–34 years	1,150	26.08	43.93	457	32.11	46.74	6.022**
35–44 years	1,150	10.95	31.24	457	18.70	39.04	7.755***
45–64 years	1,150	14.04	34.75	457	14.92	35.67	0.882
Education (%)							
No education	1,150	0.62	7.88	457	5.67	23.15	5.043***
Primary education	1,150	9.44	29.25	457	23.18	42.24	13.737***
JHS education	1,150	31.52	46.48	457	54.44	49.86	22.920***
SHS education	1,150	37.03	48.31	457	15.87	36.58	−21.159***
Tertiary education	1,150	21.39	41.02	457	0.85	9.19	−20.541***
Received ECE	1,141	81.54	38.81	453	70.84	45.50	−10.699***
Language spoken at work (%)							
Akan	806	78.92	40.81	370	88.20	32.30	9.278***
Ewe	806	7.34	26.10	370	7.83	26.90	0.486
Ga-Adangme	806	14.84	35.57	370	9.65	29.57	−5.191**
Mole-Dagbani	806	2.83	16.60	370	3.60	18.65	0.767
English	806	74.40	43.67	370	33.14	47.14	−41.256***
Others	806	7.83	26.88	370	9.48	29.34	1.658

table continues next page

Table F.1 Difference in Mean of Self-Reported Readers Who Passed and Who Failed the Reading Assessment Core Literacy Test *(continued)*

	Y1: Read and passed Core			Y2: Read and failed Core			
	Obs	Mean	SD	Obs	Mean	SD	Difference: Y2–Y1
Language spoken at home (%)							
Akan	1,150	65.56	47.54	457	72.80	44.55	7.239**
Ewe	1,150	9.04	28.69	457	6.54	24.75	−2.504
Ga-Adangme	1,150	9.67	29.57	457	3.34	17.98	−6.338***
Mole-Dagbani	1,150	5.22	22.25	457	5.00	21.82	−0.217
English	1,150	2.04	14.15	457	0.25	4.99	−1.794***
Others	1,150	8.47	27.85	457	12.08	32.63	3.615*
Labor status (%)							
Employed	1,150	45.20	49.79	457	62.44	48.48	17.235***
Unemployed	1,150	6.40	24.49	457	3.38	18.08	−3.029**
NEET	1,150	7.52	26.38	457	9.93	29.93	2.411
Inactive	1,150	40.88	49.18	457	24.26	42.91	−16.617***
Employment status (%)							
Formal employee	587	35.46	47.88	310	8.36	27.72	−27.103***
Informal employee	587	27.71	44.79	310	17.58	38.13	−10.125***
Self-employed	587	36.83	48.28	310	74.06	43.90	37.228***
Occupation (%)							
Low-skilled occupation	587	23.85	42.65	310	46.61	49.97	22.758***
Mid-skilled occupation	587	41.11	49.24	310	49.80	50.08	8.690**
High-skilled occupation	587	35.04	47.75	310	3.59	18.64	−31.448***
Economic sector (%)							
Agriculture fishing, and mining	587	5.18	22.18	310	10.10	30.18	4.916*
Manufacturing	587	8.82	28.39	310	13.76	34.50	4.935
Low- to mid-value-added	587	45.55	49.84	310	66.55	47.26	20.993***
High-value-added	587	40.44	49.12	310	9.60	29.51	−30.844***
Earnings							
Monthly earnings	648	678.52	2,091.11	304	401.69	970.30	−276.839**
Socioemotional skills							
Extraversion (score)	1,135	2.59	0.59	344	2.43	0.59	−0.163***
Missing extraversion	1,150	1.11	10.46	457	27.99	44.95	26.887***
Conscientiousness (score)	1,135	3.32	0.52	340	2.96	0.63	−0.361***
Missing conscientiousness	1,150	1.11	10.46	457	28.45	45.17	27.343***
Openness (score)	1,135	3.22	0.52	343	2.86	0.62	−0.359***
Missing openness	1,150	1.11	10.46	457	28.11	45.00	27.000***
Emotional stability (score)	1,133	2.75	0.55	340	2.65	0.57	−0.099**
Missing stability	1,150	1.47	12.02	457	28.51	45.20	27.049***
Agreeableness (score)	1,135	3.15	0.58	341	2.81	0.69	−0.342***
Missing agreeableness	1,150	1.11	10.46	457	28.40	45.14	27.293***

table continues next page

Table F.1 Difference in Mean of Self-Reported Readers Who Passed and Who Failed the Reading Assessment Core Literacy Test *(continued)*

	Y1: Read and passed Core			Y2: Read and failed Core			
	Obs	Mean	SD	Obs	Mean	SD	Difference: Y2–Y1
Self-reported skills (%)							
Reading							
Don't use reading skill	1,131	0.00	0.00	448	0.00	0.00	n.a.
Read with low intensity	1,131	30.46	46.04	448	66.28	47.33	35.822***
Read with medium intensity	1,131	28.23	45.03	448	20.17	40.17	−8.061***
Read with high intensity	1,131	41.31	49.26	448	13.55	34.26	−27.761***
Writing							
Don't use writing skill	1,136	5.26	22.33	455	17.38	37.93	12.120***
Write with low intensity	1,136	60.25	48.96	455	67.05	47.05	6.800**
Write with medium intensity	1,136	18.40	38.77	455	8.78	28.33	−9.626***
Write with high intensity	1,136	16.08	36.76	455	6.79	25.19	−9.294***
Numeracy							
Don't use numeracy skill	1,150	3.96	19.52	457	4.25	20.21	0.292
Numeracy with low intensity	1,150	10.85	31.12	457	31.45	46.48	20.592***
Numeracy with medium intensity	1,150	59.51	49.11	457	58.94	49.25	−0.569
Numeracy with high intensity	1,150	25.68	43.70	457	5.36	22.55	−20.314***
Computer							
Don't use computer skill	1,126	43.00	49.53	453	86.03	34.70	43.038***
Computer with low intensity	1,126	18.56	38.90	453	6.68	24.99	−11.882***
Computer with medium intensity	1,126	10.29	30.39	453	1.10	10.46	−9.183***
Computer with high intensity	1,126	28.16	45.00	453	6.19	24.12	−21.973***
Literacy assessment							
No answer on Reading Component or Core (%)	1,150	0.00	0.00	457	0.00	0.00	n.a.
Reading Component (average) (%)							
Sentence incorrect answers	1,150	38.47	11.30	457	40.62	27.96	2.156
Sentence correct answers	1,150	46.64	9.50	457	31.70	16.63	−14.940***
Sentence no answers	1,150	14.90	11.70	457	27.68	18.61	12.785***
Passage incorrect answers	1,150	51.28	8.87	457	55.51	25.16	4.231***
Passage correct answers	1,150	44.67	7.96	457	27.59	17.80	−17.081***
Passage no answers	1,150	4.05	6.54	457	16.90	17.17	12.850***
Vocabulary incorrect answers	1,150	72.85	4.42	457	63.37	14.12	−9.482***
Vocabulary correct answers	1,150	22.84	2.39	457	18.24	6.36	−4.608***
Vocabulary no answers	1,150	4.31	5.21	457	18.39	18.53	14.089***
Core (average) (%)							
Score Core test	1,150	6.24	1.61	457	0.76	0.85	−5.478***
Passed Core test	1,150	100.00	0.00	457	0.00	0.00	−100.00***
Literacy assessment							
Reading proficiency	1,150		222.86	457		53.02	−169.841***

Note: n.a. = not applicable; NEET = Not in Employment, Education, or Training.
*** $p < 0.01$, ** $p < 0.05$, * $p < 0.1$.

Stepping Up Skills in Urban Ghana · http://dx.doi.org/10.1596/978-1-4648-1012-1

Table F.2 Unexploited Potential: Reading Skill

	Y1: Read at home and at work			Y2: Read at home but not at work			Difference: Y2–Y1
	Obs	Mean	SD	Obs	Mean	SD	
Female (%)	650	36.84	48.28	560	61.41	48.73	24.562***
Low SES (%)	646	16.24	36.91	555	21.61	41.20	5.371*
Middle SES (%)	646	61.79	48.63	555	56.43	49.63	−5.355
High SES (%)	646	21.97	41.44	555	21.96	41.43	−0.015
Age range (years) (%)	650	36.47	11.87	560	37.22	11.36	0.750
15–19 years	650	1.17	10.77	560	2.69	16.19	1.517
20–24 years	650	14.81	35.55	560	10.70	30.93	−4.113
25–34 years	650	36.81	48.27	560	31.37	46.44	−5.446*
35–44 years	650	20.24	40.21	560	30.33	46.01	10.089***
45–64 years	650	26.97	44.41	560	24.92	43.29	−2.046
Education (%)							
No education	650	1.92	13.72	560	6.35	24.41	4.438***
Primary education	650	4.19	20.05	560	12.22	32.78	8.031***
JHS education	650	27.30	44.59	560	57.41	49.49	30.106***
SHS education	650	37.13	48.35	560	20.80	40.62	−16.336***
Tertiary education	650	29.46	45.62	560	3.22	17.67	−26.240***
Received ECE	645	69.31	46.15	548	66.08	47.39	−3.237
Language spoken at work (%)							
Akan	649	80.75	39.45	559	85.78	34.96	5.026**
Ewe	649	7.75	26.76	559	12.26	32.83	4.509*
Ga-Adangme	649	16.14	36.82	559	12.44	33.03	−3.701
Mole-Dagbani	649	2.48	15.56	559	2.19	14.64	−0.293
English	649	76.57	42.39	559	31.36	46.44	−45.205***
Others	649	7.74	26.74	559	9.89	29.87	2.149
Language spoken at home (%)							
Akan	648	69.86	45.92	557	64.88	47.78	−4.977
Ewe	648	7.80	26.83	557	12.81	33.45	5.013**
Ga-Adangme	648	8.83	28.40	557	7.33	26.09	−1.500
Mole-Dagbani	648	4.41	20.55	557	3.06	17.23	−1.355
English	648	2.00	14.03	557	0.29	5.40	−1.713***
Others	648	7.10	25.70	557	11.63	32.09	4.532**
Labor status (%)							
Employed	650	100.00	0.00	560	100.00	0.00	n.a.
Unemployed	650	0.00	0.00	560	0.00	0.00	n.a.
NEET	650	0.00	0.00	560	0.00	0.00	n.a.
Inactive	650	0.00	0.00	560	0.00	0.00	n.a.
Employment status (%)							
Formal employee	650	36.91	48.29	560	5.96	23.69	−30.954***
Informal employee	650	24.76	43.20	560	21.64	41.22	−3.122
Self-employed	650	38.32	48.66	560	72.40	44.74	34.076***
Occupation (%)							
Low-skilled occupation	650	29.05	45.43	560	40.77	49.18	11.725***
Mid-skilled occupation	650	35.78	47.97	560	56.52	49.62	20.733***
High-skilled occupation	650	35.17	47.79	560	2.71	16.27	−32.458***

table continues next page

Table F.2 Unexploited Potential: Reading Skill (continued)

	Y1: Read at home and at work			Y2: Read at home but not at work			Difference:
	Obs	Mean	SD	Obs	Mean	SD	Y2–Y1
Economic sector (%)							
Agriculture, fishing, and mining	650	4.42	20.57	560	9.38	29.17	4.956**
Manufacturing	650	10.99	31.31	560	11.22	31.59	0.228
Low- to mid-value-added	650	42.75	49.51	560	71.56	45.15	28.815***
High-value-added	650	41.84	49.37	560	7.84	26.90	−33.998***
Earnings							
Monthly earnings	626	771.72	2,391.23	540	383.97	669.19	−387.751***
Socioemotional skills							
Extraversion (score)	596	2.58	0.57	387	2.45	0.59	−0.131***
Missing extraversion	650	8.40	27.76	560	32.17	46.75	23.773***
Conscientiousness (score)	594	3.33	0.52	385	3.13	0.61	−0.198***
Missing conscientiousness	650	8.49	27.89	560	32.46	46.86	23.973***
Openness (score)	595	3.14	0.55	385	2.92	0.63	−0.219***
Missing openness	650	8.51	27.92	560	32.34	46.82	23.826***
Emotional stability (score)	593	2.81	0.55	382	2.73	0.56	−0.078*
Missing stability	650	8.60	28.06	560	33.31	47.18	24.711***
Agreeableness (score)	594	3.09	0.60	383	2.94	0.69	−0.149***
Missing agreeableness	650	8.55	27.98	560	32.64	46.93	24.091***
Self-reported skills (%)							
Reading							
Don't use reading skill	649	0.00	0.00	547	0.00	0.00	n.a.
Read with low intensity	649	44.37	49.72	547	70.70	45.55	26.333***
Read with medium intensity	649	24.79	43.21	547	18.29	38.69	−6.501**
Read with high intensity	649	30.84	46.22	547	11.01	31.33	−19.832***
Writing							
Don't use writing skill	646	3.47	18.32	557	23.72	42.58	20.251***
Write with low intensity	646	71.84	45.01	557	67.40	46.92	−4.437
Write with medium intensity	646	14.24	34.97	557	6.88	25.34	−7.358***
Write with high intensity	646	10.45	30.62	557	1.99	13.99	−8.456***
Numeracy							
Don't use numeracy skill	650	2.36	15.20	560	4.81	21.41	2.446*
Numeracy with low intensity	650	17.32	37.87	560	33.84	47.36	16.523***
Numeracy with medium intensity	650	68.90	46.32	560	59.96	49.04	−8.940**
Numeracy with high intensity	650	11.42	31.82	560	1.39	11.70	−10.029***
Computer							
Don't use computer skill	641	55.66	49.72	556	90.23	29.72	34.571***
Computer with low intensity	641	9.30	29.07	556	4.08	19.81	−5.220***
Computer with medium intensity	641	6.50	24.66	556	2.39	15.30	−4.101***
Computer with high intensity	641	28.54	45.20	556	3.29	17.86	−25.251***
Literacy assessment							
No answer on Reading Component or Core (%)	650	18.54	38.89	560	36.87	48.29	18.335***

table continues next page

Table F.2 Unexploited Potential: Reading Skill (continued)

	Y1: Read at home and at work			Y2: Read at home but not at work			Difference:
	Obs	Mean	SD	Obs	Mean	SD	Y2–Y1
Reading Component (average) (%)							
Sentence incorrect answers	527	39.98	15.20	353	42.80	24.52	2.814
Sentence correct answers	527	44.30	12.34	353	37.26	17.06	−7.045***
Sentence no answers	527	15.72	13.39	353	19.95	16.23	4.230***
Passage incorrect answers	527	52.79	13.62	353	56.04	21.32	3.242**
Passage correct answers	527	41.61	12.54	353	33.54	17.82	−8.074***
Passage no answers	527	5.59	9.71	353	10.42	13.56	4.832***
Vocabulary incorrect answers	527	71.40	8.17	353	68.35	12.03	−3.052***
Vocabulary correct answers	527	22.24	3.63	353	20.54	5.42	−1.698***
Vocabulary no answers	527	6.36	10.45	353	11.11	15.70	4.750***
Core (average)							
Score Core test	527	5.29	2.74	353	2.97	2.71	−2.320***
Passed Core test	527	78.76	40.94	353	49.42	50.07	−29.338***
Literacy assessment							
Reading proficiency	650		176	560		107	−69.405***

Note: n.a. = not applicable; NEET = Not in Employment, Education, or Training.
*** $p < 0.01$, ** $p < 0.05$, * $p < 0.1$.

Table F.3 Unexploited Potential: Writing Skill

	Y1: Write at home and at work			Y2: Write at home but not at work			Difference:
	Obs	Mean	SD	Obs	Mean	SD	Y2–Y1
Female (%)	812	42.82	49.51	248	55.20	49.83	12.383***
Low SES (%)	808	17.56	38.07	245	22.07	41.56	4.514
Middle SES (%)	808	62.38	48.47	245	51.68	50.07	−10.700**
High SES (%)	808	20.06	40.07	245	26.24	44.08	6.186
Age range (years) (%)	812	37.36	11.81	248	35.29	10.86	−2.065**
15–19 years	812	1.21	10.95	248	3.54	18.51	2.325*
20–24 years	812	12.16	32.70	248	13.69	34.44	1.533
25–34 years	812	34.79	47.66	248	35.76	48.03	0.974
35–44 years	812	23.65	42.52	248	26.76	44.36	3.114
45–64 years	812	28.19	45.02	248	20.25	40.27	−7.946**
Education (%)							
No education	812	1.93	13.75	248	7.56	26.49	5.633***
Primary education	812	4.70	21.19	248	12.95	33.64	8.243***
JHS education	812	34.91	47.70	248	53.19	50.00	18.276***
SHS education	812	33.94	47.38	248	23.25	42.33	−10.684***
Tertiary education	812	24.52	43.05	248	3.05	17.24	−21.467***
Received ECE	805	67.32	46.93	243	62.77	48.44	−4.555

table continues next page

Table F.3 Unexploited Potential: Writing Skill *(continued)*

	Y1: Write at home and at work			Y2: Write at home but not at work			Difference:
	Obs	Mean	SD	Obs	Mean	SD	Y2–Y1
Language spoken at work (%)							
Akan	810	80.21	39.86	248	84.73	36.04	4.516
Ewe	810	9.47	29.30	248	12.00	32.56	2.525
Ga-Adangme	810	17.33	37.88	248	11.61	32.10	−5.724**
Mole-Dagbani	810	2.38	15.25	248	4.91	21.65	2.530
English	810	68.95	46.30	248	24.60	43.15	−44.346***
Others	810	8.02	27.18	248	10.41	30.60	2.389
Language spoken at home (%)							
Akan	808	68.53	46.47	247	63.61	48.21	−4.912
Ewe	808	9.66	29.56	247	10.97	31.32	1.316
Ga-Adangme	808	9.72	29.65	247	5.92	23.64	−3.807*
Mole-Dagbani	808	3.49	18.37	247	5.72	23.26	2.222
English	808	1.64	12.69	247	0.76	8.68	−0.879
Others	808	6.96	25.47	247	13.02	33.73	6.060*
Labor status (%)							
Employed	812	100.00	0.00	248	100.00	0.00	n.a.
Unemployed	812	0.00	0.00	248	0.00	0.00	n.a.
NEET	812	0.00	0.00	248	0.00	0.00	n.a.
Inactive	812	0.00	0.00	248	0.00	0.00	n.a.
Employment status (%)							
Formal employee	812	31.27	46.39	248	4.87	21.56	−26.403***
Informal employee	812	20.55	40.43	248	24.75	43.24	4.203
Self-employed	812	48.18	50.00	248	70.38	45.75	22.200***
Occupation (%)							
Low-skilled occupation	812	32.62	46.91	248	43.42	49.67	10.803**
Mid-skilled occupation	812	39.66	48.95	248	54.58	49.89	14.914***
High-skilled occupation	812	27.72	44.79	248	2.00	14.02	−25.717***
Economic sector (%)							
Agriculture, fishing, and mining	812	4.60	20.95	248	15.44	36.20	10.842***
Manufacturing	812	14.54	35.28	248	4.85	21.53	−9.691***
Low- to mid-value-added	812	46.75	49.92	248	72.88	44.55	26.135***
High-value-added	812	34.11	47.44	248	6.83	25.27	−27.286***
Earnings							
Monthly earnings	783	704.36	2,110.72	236	315.79	457.89	−388.565***
Socioemotional skills							
Extraversion (score)	698	2.56	0.58	178	2.43	0.59	−0.134**
Missing extraversion	812	13.81	34.52	248	30.64	46.19	16.837***
Conscientiousness (score)	695	3.32	0.51	176	3.04	0.67	−0.281***
Missing conscientiousness	812	14.10	34.82	248	31.30	46.46	17.198***
Openness (score)	695	3.06	0.60	177	3.03	0.57	−0.030

table continues next page

Table F.3 Unexploited Potential: Writing Skill (continued)

	Y1: Write at home and at work			Y2: Write at home but not at work			Difference:
	Obs	Mean	SD	Obs	Mean	SD	Y2–Y1
Missing openness	812	14.17	34.90	248	30.86	46.29	16.689***
Emotional stability (score)	693	2.81	0.55	175	2.77	0.54	−0.039
Missing stability	812	14.27	34.99	248	32.36	46.88	18.092***
Agreeableness (score)	692	3.09	0.61	176	2.93	0.69	−0.168**
Missing agreeableness	812	14.49	35.22	248	31.34	46.48	16.849***
Self-reported skills (%)							
Reading							
Don't use reading skill	806	4.40	20.52	245	12.69	33.35	8.285***
Read with low intensity	806	46.12	49.88	245	58.20	49.42	12.086***
Read with medium intensity	806	24.00	42.73	245	19.14	39.42	−4.864
Read with high intensity	806	25.48	43.60	245	9.98	30.03	−15.507***
Writing							
Don't use writing skill	809	0.00	0.00	244	0.00	0.00	n.a.
Write with low intensity	809	77.14	42.02	244	89.66	30.50	12.529***
Write with medium intensity	809	13.33	34.01	244	9.58	29.49	−3.752
Write with high intensity	809	9.53	29.38	244	0.76	8.68	−8.777***
Numeracy							
Don't use numeracy skill	812	3.06	17.24	248	4.58	20.95	1.519
Numeracy with low intensity	812	18.59	38.92	248	35.98	48.09	17.393***
Numeracy with medium intensity	812	68.91	46.31	248	57.71	49.50	−11.208**
Numeracy with high intensity	812	9.44	29.25	248	1.73	13.08	−7.704***
Computer							
Don't use computer skill	800	64.05	48.01	247	90.57	29.28	26.519***
Computer with low intensity	800	8.11	27.31	247	2.50	15.63	−5.611***
Computer with medium intensity	800	6.19	24.11	247	1.62	12.64	−4.574***
Computer with high intensity	800	21.65	41.21	247	5.31	22.48	−16.334***
Literacy assessment							
No answer on Reading Component or Core (%)	812	24.30	42.92	248	32.46	46.92	8.157**
Reading Component (average) (%)							
Sentence incorrect answers	611	40.06	15.84	165	42.09	24.57	2.034
Sentence correct answers	611	43.51	12.83	165	37.73	17.31	−5.782***
Sentence no answers	611	16.43	13.83	165	20.18	16.53	3.748**
Passage incorrect answers	611	53.18	14.91	165	55.94	21.38	2.755
Passage correct answers	611	40.93	13.37	165	33.52	17.78	−7.404***
Passage no answers	611	5.89	9.85	165	10.54	14.23	4.649***
Vocabulary incorrect answers	611	71.57	7.80	165	68.44	10.10	−3.132***
Vocabulary correct answers	611	22.18	3.67	165	20.46	5.42	−1.718***
Vocabulary no answers	611	6.25	9.88	165	11.10	13.74	4.850***

table continues next page

Table F.3 Unexploited Potential: Writing Skill (continued)

	Y1: Write at home and at work			Y2: Write at home but not at work			Difference: Y2–Y1
	Obs	Mean	SD	Obs	Mean	SD	
Core (average)							
Score Core test	611	5.01	2.80	165	2.80	2.60	−2.207***
Passed Core test	611	75.95	42.77	165	47.20	50.07	−28.749***
Literacy assessment							
Reading proficiency	812		164	248		109	−54.538***

Note: n.a. = not applicable; NEET = Not in Employment, Education, or Training.
*** *p* < 0.01, ** *p* < 0.05, * *p* < 0.1.

Table F.4 Unexploited Potential: Numeracy Skill

	Y1: Use mathematics at home and at work			Y2: Use mathematics at home but not at work			Difference: Y2–Y1
	Obs	Mean	SD	Obs	Mean	SD	
Female (%)	1,603	58.30	49.32	88	39.40	49.14	−18.905***
Low SES (%)	1,591	25.27	43.47	88	31.19	46.59	5.916
Middle SES (%)	1,591	55.57	49.70	88	49.81	50.29	−5.764
High SES (%)	1,591	19.15	39.36	88	19.00	39.46	−0.152
Age range (years) (%)	1,603	37.41	11.61	88	36.92	12.18	−0.497
15–19 years	1,603	1.80	13.32	88	0.65	8.06	−1.158
20–24 years	1,603	11.78	32.25	88	13.00	33.82	1.217
25–34 years	1,603	32.05	46.68	88	41.38	49.53	9.329
35–44 years	1,603	27.47	44.65	88	18.62	39.15	−8.855*
45–64 years	1,603	26.89	44.35	88	26.36	44.31	−0.533
Education (%)							
No education	1,603	25.58	43.64	88	25.16	43.64	−0.417
Primary education	1,603	9.96	29.95	88	7.95	27.21	−2.003
JHS education	1,603	34.33	47.49	88	27.04	44.67	−7.289
SHS education	1,603	19.54	39.67	88	20.46	40.57	0.911
Tertiary education	1,603	10.60	30.79	88	19.40	39.77	8.799
Received ECE	1,585	55.63	49.70	87	56.09	49.92	0.459
Language spoken at work (%)							
Akan	1,599	80.59	39.56	88	70.73	45.76	−9.862
Ewe	1,599	6.15	24.03	88	17.59	38.29	11.435*
Ga-Adangme	1,599	13.17	33.83	88	14.51	35.43	1.345
Mole-Dagbani	1,599	7.85	26.90	88	6.72	25.17	−1.131
English	1,599	38.72	48.73	88	48.77	50.27	10.049
Others	1,599	12.16	32.70	88	12.14	32.85	−0.023
Language spoken at home (%)							
Akan	1,598	64.12	47.98	88	61.81	48.86	−2.307
Ewe	1,598	6.71	25.03	88	12.13	32.84	5.420

table continues next page

Table F.4 Unexploited Potential: Numeracy Skill *(continued)*

	Y1: Use mathematics at home and at work			Y2: Use mathematics at home but not at work			Difference: Y2–Y1
	Obs	Mean	SD	Obs	Mean	SD	
Ga-Adangme	1,598	6.89	25.34	88	6.04	23.96	−0.847
Mole-Dagbani	1,598	8.00	27.13	88	11.02	31.49	3.021
English	1,598	0.84	9.11	88	0.00	0.00	−0.835***
Others	1,598	13.44	34.12	88	8.99	28.77	−4.451
Labor status (%)							
Employed	1,603	100.00	0.00	88	100.00	0.00	n.a.
Unemployed	1,603	0.00	0.00	88	0.00	0.00	n.a.
NEET	1,603	0.00	0.00	88	0.00	0.00	n.a.
Inactive	1,603	0.00	0.00	88	0.00	0.00	n.a.
Employment status (%)							
Formal employee	1,603	13.44	34.12	88	37.91	48.79	24.468***
Informal employee	1,603	17.85	38.31	88	45.14	50.05	27.282***
Self-employed	1,603	68.71	46.38	88	16.95	37.74	−51.750***
Occupation (%)							
Low-skilled occupation	1,603	38.82	48.75	88	40.95	49.46	2.123
Mid-skilled occupation	1,603	48.24	49.98	88	28.93	45.60	−19.314***
High-skilled occupation	1,603	12.93	33.57	88	30.12	46.14	17.191**
Economic sector (%)							
Agriculture, fishing, and mining	1,603	11.12	31.45	88	11.06	31.55	−0.061
Manufacturing	1,603	11.10	31.42	88	3.29	17.94	−7.807***
Low- to mid-value-added	1,603	62.73	48.37	88	35.03	47.98	−27.707***
High-value-added	1,603	15.05	35.76	88	50.62	50.28	35.575***
Earnings							
Monthly earnings	1,560	566.46	1,770.94	82	315.20	490.52	−251.257***
Socioemotional skills							
Extraversion (score)	931	2.51	0.60	56	2.61	0.54	0.102
Missing extraversion	1,603	44.55	49.72	88	33.74	47.55	−10.818
Conscientiousness (score)	925	3.23	0.57	56	3.39	0.53	0.161
Missing conscientiousness	1,603	44.95	49.76	88	33.74	47.55	−11.218
Openness (score)	924	3.04	0.60	56	3.05	0.61	0.009
Missing openness	1,603	44.91	49.76	88	33.74	47.55	−11.180
Emotional stability (score)	918	2.77	0.56	56	2.74	0.57	−0.032
Missing stability	1,603	45.30	49.79	88	33.74	47.55	−11.563
Agreeableness (score)	919	3.02	0.64	56	3.12	0.55	0.099
Missing agreeableness	1,603	45.16	49.78	88	33.74	47.55	−11.422
Self-reported skills (%)							
Reading							
Don't use reading skill	1,593	37.74	48.49	88	30.28	46.21	−7.464
Read with low intensity	1,593	35.92	47.99	88	39.41	49.15	3.489

table continues next page

Table F.4 Unexploited Potential: Numeracy Skill (continued)

	Y1: Use mathematics at home and at work			Y2: Use mathematics at home but not at work			Difference:
	Obs	Mean	SD	Obs	Mean	SD	Y2–Y1
Read with medium intensity	1,593	14.01	34.72	88	12.36	33.10	−1.650
Read with high intensity	1,593	12.32	32.88	88	17.95	38.60	5.625
Writing							
Don't use writing skill	1,596	40.78	49.16	88	32.45	47.09	−8.325
Write with low intensity	1,596	48.11	49.98	88	52.27	50.23	4.160
Write with medium intensity	1,596	6.98	25.48	88	9.97	30.14	2.998
Write with high intensity	1,596	4.13	19.91	88	5.30	22.53	1.167
Numeracy							
Don't use numeracy skill	1,603	0.00	0.00	88	0.00	0.00	n.a.
Numeracy with low intensity	1,603	29.59	45.66	88	43.38	49.84	13.786*
Numeracy with medium intensity	1,603	65.55	47.53	88	54.51	50.08	−11.044
Numeracy with high intensity	1,603	4.86	21.51	88	2.12	14.48	−2.741
Computer							
Don't use computer skill	1,590	81.99	38.44	88	74.34	43.92	−7.650
Computer with low intensity	1,590	4.26	20.20	88	4.93	21.77	0.667
Computer with medium intensity	1,590	3.27	17.79	88	1.49	12.20	−1.775
Computer with high intensity	1,590	10.48	30.63	88	19.23	39.64	8.758
Literacy assessment							
No answer on Reading Component or Core (%)	1,603	46.91	49.92	88	45.95	50.12	−0.962
Reading Component (average) (%)							
Sentence incorrect answers	843	43.19	23.48	51	44.15	19.78	0.964
Sentence correct answers	843	38.34	17.12	51	42.38	15.53	4.038
Sentence no answers	843	18.47	16.27	51	13.47	11.85	−5.003**
Passage incorrect answers	843	55.78	20.31	51	54.78	17.14	−1.007
Passage correct answers	843	35.11	17.65	51	40.02	15.18	4.908*
Passage no answers	843	9.11	14.14	51	5.21	7.93	−3.901***
Vocabulary incorrect answers	843	67.41	14.25	51	69.97	11.44	2.559
Vocabulary correct answers	843	20.20	6.12	51	22.05	4.09	1.849***
Vocabulary no answers	843	12.38	18.97	51	7.97	14.92	−4.408*
Core (average)							
Score Core test	843	3.86	3.09	51	5.15	2.52	1.286***
Passed Core test	843	58.99	49.21	51	83.36	37.62	24.364***
Literacy assessment							
Reading proficiency	1,603		120	88		144	24.144**

Note: NEET = Not in Employment, Education, or Training.
*** $p < 0.01$, ** $p < 0.05$, * $p < 0.1$.

Stepping Up Skills in Urban Ghana · http://dx.doi.org/10.1596/978-1-4648-1012-1

Table F.5 Unexploited Potential: Computer Skill

	Y1: Use computer at home and at work			Y2: Use computer at home but not at work			Difference:
	Obs	Mean	SD	Obs	Mean	SD	Y2–Y1
Female (%)	172	27.59	44.83	190	28.29	45.16	0.706
Low SES (%)	172	8.74	28.32	190	18.68	39.08	9.943**
Middle SES (%)	172	60.85	48.95	190	60.05	49.11	−0.801
High SES (%)	172	30.41	46.14	190	21.27	41.03	−9.143
Age (%)	172	34.81	11.41	190	29.81	8.94	−4.996***
15–19 years	172	0.70	8.33	190	3.72	18.97	3.024
20–24 years	172	17.94	38.48	190	30.88	46.32	12.944**
25–34 years	172	43.71	49.75	190	39.11	48.93	−4.605
35–44 years	172	14.59	35.40	190	20.91	40.77	6.318
45–64 years	172	23.07	42.25	190	5.39	22.64	−17.681***
Education (%)							
No education	172	0.00	0.00	190	1.34	11.53	1.339*
Primary education	172	0.31	5.58	190	4.76	21.35	4.451**
JHS education	172	2.25	14.88	190	22.63	41.95	20.376***
SHS education	172	33.01	47.16	190	48.84	50.12	15.831**
Tertiary education	172	64.43	48.01	190	22.43	41.82	−41.997***
Received ECE	170	77.06	42.17	187	81.95	38.56	4.892
Language spoken at work (%)							
Akan	172	73.33	44.36	190	76.25	42.67	2.928
Ewe	172	4.93	21.71	190	7.95	27.12	3.018
Ga-Adangme	172	17.47	38.08	190	19.61	39.81	2.143
Mole-Dagbani	172	1.42	11.86	190	3.29	17.87	1.867
English	172	95.74	20.25	190	75.46	43.14	−20.279***
Others	172	8.68	28.24	190	7.60	26.57	−1.086
Language spoken at home (%)							
Akan	172	69.39	46.22	190	58.82	49.35	−10.570*
Ewe	172	6.90	25.42	190	12.73	33.42	5.829
Ga-Adangme	172	10.73	31.04	190	11.16	31.57	0.424
Mole-Dagbani	172	3.40	18.18	190	7.64	26.63	4.233
English	172	4.25	20.22	190	3.07	17.31	−1.173
Others	172	5.33	22.53	190	6.59	24.87	1.256
Labor status (%)							
Employed	172	100.00	0.00	190	100.00	0.00	n.a.
Unemployed	172	0.00	0.00	190	0.00	0.00	n.a.
NEET	172	0.00	0.00	190	0.00	0.00	n.a.
Inactive	172	0.00	0.00	190	0.00	0.00	n.a.
Employment status (%)							
Formal employee	172	58.89	49.35	190	26.12	44.04	−32.774***
Informal employee	172	20.93	40.80	190	40.21	49.16	19.282***
Self-employed	172	20.18	40.25	190	33.67	47.38	13.492**

table continues next page

Table F.5 Unexploited Potential: Computer Skill (continued)

	Y1: Use computer at home and at work			Y2: Use computer at home but not at work			Difference: Y2–Y1
	Obs	Mean	SD	Obs	Mean	SD	
Occupation (%)							
Low-skilled occupation	172	7.31	26.11	190	28.23	45.13	20.921***
Mid-skilled occupation	172	28.27	45.16	190	39.73	49.06	11.458*
High-skilled occupation	172	64.41	48.02	190	32.04	46.78	−32.380***
Economic sector (%)							
Agriculture, fishing, and mining	172	1.42	11.89	190	3.33	18.00	1.909
Manufacturing	172	4.25	20.22	190	8.52	27.99	4.270
Low- to mid-value-added	172	33.74	47.42	190	53.53	50.01	19.795***
High-value-added	172	60.59	49.01	190	34.62	47.70	−25.975***
Earnings							
Monthly earnings	163	1,360.81	4,175.78	184	514.12	703.04	−846.695*
Socioemotional skills							
Extraversion (score)	171	2.72	0.56	182	2.62	0.54	−0.097
Missing extraversion	172	0.31	5.58	190	4.25	20.22	3.937**
Conscientiousness (score)	171	3.40	0.46	182	3.34	0.50	−0.060
Missing conscientiousness	172	0.31	5.58	190	4.25	20.22	3.937**
Openness (score)	171	3.27	0.48	182	3.18	0.58	−0.084
Missing openness	172	0.31	5.58	190	4.25	20.22	3.937**
Emotional stability (score)	171	2.85	0.54	182	2.75	0.52	−0.091
Missing stability	172	0.31	5.58	190	4.25	20.22	3.937**
Agreeableness (score)	171	3.19	0.57	182	3.12	0.60	−0.077
Missing agreeableness	172	0.31	5.58	190	4.25	20.22	3.937**
Self-reported skills (%)							
Reading							
Don't use reading skill	172	0.00	0.00	189	4.20	20.12	4.205***
Read with low intensity	172	20.51	40.50	189	36.49	48.27	15.976***
Read with medium intensity	172	32.86	47.11	189	32.65	47.02	−0.213
Read with high intensity	172	46.62	50.03	189	26.66	44.33	−19.967***
Writing							
Don't use writing skill	170	2.46	15.53	189	9.50	29.40	7.040**
Write with low intensity	170	50.99	50.14	189	67.14	47.10	16.153**
Write with medium intensity	170	25.82	43.89	189	17.21	37.85	−8.609*
Write with high intensity	170	20.74	40.66	189	6.15	24.09	−14.583***
Numeracy							
Don't use numeracy skill	172	4.24	20.22	190	3.45	18.30	−0.795
Numeracy with low intensity	172	10.67	30.96	190	10.68	30.97	0.013
Numeracy with medium intensity	172	56.19	49.76	190	77.78	41.68	21.597***
Numeracy with high intensity	172	28.90	45.46	190	8.08	27.33	−20.815***
Computer							
Don't use computer skill	172	0.00	0.00	178	0.00	0.00	n.a.
Computer with low intensity	172	6.75	25.17	178	42.17	49.52	35.413***

table continues next page

Table F.5 Unexploited Potential: Computer Skill *(continued)*

	Y1: Use computer at home and at work			Y2: Use computer at home but not at work			Difference: Y2–Y1
	Obs	Mean	SD	Obs	Mean	SD	
Computer with medium intensity	172	8.47	27.92	178	26.07	44.02	17.602***
Computer with high intensity	172	84.78	36.02	178	31.77	46.69	−53.015***
Literacy assessment							
No answer on Reading Component or Core (%)	172	8.15	27.45	190	11.03	31.40	2.871
Reading Component (average) (%)							
Sentence incorrect answers	153	40.62	7.64	162	38.19	14.12	−2.439*
Sentence correct answers	153	49.07	7.19	162	44.25	11.82	−4.825***
Sentence no answers	153	10.30	10.12	162	17.57	14.20	7.264***
Passage incorrect answers	153	51.48	6.76	162	50.63	12.24	−0.846
Passage correct answers	153	45.91	5.60	162	42.69	10.84	−3.214***
Passage no answers	153	2.62	5.33	162	6.68	12.35	4.060***
Vocabulary incorrect answers	153	73.63	3.87	162	71.35	9.03	−2.282**
Vocabulary correct answers	153	23.30	1.85	162	22.19	3.90	−1.111***
Vocabulary no answers	153	3.06	4.20	162	6.46	11.99	3.393***
Core (average)							
Score Core test	153	6.63	1.72	162	5.65	2.54	−0.984***
Passed Core test	153	95.87	19.97	162	85.11	35.71	−10.763***
Literacy assessment							
Reading proficiency	172		233	190		199	−33.236***

Note: n.a. = not applicable; NEET = Not in Employment, Education, or Training; Obs = number of observations.
*** $p < 0.01$, ** $p < 0.05$, * $p < 0.1$.

Effect of Socioemotional Skills on Education and Labor Outcomes

Table G.1 Years of Education, Controlling for Socioemotional Skills

	Time preference	Risk	Hostile bias	Grit	Big five
Socioemotional skills					
Time preference (score)	−0.4006***				
	(0.0964)				
Risk aversion (score)		0.2359**			
		(0.0981)			
Hostile bias (score)			−0.8940***		
			(0.1348)		
Grit (score)				0.3309*	
				(0.1751)	
Openness (score)					0.6430***
					(0.1853)
Conscientiousness (score)					1.0076***
					(0.1757)
Extraversion (score)					0.6508***
					(0.1502)
Agreeableness (score)					0.4639***
					(0.1668)
Emotional stability (score)					0.2862*
					(0.1684)
Controls					
Female (%)	−0.4034**	−0.3887*	−0.3431*	−0.3654*	−0.0660
	(0.1992)	(0.2005)	(0.1981)	(0.2002)	(0.1967)
Age	0.0812***	0.0869***	0.0881***	0.0841***	0.0788***
	(0.0096)	(0.0094)	(0.0095)	(0.0096)	(0.0094)
Middle socioeconomic status (%)	0.7723**	0.7370**	0.6398**	0.7660**	0.7546**
	(0.3175)	(0.3092)	(0.2921)	(0.3114)	(0.2966)

table continues next page

Table G.1 Years of Education, Controlling for Socioemotional Skills *(continued)*

	Time preference	Risk	Hostile bias	Grit	Big five
High socioeconomic status (%)	0.8857**	0.8384**	0.7284**	0.8551**	0.6907**
	(0.3612)	(0.3568)	(0.3362)	(0.3609)	(0.3414)
Mother's education					
Primary	−0.8607	−0.9151	−0.9787	−0.9161	−0.6848
	(0.6032)	(0.6176)	(0.6097)	(0.6239)	(0.6082)
Secondary	0.8415**	0.8650**	0.8621**	0.8787**	0.8963**
	(0.3500)	(0.3517)	(0.3433)	(0.3537)	(0.3489)
Tertiary	1.9081***	1.9352***	1.9516***	1.8942***	1.8244***
	(0.6603)	(0.6487)	(0.5916)	(0.6696)	(0.6760)
Dummy for region	x	x	x	x	X
Number of observations	1,868	1,868	1,868	1,868	1,868
R^2	0.144	0.137	0.163	0.135	0.209

Note: All models estimated using ordinary least squares. Robust standard errors are in parentheses. Controls include gender, age, socioeconomic status at age 15 years, mother's education, and dummies for region. Dependent variable equals years of education.
***$p < 0.01$, **$p < 0.05$, *$p < 0.1$

Table G.2 Linear Probability Model of Completing SHS or Tertiary Education, Controlling for Socioemotional Skills

	Time preference	Risk	Hostile bias	Grit	Big five
Socioemotional skills					
Time preference (score)	−0.0515***				
	(0.0137)				
Risk aversion (score)		0.0360***			
		(0.0124)			
Hostile bias (score)			−0.1149***		
			(0.0193)		
Grit (score)				0.0293	
				(0.0238)	
Openness (score)					0.0783***
					(0.0255)
Conscientiousness (score)					0.1410***
					(0.0247)
Extraversion (score)					0.0850***
					(0.0221)
Agreeableness (score)					0.0518**
					(0.0234)
Emotional stability (score)					0.0525**
					(0.0232)

table continues next page

Table G.2 Linear Probability Model of Completing SHS or Tertiary Education, Controlling for Socioemotional Skills *(continued)*

	Time preference	Risk	Hostile bias	Grit	Big five
Controls					
Female (%)	−0.0499*	−0.0479*	−0.0421	−0.0461	−0.0026
	(0.0282)	(0.0283)	(0.0280)	(0.0283)	(0.0278)
Age	0.0074***	0.0082***	0.0083***	0.0079***	0.0070***
	(0.0013)	(0.0013)	(0.0013)	(0.0013)	(0.0013)
Middle socioeconomic status (%)	0.0776	0.0729	0.0605	0.0758	0.0759*
	(0.0478)	(0.0468)	(0.0440)	(0.0468)	(0.0435)
High socioeconomic status (%)	0.0809	0.0742	0.0606	0.0772	0.0557
	(0.0537)	(0.0532)	(0.0497)	(0.0536)	(0.0504)
Mother's education					
Primary	−0.0869	−0.0940	−0.1021	−0.0940	−0.0670
	(0.0752)	(0.0772)	(0.0760)	(0.0770)	(0.0728)
Secondary	0.0877	0.0903*	0.0904*	0.0927*	0.0926*
	(0.0541)	(0.0544)	(0.0535)	(0.0546)	(0.0542)
Tertiary	0.1745*	0.1782*	0.1801**	0.1739*	0.1612
	(0.0974)	(0.0960)	(0.0899)	(0.0983)	(0.1007)
Dummy for region	x	x	x	x	x
Number of observations	1,868	1,868	1,868	1,868	1,868
R^2	0.087	0.082	0.106	0.078	0.152

Note: All models estimated using ordinary least squares. Robust standard errors in parentheses. Controls include gender, age, socioeconomic status at age 15 years, mother's education, and dummies for region. Dependent variable equals 1 if highest level of education completed is senior high school (SHS) or tertiary, and 0 otherwise.
***$p < 0.01$, **$p < 0.05$, *$p < 0.1$.

Table G.3 Linear Probability Model of Being Employed, Controlling for Socioemotional Skills

	Time preference	Risk	Hostile bias	Grit	Big five
Socioemotional skills					
Time preference (score)	−0.0108				
	(0.0150)				
Risk aversion (score)		−0.0047			
		(0.0130)			
Hostile bias (score)			−0.0023		
			(0.0201)		
Grit (score)				−0.0194	
				(0.0240)	
Openness (score)					−0.0006
					(0.0281)
Conscientiousness (score)					0.0254
					(0.0280)

table continues next page

Table G.3 Linear Probability Model of Being Employed, Controlling for Socioemotional Skills (continued)

	Time preference	Risk	Hostile bias	Grit	Big five
Extraversion (score)					−0.0228
					(0.0267)
Agreeableness (score)					−0.0402*
					(0.0237)
Emotional stability (score)					−0.0083
					(0.0257)
Controls					
Female (%)	−0.1072***	−0.1067***	−0.1065***	−0.1086***	−0.1048***
	(0.0302)	(0.0302)	(0.0301)	(0.0303)	(0.0304)
Age	0.0068***	0.0068***	0.0068***	0.0069***	0.0070***
	(0.0015)	(0.0015)	(0.0015)	(0.0015)	(0.0015)
Middle socioeconomic status (%)	0.0677	0.0677	0.0673	0.0654	0.0690
	(0.0483)	(0.0483)	(0.0479)	(0.0469)	(0.0480)
High socioeconomic status (%)	0.0795	0.0794	0.0785	0.0794	0.0816
	(0.0518)	(0.0517)	(0.0512)	(0.0517)	(0.0526)
Mother's education					
Primary	−0.1510*	−0.1518*	−0.1520*	−0.1536*	−0.1592*
	(0.0895)	(0.0906)	(0.0904)	(0.0902)	(0.0893)
Secondary	−0.0908	−0.0889	−0.0892	−0.0892	−0.0929*
	(0.0568)	(0.0564)	(0.0564)	(0.0563)	(0.0558)
Tertiary	−0.2269*	−0.2259*	−0.2256*	−0.2238*	−0.2247*
	(0.1359)	(0.1360)	(0.1334)	(0.1337)	(0.1365)
Dummy for region	x	x	x	x	x
Number of observations	1,362	1,362	1,362	1,362	1,362
R^2	0.091	0.091	0.091	0.092	0.096

Note: All models estimated using ordinary least squares. Robust standard errors in parentheses. Controls include gender, age, socioeconomic status at age 15 years, mother's education, and dummies for region. Dependent variable equals 1 if employed and 0 if not employed and not in education.
***$p < 0.01$, **$p < 0.05$, *$p < 0.1$.

Table G.4 Linear Probability Model of Being Self-Employed, Controlling for Socioemotional Skills

	Time preference	Risk	Hostile bias	Grit	Big five
Socioemotional skills					
Time preference (score)	−0.0007				
	(0.0190)				
Risk aversion (score)		−0.0408***			
		(0.0158)			
Hostile bias (score)			0.0878***		
			(0.0223)		
Grit (score)				0.0077	
				(0.0313)	
Openness (score)					0.0308
					(0.0314)
Conscientiousness (score)					−0.0882***
					(0.0342)
Extraversion (score)					−0.0712**
					(0.0282)
Agreeableness (score)					−0.0328
					(0.0297)
Emotional stability (score)					−0.0516*
					(0.0307)
Controls					
Female (%)	0.2829***	0.2805***	0.2765***	0.2840***	0.2621***
	(0.0363)	(0.0361)	(0.0362)	(0.0366)	(0.0367)
Age	0.0056***	0.0053***	0.0053***	0.0056***	0.0068***
	(0.0018)	(0.0018)	(0.0017)	(0.0018)	(0.0017)
Middle socioeconomic status (%)	−0.0159	−0.0187	−0.0093	−0.0160	−0.0099
	(0.0478)	(0.0479)	(0.0470)	(0.0478)	(0.0468)
High socioeconomic status (%)	0.1039*	0.1070*	0.1049*	0.1026*	0.1139**
	(0.0554)	(0.0554)	(0.0547)	(0.0557)	(0.0535)
Mother's education					
Primary	0.0343	0.0332	0.0401	0.0350	0.0272
	(0.1002)	(0.0993)	(0.0979)	(0.0999)	(0.0979)
Secondary	−0.0321	−0.0377	−0.0323	−0.0324	−0.0219
	(0.0660)	(0.0644)	(0.0676)	(0.0659)	(0.0658)
Tertiary	0.0096	0.0167	0.0057	0.0083	0.0264
	(0.1073)	(0.1037)	(0.1030)	(0.1070)	(0.1025)
Dummy for region	x	x	x	x	x
Number of observations	1,089	1,089	1,089	1,089	1,089
R^2	0.121	0.128	0.137	0.121	0.144

Note: All models estimated using ordinary least squares. Robust standard errors in parentheses. Controls include gender, age, socioeconomic status at age 15 years, mother's education, and dummies for region. Dependent variable equals 1 if selfemployed and 0 if wage employed.
***$p < 0.01$, **$p < 0.05$, *$p < 0.1$.

Table G.5 Linear Probability Model of Working in a Medium- to High-Skilled Occupation, Controlling for Socioemotional Skills

	Time preference	Risk	Hostile bias	Grit	Big five
Socioemotional skills					
Time preference (score)	−0.0113				
	(0.0179)				
Risk aversion (score)		0.0144			
		(0.0153)			
Hostile bias (score)			−0.0244		
			(0.0232)		
Grit (score)				0.0388	
				(0.0286)	
Openness (score)					0.0366
					(0.0346)
Conscientiousness (score)					0.0351
					(0.0331)
Extraversion (score)					0.0261
					(0.0282)
Agreeableness (score)					0.0481
					(0.0305)
Emotional stability (score)					0.0722**
					(0.0317)
Controls					
Female (%)	0.2295***	0.2314***	0.2323***	0.2358***	0.2571***
	(0.0357)	(0.0355)	(0.0357)	(0.0361)	(0.0353)
Age	−0.0004	−0.0002	−0.0003	−0.0004	−0.0011
	(0.0018)	(0.0018)	(0.0017)	(0.0018)	(0.0018)
Middle socioeconomic status (%)	0.0951*	0.0957*	0.0929*	0.0944*	0.0898*
	(0.0492)	(0.0492)	(0.0495)	(0.0491)	(0.0509)
High socioeconomic status (%)	0.0988*	0.0970*	0.0979*	0.0916*	0.0784
	(0.0546)	(0.0545)	(0.0550)	(0.0550)	(0.0565)
Mother's education					
Primary	−0.0877	−0.0841	−0.0861	−0.0822	−0.0718
	(0.0907)	(0.0918)	(0.0898)	(0.0894)	(0.0848)
Secondary	−0.0226	−0.0179	−0.0199	−0.0223	−0.0289
	(0.0548)	(0.0541)	(0.0549)	(0.0545)	(0.0532)
Tertiary	−0.1785	−0.1808	−0.1772	−0.1846	−0.1919*
	(0.1160)	(0.1146)	(0.1149)	(0.1148)	(0.1071)
Dummy for region	x	x	x	x	x
Number of observations	1,089	1,089	1,089	1,089	1,089
R^2	0.091	0.091	0.092	0.092	0.113

Note: All models estimated using ordinary least squares. Robust standard errors in parentheses. Controls include gender, age, socioeconomic status at age 15 years, mother's education, and dummies for region. Dependent variable equals 1 if working in medium- or high-skilled occupation and 0 if working in low-skilled occupation.
***$p < 0.01$, **$p < 0.05$, *$p < 0.1$.

Environmental Benefits Statement

The World Bank Group is committed to reducing its environmental footprint. In support of this commitment, we leverage electronic publishing options and print-on-demand technology, which is located in regional hubs worldwide. Together, these initiatives enable print runs to be lowered and shipping distances decreased, resulting in reduced paper consumption, chemical use, greenhouse gas emissions, and waste.

We follow the recommended standards for paper use set by the Green Press Initiative. The majority of our books are printed on Forest Stewardship Council (FSC)–certified paper, with nearly all containing 50–100 percent recycled content. The recycled fiber in our book paper is either unbleached or bleached using totally chlorine-free (TCF), processed chlorine–free (PCF), or enhanced elemental chlorine–free (EECF) processes.

More information about the Bank's environmental philosophy can be found at http://www.worldbank.org/corporateresponsibility.

green press INITIATIVE

www.ingramcontent.com/pod-product-compliance
Lightning Source LLC
Chambersburg PA
CBHW071958220326
41599CB00032BA/6437